The Best of  Family Cooking

The Best of woman Family Cooking

Joy Davies

GRAFTON BOOKS

A Division of the Collins Publishing Group

LONDON GLASGOW
TORONTO SYDNEY AUCKLAND

Grafton Books
A Division of the Collins Publishing Group
8 Grafton Street, London W1X 3LA

Published by Grafton Books 1987

British Library Cataloguing in Publication Data

Davies, Joy
    The best of Woman family cooking.
    1. Cookery, International
    I. Title
    641.5   TX725.A1

ISBN 0-246-13198-5

Photographers: With special thanks to Laurie Evans and Jan Baldwin.
Contributing photographers: Tom Belshaw, Ken Christie, Martin
Brigdale, James Duncan, Alan Duns, Melvin Grey, James Jackson,
Vernon Morgan, Ian O'Leary, Bill Richmond, Christian Teubner,
Roger Tuff, Andrew Whittuck

Stylists: Bobby Baker, Gina Carminati, Rhana Flett, Katie Gibbs, Maggie
Heinz, Lesley Richardson, Carolyn Russell, Sue Russell, Cathy
Sinker

Home Economists: Liz and Pete, Jane Suthering

With thanks to past and present members of the Woman Cookery
Department: Coralie Dorman, Juliet Holmes, Chris Ingram, Wendy Jones,
Elizabeth Martin, and Catherine Redington, and continued freelance
help from Helen Dore

China, glass and cutlery borrowed from David Mellor, London WC2,
Divertimenti, London W1, and The Conran Shop, London SW3

Design: Graham Davis Associates
Designer: Graham Davis
Illustrations: Michael A. Hill
Typeset by I.C. Dawkins Ltd, London EC1
Printed and bound by New Interlitho spa, Milan

Introduction

Whether it's an avocado pear dressed with a simple vinaigrette, a succulently roasted chicken or a fillet of grilled fish, simplicity is the key to success, for the essence of good cooking is no more than selecting the best quality ingredients you can find and treating them with care. They deserve it and so do you, for food is more than just fuel; it is a way of expressing how we feel about ourselves and each other, and it should always be a pleasure and not a chore.

The recipes in this book are a selection of cookery features that have appeared in *Woman* over the last few years, chosen to cover everyday eating as well as special occasions. Some of them may be familiar to you, others less so, but I hope they all will provide you with a constant source of inspiration and enjoyment.

There's a great new awareness of food, and certainly the relationship between diet and health has become of paramount importance. Healthy eating is about balance, about moderation not about mediocrity. This is the culinary philosophy that we have adopted in the *Woman* Cookery Department, and you will find it reflected in all our recipes.

Current guidelines for a healthy diet point towards a reduction in intake of fats, salt and sugar, with an increase in consumption of fibre. This means cutting down on heavily sweetened and seasoned foods, and eating more fruit, vegetables and cereals, especially bread. To reduce the fat in your diet, and especially saturated animal fat, try and cut down on meat and animal products and adopt cooking methods such as grilling, roasting and steaming instead of frying. Substitute polyunsaturated margarine and oils for butter, and use yogurt or skimmed milk cheeses such as quark and *fromage frais* for cream. By not eating over-seasoned processed foods, our consumption of salt

and sugar will automatically drop, and incorporating more vegetables, pulses and fruit into the diet boosts fibre intake, as does eating bread, especially if it's wholemeal.

If this sounds like changing the eating habits of a lifetime, it will come as a surprise to find just how easy it can be, with the huge variety of foods that are now available. Healthy eating need not become an obsession, since it does not involve abstinence or deprivation, but variety. It is a way of eating food in its natural state, cutting out artificial flavours and additives.

Cooking should always enhance rather than mask, alter or destroy natural flavours and textures. It is an art as well as a science, and what's to be learned are techniques rather than rules. There must always be ample space for creativity, imagination and experiment — and for sheer fun, too. I hope that this book will help you to share my own personal love of cooking, and that you will get as much enjoyment from using the recipes as I have had in creating them for you.

Soups and Starters

Soup, be it a light and fragrant broth or a chilled fruit purée, is the perfect starter — winter or summer — and a hearty soup can be almost a meal in itself. A good, home-made stock is the essential base, well worth the time and effort you put into making it. Stock cubes really are no substitute — high in salt and added flavours which mask rather than enhance food, although you can buy additive-and-salt-free stock cubes from health food shops. You don't have to spend hours over a pot of bones, however, to get a stock that will make all the difference to your finished soup: vegetable stocks are quick and simple and, like meat stocks, can be made in large quantities then reduced by rapid boiling for freezing in small amounts.

● If time *really* doesn't allow for even the simplest of stock-making, use water with a dash of soy sauce, mushroom ketchup, fruit juice, wine or sherry, and rely on garlic, herbs and spices to make up the flavour. Made the day before to allow flavours to develop, soups certainly take the sweat out of entertaining, and your food processor or liquidiser can take over much of the hard work. Serve your soups with fresh chopped herbs, a swirl of yogurt and plenty of warm crusty bread or croûtons.

● Whether it's a soup, a simple salad of mixed leaves, fruit and vegetables served with a piquant dressing or a delicate fish pâté, the role of the starter is to act as an appetite-teaser. Colour, texture and flavour are all-important. Marry pale with vibrant: milky white Mozzarella with scarlet red pepper; smooth with crunchy: avocado with crispy bacon; rich with sharp: smoked salmon with fresh lemon juice.

● Keep all starters small and delicate so as not to spoil appetites for what is to come and, for entertaining, choose a starter that can be assembled in advance or, if at the last minute, literally in moments, and do allow some time and thought for presentation and garnish. Fresh herbs, flowers, toasted nuts, fruit or fine strips of citrus rind can all improve the appetising finish of a dish, but don't over-garnish, and never fall into traps like trying to make chrysanthemums out of carrots.

CABBAGE AND LENTIL SOUP

1 tablespoon/15 ml oil
2 sticks celery, sliced
1 onion, sliced
1 leek, sliced
1 carrot, sliced
2 rashers smoky bacon, derinded, chopped
1 oz/25 g split lentils
1 oz/25 g long grain rice
2 pints/1.2 litres chicken stock
4 tablespoons/60 ml tomato purée
1 tablespoon/15 ml Worcestershire sauce
1 small head cabbage, shredded
4 oz/125 g sprouts, trimmed and sliced
To garnish: fresh pesto sauce (from supermarkets and delicatessens)

Heat the oil in a large pan and fry the celery, onion, leek, carrot and bacon for 10 minutes. Stir in the lentils, rice, stock, tomato purée, Worcestershire sauce and plenty of freshly ground black pepper. Bring to the boil. Cover and simmer for 1½ hours. Add the cabbage and sprouts and simmer for another 10 minutes. Garnish with pesto if liked.   *Serves 4-6*

TOMATO AND RASPBERRY SOUP

1 tablespoon/15 ml olive oil
1 onion chopped
1½ lb/700 g tomatoes, roughly chopped
8 oz/225 g raspberries
1 tablespoon/15 ml red wine vinegar
1 teaspoon/5 ml caster sugar
1 pint/600 ml chicken stock
1 tablespoon/15 ml chopped fresh chervil

Heat oil in a large pan. Add onion and tomatoes, cook for 5 minutes. Add raspberries, vinegar, sugar, stock and seasoning. Simmer for 30 minutes, then sieve. Chill. Stir in chervil, serve.
Serves 4

CABBAGE AND LENTIL SOUP

GAZPACHO

A deliciously refreshing chilled Spanish soup.

1 thick slice wholewheat bread, crusts
   removed and chopped
2 cloves garlic, peeled and crushed
4 spring onions, trimmed and finely
   chopped
1 teaspoon/5 ml chopped fresh coriander
1½ pints/900 ml tomato juice
2 tablespoons/30 ml wine vinegar
1 red and ½ green pepper, cored,
   deseeded and finely diced
1 cucumber, peeled and finely diced
4 ripe tomatoes, diced
To garnish: **parsley**

Blend the bread, garlic, spring onions,
coriander, tomato juice and vinegar until
smooth. Add the remaining ingredients
and chill. Just before serving, float ice
cubes in the soup and garnish with
parsley. **Serves 6**

SAXE-COBURG

1 onion, finely chopped
2 tablespoons/30 ml oil
12 oz/350 g sprouts, trimmed and finely
   sliced
2 oz/50g ham, finely chopped
1 tablespoon/15 ml flour
½ teaspoon/2.5 ml ground nutmeg
2 pints/1.2 litres chicken stock
2 oz/50 g cooked ham, cut into strips
To garnish: **Greek yogurt, pine kernels,
   fresh parsley sprigs**

Fry onion in oil in a large pan for 5
minutes. Add sprouts and ham. Cook for a
further 5 minutes. Add flour, nutmeg and
seasoning. Gradually stir in stock, bring
to the boil, cover, then simmer for 10
minutes. Place in a liquidiser or processor
and blend until smooth. Reheat gently
without boiling. Stir in ham strips just
before serving. Garnish each soup bowl
with a spoonful of yogurt, a few pine
kernels and a sprig of parsley. **Serves 8**

STILTON AND CHESTNUT SOUP

1 lb/450 g chestnuts
3 sticks celery, chopped
1 onion, chopped
1 tablespoon/15 ml oil
1 pint/600 ml chicken stock
1 pint/600 ml milk
4 oz/125 g Stilton cheese, crumbled
1 tablespoon/15 ml lemon juice
few drops Tabasco sauce
To garnish: **few sprigs coriander**

Nick chestnuts with a sharp knife. Place
on a baking tray and cook at Mark 6 —
200°C — 400°F for 30 minutes. Shell and
skin. Fry celery and onion in oil for 10
minutes without browning. Add
chestnuts, stock and milk. Cook for 15
minutes. Blend in a liquidiser with Stilton,
lemon juice and Tabasco. Serve hot,
garnished. **Serves 6-7**

BELOW: GAZPACHO

FROM THE BACK: STILTON AND CHESTNUT SOUP,
COCK-A-LEEKIE, MULLIGATAWNY, SAXE-COBURG

COCK-A-LEEKIE

2 tablespoons/30 ml oil
1 small boiling chicken, cut into portions
2lb/900 g leeks, thickly sliced
4 pints/2.25 litres chicken stock
12 prunes
1 bouquet garni

Heat oil in a large pan. Add chicken portions and fry until golden on all sides. Add leeks, stock, prunes, bouquet garni and seasoning. Bring to the boil. Skim. Simmer for 2 hours. Remove bouquet garni. Cut meat from bones and return to soup. Adjust seasoning. Serve hot.

Serves 10-12

MULLIGATAWNY

2 onions, finely chopped
1 carrot, diced
1 dessert apple, diced
2 tablespoons/30 ml oil
1½ tablespoons/25 ml curry powder
2 pints/1.2 litres beef or chicken stock
5 oz/150 g natural yogurt
2 roast turkey drumsticks, skinned, boned and diced
4 oz/125 g green beans, cut into 1-inch/ 2.5 cm lengths
To garnish: fresh chopped parsley

Fry onions, carrot, apple and curry powder in oil for 5 minutes. Add stock and yogurt. Simmer for 1 hour. Add turkey and beans. Simmer for 15 minutes. Serve hot with parsley.

Serves 8

LETTUCE AND AVOCADO SOUP

1½ pints/900 ml chicken stock
2 lettuces, roughly chopped
2 avocados, stoned and peeled
2 fl oz/60 ml dry white wine
1 green chilli, seeded and finely chopped
5 fl oz/150 ml soured cream
To garnish: finely shredded lettuce

Boil stock and plunge in lettuces. Leave for 2 minutes. Allow to cool. Mash avocados with a fork, stir in wine, chilli and seasoning. Add lettuces and stock and blend in a liquidiser or food processor until smooth. Stir in soured cream. Chill, garnish and serve the same day.

Serves 8

FRENCH ONION SOUP

Cook the onions until they are very brown, to give a rich, caramel-flavoured soup.

2 oz/50 g butter
1 lb/450 g onions, thinly sliced into rings
1 tablespoon/15 ml plain flour
2½ pints/1.5 litres beef stock
1 small French loaf
1½ oz/40 g Emmental cheese, grated
1½ oz/40 g fresh Parmesan or mature Cheddar, grated

Melt the butter in a flameproof casserole or heavy pan and when foaming add the onions. Cook over a moderate heat until transparent then cover and cook for a further 10-15 minutes until well browned, stirring the onions occasionally to prevent burning. Add the flour and cook, stirring for 2 minutes. Blend in stock, bring to the boil, cover and simmer for 20-30 minutes. Taste and adjust seasoning.

Slice French bread and lay in a large earthenware casserole. Pour soup over bread, then sprinkle the top with the grated cheese. Place in a very hot oven (Mark 7 — 220°C — 425°F) for 5-10 minutes to brown top.

Serves 6

BORSCH

A real hearty Russian classic, traditionally served with dumplings.

1 lb/450 g fresh, uncooked beetroot, peeled
½ celeriac, peeled
1 oz/25 g butter
1 onion, roughly chopped
1 clove garlic, peeled and crushed
½ teaspoon/2.5 ml sugar
4 tablespoons/60 ml red wine vinegar
3 pints/1.75 litres ham stock
3 oz/75 g white cabbage
3 oz/75 g cooked ham
5 oz/150 g thick yogurt

Cut beetroot and celeriac into matchsticks. Melt butter in a large heavy saucepan and fry onion until just softened. Add beetroot, celeriac and garlic and cook gently for 2-3 minutes. Sprinkle with sugar and add vinegar. Boil for 1 minute then stir in stock and seasoning. Boil, cover and simmer for 40 minutes until vegetables are tender.

Meanwhile, finely shred cabbage and roughly chop ham. Add to soup and cook for a further 10 minutes. Adjust seasoning. Pour into heated tureen. Garnish with yogurt.

Serves 6-8

ASPARAGUS WITH ORANGE HOLLANDAISE

ORIENTAL MINCED PORK

Deliciously light and tender meat balls with a slightly oriental flavour. Chicken or lamb can be used just as successfully as pork.

1 lb/450 g minced pork
2 tablespoons/30 ml fresh parsley, chopped
¼ inch/5 mm piece root ginger, peeled and shredded
½ tablespoon/7.5 ml soy sauce
1 teaspoon/5 ml dry sherry
2 teaspoons/10 ml cornflour
1 ½ tablespoons/25 ml water
1 small egg, beaten
½ Savoy cabbage, washed
½ head Chinese leaves, washed

Mix together the pork, parsley, ginger, soy sauce and sherry. Blend the cornflour and water and add the beaten egg. Gently mix into the pork. Leave to rest for 1 hour. Meanwhile, slice the cabbage into 1½-inch/3.5-cm wedges. Divide the pork into walnut sized pieces and roll into balls. Place well spaced apart on a plate. Steam for 4-5 minutes in batches. Remove and keep warm. Place the Savoy cabbage in the steamer and steam for 3 minutes. Add the Chinese leaves and return the pork to the steamer. Cook for a further 2 minutes. Serve immediately.   **Serves 4-5**

SALADE FRISEE

½ curly endive, trimmed
4 oz/125 g streaky bacon
4 thick slices white bread, crusts removed
1 ½ tablespoons/25 ml olive oil
1 tablespoon/15 ml wine vinegar

Put the endive in a bowl. Remove rinds from bacon, reserve. Chop bacon and fry with the rinds in a frying pan for 5 minutes. Discard the bacon rinds. Cut bread into cubes. Add bread and olive oil to the pan. Fry bread for 2 minutes until crisp. Remove with a slotted spoon. Add the vinegar to the pan and boil rapidly. Spoon the bacon and croûtons over the endive. Pour over the pan juices and toss well.   **Serves 6**

ORIENTAL MINCED PORK

ASPARAGUS AND ORANGE HOLLANDAISE

1 lb/450 g asparagus
2 tablespoons/30 ml white wine vinegar
4 oz/125 g unsalted butter
1 tablespoon/15 ml orange juice
grated rind 1 orange
3 egg yolks
2 oz/50 g Parma ham

Cut 1-inch/2.5-cm off the bottom of the asparagus and pare the first 2-inches/5-cm with a sharp knife. Place the asparagus, tips uppermost, in a steamer over boiling water. Cover and steam for 12 or 15 minutes until the tips are just tender.

Boil the vinegar to reduce by half. Melt the butter. Blend the orange juice, rind, egg yolks and boiling vinegar in a liquidiser. With blender running, add the butter in a thin stream. Blend until thick. Serve the sauce warm with the asparagus and a little Parma ham.   **Serves 4**

ST DAVID'S TARTLETS

8 oz/225 g shortcrust pastry
8 oz/225 g potatoes, peeled and chopped
8 oz/225 g celeriac, peeled and roughly
    chopped
2 oz/50 g butter
1 lb/450 g leeks, trimmed and sliced

Roll out pastry to ⅛-inch/2-mm thick and use to line four 4-inch/10-cm shallow tartlet tins. Bake blind at Mark 5 — 190°C — 375°F for 10 to 15 minutes. Meanwhile, cook the potatoes and celeriac in boiling salted water for 15 minutes, or until soft. Drain. Sieve. Stir in 1 oz/25 g butter and season with salt and freshly ground white pepper. Fill pastry cases. Melt the remaining butter in a pan and cook the leeks for 10 minutes. Spoon into the tarts and cook at Mark 4 — 180°C — 350°F for 10 minutes. **Serves 4**

HAM AND MUSHROOM HEARTS

1 small carrot, peeled
1 small leek, washed and trimmed
1 tablespoon/15 ml chopped parsley
1 garlic clove, peeled and chopped
grated rind of 1 lemon
4 large cap mushrooms, wiped, stalks
    trimmed
4 thick slices cooked ham
To serve: Greek yogurt

Take 4 (10-inch/25-cm) squares of greaseproof paper and cut each to form a heart. Cut carrot and leek into 2-inch/5-cm strips. Mix parsley, garlic and lemon rind together and place in mushroom caps. Taking one paper heart, fold in half lengthways. Place a slice of ham on the left hand side of the paper. Top with a mushroom and a few vegetables. Season, dot with butter and seal to form a packet. Repeat with other hearts. Cook in a moderately hot oven (Mark 5 — 190°C — 375°F) for 15 to 20 minutes. Serve with a spoonful of Greek yogurt. **Serves 4**

ST DAVID'S TARTLETS

MOZZARELLA PEPPER SALAD

Mozzarella cheese is soft and white, originally made from buffalo milk but now produced mostly from cows' milk. This is a variation of the classic Italian tomato, mozzarella and basil salad.

2 mozzarella cheeses — about 12 oz/
    350 g
1 (14 oz/397 g) can red pimientos
3 tablespoons/45 ml olive oil
1 tablespoon/15 ml white wine
    vinegar
freshly crushed black peppercorns
To garnish: fresh coriander leaves

Slice cheese ¼-inch/5-mm thick. Drain pimientos and cut into 1-inch/2.5-cm pieces. Arrange the cheese and pepper on individual plates. Mix the oil, vinegar and peppercorns together, season and spoon a little over each serving. Garnish with fresh coriander leaves. **Serves 6**

FENNEL PLAICE SPIRALS

4 plaice fillets, skinned
1 garlic clove, peeled and crushed
2 oz/50 g melted butter
½ fennel bulb, shredded
4 spring onions, cut into strips
juice of half a lemon
2 tablespoons/30 ml dry white wine
fresh fennel sprigs

Cut the fillets in half lengthways to make two long strips. Turn over. Blend garlic and melted butter, brush over fish. Place a few strips of fennel and spring onion at one end of each fillet strip. Season with black pepper and a squeeze of lemon juice. Secure each roll with a cocktail stick. Place each in the centre of a 6-inch/15-cm foil square, draw the sides up. Sprinkle fish with a little wine, top with a fennel sprig and secure parcel. Cook in a moderately hot oven (Mark 5 — 190°C — 375°F) for 10 minutes. **Serves 4**

STUFFED CABBAGE

8 medium Savoy cabbage leaves
Filling:
2 oz/50 g cooked long grain rice
1 tablespoon/15 ml sultanas
2 tomatoes, skinned, deseeded and chopped
1 oz/25 g blanched almonds, chopped
2 tablespoons/30 ml fresh chopped parsley
squeeze of lemon juice
5 fl oz/150 ml chicken stock
***To garnish:* tomato sauce recipe (p.30)**

Blanch cabbage leaves for 2 minutes, trim thick stalk bases. Mix all filling ingredients (not stock). Make parcels as on page 53. Place rolls, snugly, in a buttered dish. Pour over chicken stock, cover with foil and cook in a moderately hot oven (Mark 5 — 190°C — 375°F) for 20 minutes. **Serves 4**

CHINESE CHICKEN PARCELS

4 oz/125 g chicken breast, skinned and boned
3 oz/75 g thickly sliced cooked ham
1 large carrot, peeled
few sprigs of parsley
1 (8 oz/225 g) can bamboo shoots
4 spring onions, finely shredded

Cut cellophane, or greaseproof paper, into 6-inch/15-cm squares. Thinly slice the chicken breast on the diagonal into 1½-inch/3.5-cm by 1-inch/2.5-cm pieces. Cut the ham and carrot similarly. Place a sprig of parsley in the centre of each piece of cellophane. Cover with carrot, ham, bamboo shoots, spring onions, chicken breast and seasoning. Fold the cellophane around the chicken to form small envelopes. Deep fry at 190°C — 375°F for 2 minutes.

Makes 12 to 15

BUTTERFLY PRAWNS

4 Pacific prawns, preferably uncooked
1 tablespoon/15 ml soy sauce
1 garlic clove, peeled and crushed
2 thin slices root ginger, peeled and shredded
1 tablespoon/15 ml sherry
4 (4-inch/10-cm) squares of rice paper

Peel prawns and cut into 1-inch/2.5-cm pieces. Mix together soy sauce, garlic, ginger and sherry. Add prawns and marinate for 30 minutes. Brush rice paper lightly with water, place prawn in middle of each and gently draw edges to centre. Squeeze together carefully. Deep fry for 2 minutes at 190°C — 375°F turning occasionally. Drain. **Serves 4**

FILO SPINACH TRIANGLES

4 oz/125 g frozen leaf spinach, chopped
4 oz/125 g cottage cheese, sieved
1 tablespoon/15 ml fresh chopped parsley
pinch freshly grated nutmeg
1 small egg, beaten
4 sheets filo pastry
2 tablespoons/30 ml oil

Drain spinach. Place in a bowl. Stir in cheese, parsley, nutmeg, egg and seasoning. Cut filo pastry in half widthways, then into 2-inch/5-cm wide strips. Brush lightly with oil. Put a teaspoon of the mixture at the base of each strip. Fold over to make small triangles. Brush with oil and bake at Mark 6 — 200°C — 400°F for 15-20 minutes. **Makes 40**

CHEESE DOLMADES

1 packet preserved vine leaves
6 (1-inch/2.5-cm) cubes Edam cheese
6 (1-inch/2.5-cm) cubes Camembert

Rinse vine leaves in water, pat dry on tea towel. Remove rind from both cheeses. Wrap in vine leaves to form small parcels (as for cabbage on page 53). Arrange parcels in an oiled ovenproof dish, with the ends underneath. Brush with olive oil. Cook in a hot oven (Mark 7 — 220°C — 425°F) for 10 to 12 minutes, or until the leaves start to darken and parcel feels soft. Serve with crusty bread. **Serves 4-6**

CLOCKWISE FROM THE LEFT; BUTTERFLY PRAWNS, FILO SPINACH TRIANGLES, HAM AND MUSHROOM HEARTS, FENNEL PLAICE SPIRALS, CHEESE DOLMADES, STUFFED CABBAGE, CHINESE CHICKEN PARCELS

Eggs and Cheese

Eggs perform a magical role in cooking. They are able to alter their own structure and that of other food: they thicken sauces, set custards, lighten soufflés and mousses and transform flour, butter and sugar into airy cakes and sponges. They are also a valuable and cheap source of protein, vitamins and minerals as well as a favourite ingredient for quick, simple snacks and for entertaining.

● As with most foods, fresh is best. The fresher an egg the better it holds its shape, which is most important for an egg which is to be poached; slightly older eggs, on the other hand, are better for boiling as they are easier to peel. Store eggs, pointed end downwards in a cool place away from strong flavours and if you keep them in the fridge allow them to come to room temperature before using.

● Cheese, like eggs, demands care and respect in cooking since over-cooking toughens the proteins. On the whole, cheeses are interchangeable in cooking, though obviously flavours will vary, but for grilling and adding to sauces you should choose cheeses with good melting properties: Leicester is top of the list for grilling, and the traditional cheese for Welsh Rarebit; Cheshire is good for adding to sauces.

● As with all dairy produce, cheese is high in animal fat, so choose mature, well-flavoured ones for cooking so that you can keep the amount you need to a minimum. Although there are reduced-fat cheeses of the Cheshire and Cheddar varieties, they can be rubbery, especially when grilled. Parmesan is marvellous for cooking and, although it's expensive, it's best bought by the piece to grate finely whenever you need it; tubs of ready-grated Parmesan often have an unpleasant smell and flavour. All cheeses to be kept in the fridge should be wrapped in foil or greaseproof paper and stored in the coolest part. While freezing cheese is possible, it does impair texture and flavour.

● Skimmed-milk cheeses such as German quark and French *fromage frais* are, unlike hard cheeses, very low in fat and perfect substitutes for cream cheese.

BOILED EGGS

How often do people complain about their breakfast boiled egg? Well, here's the perfect guide for soft-boiled eggs. There are two methods but whichever you choose, timing is crucial. Use the guide for hard-boiled eggs too, and again watch the timing.

Using size 3 eggs, either:

1 Start the eggs off in cold water and bring to the boil. The second that bubbles start to rise to the surface, start timing — allow 3 minutes, simmering.

2 Bring water to the boil, turn down the heat, lower eggs into the pan and simmer for 4½ minutes.

In either case, do not allow the water to boil once the eggs are in the pan. This not only toughens the whites but may cause the eggs to crack by knocking against each other and the pan.

For hard-boiled eggs, allow 10 minutes for the first method, 12 minutes for the second. Longer cooking will produce a dark ring around the yolk. After cooking plunge the eggs into cold water to arrest the cooking. When cool enough to handle, crack the shell with a spoon handle and peel carefully. Peeled boiled eggs can be kept in the fridge in water for a couple of days before using.

CLOCKWISE FROM THE TOP: GOOSE, GUINEA FOWL, DUCK, QUAIL, TURKEY

POACHED EGGS

Always use very fresh eggs. Bring water to the boil in a shallow pan. Turn off heat, crack eggs into water as near to the surface as possible. Cover with lid and cook undisturbed for about 5 minutes until whites set. The water should hardly simmer — boiling water will distort the egg shape. Remove with a slotted spoon and drain. Trim neatly with a small knife.

POACHED EGGS ASPARAGUS

4 oz/125 g shortcrust pastry
1 (12 oz/350 g) tin asparagus
1 oz/25 g butter, melted
6 eggs

Roll out pastry to ⅛-inch/3-mm thick, prick all over with a fork and line six 3-inch/7.5-cm fluted tartlet tins, trim edges. Stack the tins on top of one another and place an empty one on top. Place on a baking sheet and cook in a hot oven (Mark 7 — 220°C — 425°F) for 15 minutes. Unstack the tins and cook for a further 10 minutes until golden. Allow to cool. Place the tinned asparagus and juices in a saucepan. Simmer gently for 2 minutes, drain. Toss lightly in melted butter. Poach eggs (see above). Cut asparagus into 1-inch/2.5-cm pieces. Divide between the pastry cases and top with a poached egg. Serve immediately.   ***Serves 6***

QUAIL EGGS IN ASPIC

A beautiful starter with a flower garnish set in aspic.

1 dozen quail eggs
¾ oz/20 g aspic jelly powder
2 tablespoons/30 ml white wine
1 (7 oz/200 g) can pimientos
cucumber skin

Boil eggs for 4 minutes. Drain and cover with cold water. Gently crack the shells with spoon handle, peel. Dissolve aspic powder in 16 fl oz/480 ml boiling water. Add the wine and allow to cool. Pour a very thin layer of aspic into each of four ramekin dishes. Leave in a cool place to set. Meanwhile, cut small flower shapes from pimientos with a small knife or aspic cutters. Cut very thin strips from cucumber

skin for stalks. Dip both into aspic and arrange in a flower pattern in each ramekin. Leave to set. Cover each with 1 tablespoon/15 ml of aspic and set again. Place three eggs in each dish, cover with aspic and allow to set. To serve, dip ramekins in boiling water for a few seconds. Turn out and garnish with watercress and flower shapes cut from remaining pimiento. **Serves 4**

FLOATING ISLANDS

This is a pretty dessert with the contrasting but complementary tastes and textures of custard, meringue and crunchy caramel.

Custard:
3 egg yolks
2 oz/50 g caster sugar
10 fl oz/300 ml milk
few drops of vanilla essence
Meringue:
3 egg whites
6 oz/175 g caster sugar
rice paper
Caramel:
1 lb/450 g caster sugar
5 fl oz/150 ml water

Whisk egg yolks and sugar together until thick and light. Heat milk until boiling, pour gradually on to eggs, whisking constantly. Return to pan and cook very gently, stirring until custard coats back of spoon. Do not allow to boil. Add vanilla essence, strain. Divide between four small dessert dishes. Chill.

Cut 16 1½-inch/3.5-cm diameter circles from rice paper. Whisk egg whites until stiff, gradually whisk in the sugar, until the meringue is very stiff and glossy. Fill a piping bag fitted with a large star nozzle. Pipe rosettes on to rice paper. Half fill a large frying pan with water. Bring water to the boil, then turn down heat. Place piped rosettes in water and poach for 5 to 6 minutes. Remove with a slotted spoon, drain and place on custard.

Dissolve sugar in the water over medium heat, bring to boil and boil until caramel coloured. Spoon most of the caramel over the meringues. To finish the dessert, use a fork to pull threads of caramel from the pan. Decorate the meringues with these strands of caramel.
Serves 4

CLOCKWISE FROM THE LEFT: QUAIL EGGS IN ASPIC, SOUFFLÉ OMELETTE, FLOATING ISLANDS, CRAB SOUFFLÉ, FLAMENCO EGGS, EGGS BENEDICT, POACHED EGGS ASPARAGUS

FLAMENCO EGGS

As the title suggests, this is a popular Spanish recipe. Serve for lunch or supper.

1 onion, peeled and chopped
1 garlic clove, peeled and chopped
1 red pepper, cored, deseeded and sliced
1 tablespoon/15 ml oil
1 (8 oz/225 g) can tomatoes
1 (7½ oz/200 g) can asparagus tips
   (optional)
few green beans and peas
2 oz/50 g chorizo or salami
2 thin slices cooked ham, roughly
   chopped
4 eggs

Fry onion, garlic and red pepper in oil for 5 minutes. Add tomatoes, asparagus, green beans, peas and seasoning. Cook for 1 minute. Divide mixture between two medium-sized gratin dishes. Arrange chorizo and ham on top and break two eggs into each dish. Cook in a moderate oven (Mark 4 — 180°C — 350°F) for about 25 minutes until eggs are set. **Serves 2**

CRAB SOUFFLE

1½ oz/40 g butter
½ oz/15 g Parmesan cheese
1 oz/25 g plain flour
5 fl oz/150 ml milk
5 eggs, separated
4 oz/125 g crab meat, fresh or frozen
2 oz/50 g mature Cheddar cheese,
   grated

Use ½ oz/15 g butter to grease a 2-pint/1.2-litre soufflé dish. Sprinkle with the Parmesan cheese. Melt remaining butter

BEANS MIMOSA

in a pan, add flour and cook gently for 2 minutes, stirring occasionally. Remove from heat, add milk and beat vigorously, until smooth. Cook for 1 minute, stirring. Cool slightly. Beat in egg yolks, add crab meat, cheese and seasoning.

Whisk egg whites until stiff, stir a quarter of the whites into the crab mixture, then fold in the remainder with a metal spoon. Pour into a soufflé dish, run a knife around the dish, 1-inch/2.5-cm from the edge. Cook in a hot oven (Mark 6 — 200°C — 400°F) for 25 to 30 minutes until well risen and golden brown. Serve immediately. **Serves 4**

SOUFFLE OMELETTE

Individual soufflé omelettes look most attractive. But to save time if serving two, double the quantities, use a larger frying pan and cut omelette in two after dusting with sugar.

1 (8 oz/225 g) can apricot halves in
   natural juice
1 egg, separated
2 teaspoons/10 ml caster sugar
few drops vanilla essence
dash of brandy (optional)
knob of butter
icing sugar for dusting

Roughly chop half the apricots. Purée the remainder with 2 tablespoons/30 ml juice in a food processor or liquidiser or pass through a sieve to form apricot sauce. Beat the egg yolk with the sugar. Add vanilla essence and a dash of brandy (if

using). Whisk the egg white until very stiff, fold into the egg yolk mixture with a metal spoon. Heat a knob of butter in an 8-inch/20-cm frying pan. Pour in the egg mixture and cook over a very low heat for 8 to 10 minutes until the base is golden brown and the top is starting to set. Sprinkle on the chopped apricots. Loosen the edge of the omelette and shake the pan sharply to fold the omelette in half. Dust with icing sugar and serve immediately with the apricot sauce.
  Serves 1

EGGS BENEDICT

An American favourite, perfect for brunch or lunch. You can use crisp rashers of streaky bacon instead of ham.

4 (1-inch/2.5-cm) thick slices white bread
1 oz/25 g melted butter
4 eggs
4 thin slices cooked ham
Hollandaise sauce:
1 tablespoon/15 ml warm water
3 egg yolks
1 tablespoon/15 ml lemon juice
salt and white pepper
4 oz/125 g unsalted butter

Cut four 3-inch/7.5-cm rounds from the bread slices with a pastry cutter. Brush with melted butter and cook in a moderately slow oven (Mark 3 — 160°C — 325°F) for 30 minutes until golden brown. Meanwhile poach the eggs (see page 20), cut four 3-inch/7.5-cm rounds from the ham reserving the remainder for garnish, and prepare the hollandaise

STUFFED EGGS

sauce. Place 1 tablespoon/15 ml warm water with egg yolks, lemon juice and seasoning in a liquidiser or food processor. Mix until smooth. Melt the butter until foaming hot but not browning. Pour slowly into the food processor while the machine is still turning. Continue blending until the sauce is smooth and thick. Top each bread round with ham and a poached egg. Serve with the hollandaise sauce and garnish with thin strips of ham. **Serves 4**

BEANS MIMOSA

This makes a light, tasty starter.

1 lb/450 g green beans
2 teaspoons/10 ml white wine vinegar
1 small clove garlic, peeled and crushed
½ teaspoon/2.5 ml wholegrain mustard
2 tablespoons/30 ml olive oil
4 hard-boiled eggs, peeled
To garnish: sprig of thyme

Cook the beans in boiling water for 3 to 4 minutes until still crunchy. Blend vinegar, garlic, mustard and oil together. Season. Pour over warm drained beans and cool.

Roughly chop egg whites and sieve yolks. Sprinkle over beans and garnish.
Serves 4

CHEESE AND HERB SOUFFLE

Classic hot soufflés are usually made from a thick flour-based sauce, but here we have used low fat cheese.

8 oz/ 225 g low fat soft cheese
4 oz/ 125 g mature Cheddar cheese, finely grated
pinch of dry mustard
4 eggs, separated
2 tablespoons/30 ml fresh chopped parsley
2 tablespoons/30 ml fresh chopped chives

Mix together the cheeses, mustard, egg yolks, herbs and freshly ground black pepper in a large mixing bowl. Whisk the egg whites until stiff but not dry and grainy and fold into the cheese mixture. Pour into a lightly greased 2½-pint/1½-litre soufflé dish and bake at Mark 5 — 190°C—375°F for 35 minutes until risen and golden. **Serves 4-6**

CHEESE AND HERB SOUFFLÉ

STUFFED EGGS

Never over-boil eggs as this causes discoloration of the yolks.

6 hard-boiled eggs, peeled and halved
2 oz/50 g cod's roe, skinned
2 oz/50 g low fat soft cheese
½ tablespoon/7.5 ml tomato ketchup
½ tablespoon/7.5 ml lemon juice
½ bunch watercress, trimmed and washed
2 tablespoons/30 ml fresh chopped dill
2 tablespoons/30 ml mayonnaise
10 oz/300 g Greek yogurt
To serve: mixed salad leaves

Scoop out yolks from eggs and blend with roe, cheese, ketchup and lemon juice until smooth. Chill for 2 hours until firm. Finely chop watercress and dill, then blend with remaining ingredients until smooth. Sandwich eggs back together with the cod's roe mixture and arrange on a mixed leaf salad. Coat with the sauce.
Serves 3-6

CLOCKWISE FROM THE LEFT: CHEESE PÂTÉ IN AVOCADO, COEUR À LA CRÈME, NORMANDY CHEESECAKE, FOUR-CHEESE QUICHE, ROQUEFORT PEAR SALAD, CHICKEN CORDON BLEU, DEEP-FRIED MOZZARELLA

OMELETTE ARNOLD BENNETT

6 eggs, separated
8 oz/225 g smoked haddock, cooked, skinned and flaked
3 tablespoons/45 ml low fat fromage frais
3 oz/75 g Gruyère cheese, grated
1 oz/25 g butter
2 tablespoons/30 ml single cream

Mix together well the yolks, haddock, fromage frais, 1 oz/25 g grated Gruyère and freshly ground black pepper. Whisk whites until stiff and gently fold into the fish mixture. Melt the butter in a large frying pan until foaming. Pour in egg mixture and cook for about 1 minute until almost set and base is golden. Sprinkle with remaining cheese and pour over the cream. Grill for 1 minute until golden and serve. *Serves 6*

PLUM TART

If plums are not available use eating apples, peeled, cored and thickly sliced.

Pastry:
4 oz/125 g wholemeal flour
4 oz/125 g plain flour
4 oz/125 g polyunsaturated margarine

Filling:
1½ lb/700 g plums, halved and stoned
2 oz/50 g caster sugar
2 eggs, beaten
5 fl oz/150 ml milk
4 oz/125 g Wensleydale cheese, grated
freshly ground nutmeg

Sift the flours into a bowl and fork in the margarine until the mixture resembles breadcrumbs. Bind with a little cold water. Knead lightly and roll out on a floured surface until ¼ inch/5 mm thick. Use to line a 13 by 9-inch/32 by 22-cm Swiss roll tin. Arrange the plums skin side down on the pastry and sprinkle with half the sugar. Bake at Mark 6 — 200°C — 400°F for 15 minutes. Beat the eggs, milk, cheese, remaining sugar and a pinch of nutmeg together and pour over the fruit. Reduce the oven temperature to Mark 4 — 180°C — 350°F and cook for a further 45 minutes. Serve the tart warm or cold. *Makes 14 slices*

FOUR-CHEESE QUICHE

This is the perfect quiche for using up all those left-over cheeses from the cheeseboard.

6 oz/175 g plain flour
pinch of salt
1½ oz/40 g butter
1½ oz/40g polyunsaturated margarine
Filling:
1 tablespoon/15 ml oil
1 bunch spring onions, trimmed and sliced
1 oz/25 g Lancashire, grated
1 oz/25 g Cheshire, grated
1 oz/25 g Cotswold, grated
2 oz/50 g Red Windsor, grated
3 eggs
5 fl oz/150 ml milk

Sift flour and a pinch of salt into a bowl. Rub in fats until the mixture resembles breadcrumbs. Add 2 tablespoons/30 ml water and mix to a firm dough. Knead lightly, cover and chill for 15 minutes. Roll out and use to line a 9-inch/22.5-cm flan tin. Prick with a fork, brush with a little beaten egg and bake blind in a moderately hot oven (Mark 5 — 190°C — 375°F) for 15 minutes. Heat oil in a frying pan and fry spring onions gently until soft. Place onions and grated cheeses on pastry case, reserving a little cheese. Beat eggs and milk and pour into pastry case, sprinkling top with remaining cheese. Bake in a moderately hot oven (Mark 5— 190°C—375°F) for 40 to 45 minutes until golden. *Serves 6*

CHICKEN CORDON BLEU

4 chicken or turkey breasts, boned and skinned
4 slices of ham
4 oz/125 g Emmental or Gruyère cheese
1 oz/25 g butter
5 fl oz/150 ml dry white wine

Place each chicken breast between non-PVC film, flatten with a mallet. Place a slice of ham and then a thin slice of cheese on each fillet. Season and roll up, securing with string. Melt butter in a flameproof casserole and gently fry fillets for 8 to 10 minutes until lightly brown all over. Add wine and bring to the boil, cover and cook in a moderate oven (Mark 4—180°C—350°F) for 40 minutes.

Remove fillets and keep warm. Rapidly boil cooking juices until reduced by half, strain and serve with chicken. Accompany with green vegetables. *Serves 4*

CHEESE PATE IN AVOCADO

2 oz/50 g Stilton or Danish Blue
3 oz/75 g Ricotta or quark
1 oz/25 g Cheddar, grated
4 tablespoons/60 ml Greek yogurt
½ teaspoon/2.5 ml Dijon mustard
4 avocados
juice of ½ lemon
To garnish: sprigs of mint

Mash Stilton until soft, add Ricotta and Cheddar. Mix with yogurt. Add mustard and mix well, chill. Halve avocados, sprinkle with lemon juice, place a tablespoon of pâté in each half. Add garnish. *Serves 8*

NORMANDY CHEESECAKE

1 oz/25 g sultanas
2 tablespoons/30 ml Calvados or brandy
3 oz/75 g butter
2 oz/50 g caster sugar
4 oz/125 g digestive biscuits, crushed
2 oz/50 g walnuts, finely chopped
8 oz/225 g Ricotta or curd cheese
3 eggs, separated
4 oz/125 g caster sugar
grated rind of ½ lemon
1 oz/25 g plain flour
1 large dessert apple, thinly sliced
2 tablespoons/30 ml apricot jam

Soak sultanas overnight in the Calvados. Melt butter and sugar in a small saucepan, add biscuit crumbs and nuts and stir until well mixed. Press evenly over bottom of a greased, loose-bottomed 7-inch/18-cm cake tin, chill. Soften the cheese in a large mixing bowl. Beat in egg yolks, 2 oz/50 g of the sugar, lemon rind, flour, sultanas and Calvados liquid. Whisk egg whites until stiff and whisk in remaining sugar. Fold lightly into cheese mixture and turn into prepared tin, smoothing surface. Arrange slices of apple in concentric circles on top. Bake in a moderately slow oven (Mark 3 — 160°C — 325°F) for 1½ to 1¾ hours until firm but still spongy to touch. Turn off oven, leave cheesecake to cool with door open for 1 hour. Place jam in a saucepan with 2 tablespoons/30 ml water and bring to the boil. Sieve, then brush glaze over top of cheesecake. Chill for 2 to 3 hours. Remove from tin.

DEEP FRIED MOZZARELLA

1 lb/450 g short grain rice, cooked
1 medium onion, finely grated
2 egg yolks, beaten
3 oz/75 g Mozzarella, cut into ½ -inch/
** 1-cm cubes**
4 oz/125 g fine breadcrumbs
oil for deep frying
To garnish: fresh coriander or parsley

Mix rice, onion, eggs and freshly ground black pepper. Flour your hands, put 1 tablespoon/15 ml of mixture into the palm of your hand and press a few pieces of cheese into the centre. Cover with more rice mixture, roll into a ball to enclose cheese. Roll balls in breadcrumbs and deep fry in oil heated to 180°C (350°F). Fry four or five balls at a time, turning occasionally, for 5 minutes. Drain on absorbent paper, garnish. **Makes 16**

WELSH RAREBIT

A traditional British after dinner savoury, now usually eaten as a light lunch or snack.

4 oz/125 g Red Leicester cheese, grated
2 tablespoons/30 ml milk
1 teaspoon/5 ml English mustard
cayenne pepper, optional
2 thick slices wholewheat toast

Put the cheese, milk and mustard into a small pan and stir over a low heat until melted. Season with freshly ground black pepper or a dash of cayenne pepper if wished. Place the toast on a flat,

ovenproof dish, pour over the melted cheese and grill until bubbling and golden brown. **Serves 2**

CHEDDAR RICE

1 tablespoon/15 ml oil
1 small onion, finely chopped
1 clove garlic, peeled and crushed
8 oz/225 g wholegrain rice
6 oz/175 g mushrooms, thickly sliced
15 fl oz/450 ml hot chicken stock
½ teaspoon/2.5 ml dried oregano
3 oz/75 g Cheddar, grated
3 tablespoons/45 ml fresh chopped
** parsley**

Heat the oil in a saucepan and gently fry the onion and garlic until translucent. Stir in the rice and mushrooms. Add the stock and bring to the boil, stirring. Add the oregano and cheese. Pour into a buttered casserole. Bake at Mark 4 — 180°C — 350°F, for 30 minutes or until the rice is tender. Stir in the parsley and serve with green salad. **Serves 2**

THE ULTIMATE CAULIFLOWER CHEESE

1 oz/25 g butter
2 tablespoons/30 ml flour
15 fl oz/450 ml milk
1 large cauliflower, broken into florets
1 tablespoon/15 ml oil
1 onion, finely chopped
3 rashers streaky bacon, derinded
3 oz/75 g Cheshire cheese, grated

Heat the butter in a small pan over a gentle heat until foaming. Add the flour and cook, stirring constantly for 2 minutes. Add the milk and stir until blended. Simmer for 15-20 minutes.

Meanwhile, boil or steam the cauliflower for 15-20 minutes until just tender. Heat the oil in a pan and fry the onion until golden. Grill the bacon until crisp. Chop. Drain the cauliflower very well and put into a shallow ovenproof dish. Stir the onion and 2 oz/50 g of the cheese into the white sauce. Stir well. Pour over the cauliflower and top with the bacon and remaining cheese. Grill until golden. **Serves 4**

ROQUEFORT PEAR SALAD

3 ripe pears, peeled and cored
juice of ½ lemon
1 curly endive
1 radicchio
4 oz/125 g Roquefort or crumbly blue
** cheese**
1 teaspoon/5 ml coarse-grained mustard
1 tablespoon/15 ml white wine vinegar
olive oil

Cut pears into ¼-inch/5-mm slices lengthways, sprinkle with a little lemon juice. Arrange on a bed of endive and radicchio. Crumble cheese over pears. Mix lemon juice, mustard and vinegar with seasoning. Add olive oil and mix well. Pour over cheese and pears. **Serves 4**

COEUR A LA CREME

Heart-shaped moulds are available from kitchen shops or some department stores. You can substitute half fat cream for the double cream.

8 oz/225 g cottage cheese
5 fl oz/150 ml double cream, whipped
1 egg white
½ oz/15 g caster sugar
To serve: double cream, caster sugar to
** taste, strawberries**

Rinse four cheese moulds in cold water; do not dry them. Line the bases with muslin. Press the cheese through a sieve, fold in cream. Whisk the egg white until stiff and fold into cheese mixture with the sugar. Fill moulds. Stand on a tray for 30 minutes, then freeze for 2 to 3 hours. Unmould frozen "coeurs", thaw for 15 to 20 minutes. Spoon over a little cream, sprinkle with sugar, decorate with strawberries. **Serves 4**

Pasta, Rice and Pulses

With shell shapes, butterfly bows and spirals, spinach and egg noodles, multi-coloured and wholewheat pasta crowding supermarket shelves, we've come a long way since the days pasta meant spaghetti and invariably came in long, blue packets. Even fresh pasta has emerged from the Italian deli to appear in supermarkets, and it's become fashionable to make your own, though this is an American rather than an Italian trend. Fresh or dried, pasta must be cooked *al dente* to avoid a soupy mess — see the note (right) for tips on perfect cooking. Treated like this, any pasta lends itself to simple dressing with olive oil and freshly grated Parmesan cheese as well as to rich aromatic sauces of tomatoes, mushrooms, chicken livers and seafood in addition to the classic Bolognese sauce. Baked in layers with a silky smooth cheese sauce as well as the meaty Bolognese, pasta is transformed into Lasagne al Forno.

● Some recipes turn rice into a fully orchestrated work, such as the Spanish paella, where a rich variety of meat and seafood is combined. Rice, like pasta, exists in many forms and appears in many guises. It can be simply boiled or steamed to accompany a curry or stir-fry, or cooked and tossed in with other ingredients in a pilaf or a risotto — see recipes on page 36.

● Pulses are packed with protein and fibre, so we should all be eating more of them, even though they need careful preparation, soaking and often lengthy cooking. They readily absorb flavours, so toss them warm in a vinaigrette, cook them in rich tomato sauce or layer the beans with meat and vegetables for Cassoulet. Add them to salads, stir-fries, soups and casseroles, or serve them tossed with garlic, herbs and a little melted butter, in their own right as a vegetable.

● You can also sprout beans and pulses to make a whole new range of vegetables, crunchy and high in protein for summer or winter. Mung beans make the familiar bean sprouts, and you can experiment with more delicate alfalfa, chickpeas, lentils and even pumpkin seeds — see how on page 38.

COOKING PASTA

Bring a large pan of salted water to the boil, add a spoonful of oil to stop the pasta sticking to itself, then the pasta. If it's spaghetti, push the bundle down against the bottom of the pan, then bend the ends round into the water and stir to separate the strands. Dried pasta should be cooked at a steady boil for about 12 minutes before you start testing to check if it's *al dente*, which means that the pasta should have a slight bite and not be in the least flabby. Drain thoroughly in a colander while you melt a little butter or heat olive oil in the saucepan, then add the pasta and toss quickly to evaporate any water that clings. This is important because sauce slips off still-wet pasta and ends up in the bottom of the dish.

CHINESE NOODLES WITH PRAWNS AND ALMONDS

2 tablespoons/30 ml oil
2-inch/5-cm piece fresh root ginger, peeled, finely shredded
1 clove garlic, peeled and crushed
2 oz/50 g blanched almonds, shredded
2 spring onions, shredded
½ red pepper, cored, deseeded, shredded
6 oz/175 g peeled prawns
8 oz/225 g Chinese noodles, cooked
1 tablespoon/15 ml soy sauce
1 tablespoon/15 ml dry sherry
pinch of ground cardamom
½ small head Chinese leaves, sliced

Heat the oil until very hot in a wok or large saucepan. Add the ginger, garlic and almonds and cook, stirring, for 1 minute. Add the spring onions, red pepper, prawns and noodles and stir-fry for 2 minutes. Mix the soy sauce, sherry and cardamom. Pour into the pan with the Chinese leaves. Season and cook, stirring, for a few more seconds. Serve immediately. ***Serves 4***

CHINESE NOODLES WITH PRAWNS AND ALMONDS

BASIC TOMATO SAUCE

2 tablespoons/30 ml olive oil
1 large onion, finely chopped
1 garlic clove, peeled and crushed
1 (14 oz/397 g) can Italian tomatoes, sieved, or 10 fresh tomatoes, skinned and deseeded
3 fl oz/90 ml red wine
2 tablespoons/30 ml finely chopped fresh parsley or 1 teaspoon/5 ml dried oregano

Heat the oil and fry the onion and garlic until soft, about 15-20 minutes. Do not brown. Add the remaining ingredients and seasoning. Simmer for 30 minutes, stirring often. **Serves 4**

BACON, MUSHROOM AND COURGETTE SAUCE

12 oz/350 g smoked bacon rashers
2 tablespoons/30 ml olive oil
1 oz/25 g butter
8 oz/225 g mushrooms, wiped
3 courgettes, trimmed and sliced

Remove rinds from bacon, reserve. Finely chop the bacon. Fry bacon and rinds in a frying pan, over moderate heat, until the fat runs. Remove rinds from the pan with a slotted spoon and discard. Add the oil and butter to the fat in the pan. Slice the mushrooms and add with the courgettes, fry for 5 minutes. Season and fry for a further 1 minute. Serve hot with freshly boiled pasta. **Serves 6**

LEEK AND BROCCOLI SAUCE

Peel the outer skin from the broad beans for a bright green colour.

4 oz/125 g quark
3 tablespoons/45 ml double cream
2 tablespoons/30 ml chopped watercress
1 tablespoon/15 ml fresh chopped parsley
2 oz/50 g butter
2 large leeks, trimmed and sliced
8 oz/225 g broccoli, broken into tiny florets, steamed
8 oz/225 g frozen broad beans, thawed

Mash the quark with the cream and stir in the watercress, parsley and seasoning. Melt the butter in a frying pan and fry the leeks until soft. Add the broccoli, cook for

BASIC MEAT SAUCE

If the amount of sauce is too much for one meal, freeze the rest for another day. The sauce is best made in larger quantities for maximum flavour.

1 oz/25 g butter
2 tablespoons/30 ml olive oil
2 large onions, finely chopped
2 garlic cloves, peeled and crushed
2 celery stalks, finely chopped
1 carrot, peeled and finely chopped
1½ lb/700 g lean minced beef
4 oz/125 g bacon, derinded and chopped
1 (14 oz/397 g) can Italian plum tomatoes
4 oz/125 g flat field mushrooms, chopped
3 fl oz/90 ml red wine or water
1 tablespoon/15 ml chopped fresh parsley
1 teaspoon/5 ml dried oregano or basil

Melt the butter with 1 tablespoon/15 ml of the oil and sweat the onions, garlic, celery and carrot in a large covered pan for 15-20 minutes. Remove from the pan with a slotted spoon. Fry the beef and bacon until browned all over. Add the vegetables with the rest of the ingredients, and seasoning. Mix well and bring to the boil. Reduce heat to low, cover pan and simmer for 2 hours (4 hours is best). Spoon into a large bowl and leave to cool completely. Chill overnight, then remove any fat from the surface. Reheat gently for 30 minutes, stirring. **Serves 6-8**

2 minutes. Then add the broad beans and fry, stirring, for 1 minute. Stir in the quark mixture. Serve with freshly boiled pasta.

Serves 6

SPINACH SAUCE

1 lb/450 g fresh spinach, spines removed
2 onions, peeled and finely chopped
3 tablespoons/45 ml olive oil
1 oz/25 g butter
4-6 anchovy fillets
5 fl oz/150 ml chicken stock

Wash the spinach thoroughly, then cook without added water in a large, non-stick saucepan until soft. Drain, squeeze dry and chop finely. Fry the onions in the oil and butter until soft. Chop the anchovies finely and add to the pan with the spinach. Fry for 1 minute, then purée in a blender with the chicken stock until smooth. Season with freshly ground black pepper.

TUNA, ARTICHOKE AND OLIVE SAUCE

1 onion, finely chopped
2 tablespoons/30 ml olive oil
1 (14-oz/397-g) can artichoke hearts, drained and chopped
1 (6-oz/175-g) can tuna, drained and flaked
3 oz/75 g stoned black olives

Fry the onion in the oil until soft. Add the remaining ingredients and cook, stirring carefully, for 2 minutes.

GORGONZOLA CREAM SAUCE

3 oz/75 g Gorgonzola cheese
2 oz/50 g cream cheese
1 oz/25 g butter
6 tablespoons/90 ml single cream
2 tablespoons/30 ml chopped celery leaves

Place the Gorgonzola, cream cheese and butter in a bowl over a saucepan of boiling water. Cook, stirring, until melted and well blended. Stir in the cream and celery leaves and season well with freshly ground black pepper.

SEAFOOD SAUCE

1 oz/25 g butter
½ bunch spring onions, trimmed and chopped
2 tablespoons/30 ml dry white wine
2 oz/50 g smoked salmon trimmings
4 oz/125 g peeled prawns
2 fl oz/60 ml double cream
2 tablespoons/30 ml freshly grated Parmesan

Melt the butter in a pan and gently fry the spring onions until softened slightly. Add the wine and bring to the boil. Add the remaining ingredients and toss immediately with fresh cooked pasta.

BREADCRUMB AND HERB SAUCE

3 tablespoons/45 ml oil
2 medium onions, finely chopped
1 clove garlic, peeled and crushed
4 oz/125 g wholewheat breadcrumbs
4 oz/125 g unsalted butter
6 tablespoons/90 ml fresh chopped parsley

Heat the oil and fry the onions and garlic until soft and golden. In another pan, fry the breadcrumbs in the butter until golden brown and crisp. Mix together with the parsley and toss through pasta of choice.

Serves 6

CLOCKWISE FROM THE LEFT: SEAFOOD SAUCE, SPINACH SAUCE, BREADCRUMB AND HERB SAUCE, BASIC TOMATO SAUCE, GORGONZOLA CREAM SAUCE

SEAFOOD PASTA SALAD

12 oz/350 g cooked pasta shapes
8 oz/225 g peeled prawns
1 (8½-oz/250-g) can pink salmon,
   drained, flaked
8 spring onions, trimmed and sliced
For the dressing:
8 tablespoons/120 ml salad oil
4 teaspoons/20 ml white wine vinegar
2 tablespoons/30 ml fresh lime juice
1 teaspoon/5 ml chopped fresh dill
To garnish: lime slices, dill sprigs

Place pasta, prawns, salmon and spring onions in a bowl. Thoroughly combine the dressing ingredients and season. Pour over the salad and toss lightly. Garnish with lime slices and dill and serve.

Serves 4

CHICKEN LIVER SAUCE

½ oz/15 g butter
1 tablespoon/15 ml olive oil
1 clove garlic, peeled and crushed
8 oz/225 g chicken livers, trimmed
1 onion, finely chopped
2 rashers streaky bacon, chopped
1 (14-oz/397-g) can tomatoes, sieved
2 oz/50 g button mushrooms, sliced
1 teaspoon/5 ml dried oregano

Heat the butter and oil in a medium saucepan, add the garlic and chicken livers and fry, stirring, until the livers are browned and sealed, but still pink inside. Remove with a slotted spoon and set aside. Add the onion and bacon and cook until the onion is soft. Add the tomatoes, mushrooms and oregano and simmer for 20-30 minutes. Chop the chicken livers roughly and return to the pan. Season to taste and heat through gently for 5 minutes.

SEAFOOD PASTA SALAD

COOKING RICE

Method 1: Bring a large pan of salted water to the boil, add rice and stir to separate the grains, then boil for about 15 minutes before you scoop out a grain to test with your fingernail. When the rice is cooked drain it in a sieve, pouring boiling water through it if it looks a little starchy, then spread in a dish and dry off in the oven at Mark 2 — 150°C — 300°F for 10-15 minutes. Stir in a little butter before you serve.

Method 2: Measure rice into a saucepan with a cup and then use the same cup to pour on two parts of water to one part rice. Bring to the boil, reduce heat, cover tightly and cook over low heat for 18-20 minutes until the water has been absorbed.

Method 3: Melt a little butter in a heavy-based pan, add rice and stir gently for 2-3 minutes until the grains are coated and opaque, then pour on twice the rice's volume of boiling water or stock, reduce heat, cover and cook gently for 18-20 minutes. Stir in a little more butter and serve.

FIESTA RICE SALAD

1 (15-oz/425-g) can baby sweetcorn
3 oz/75 g cooked long-grain rice
3 oz/75 g cooked brown rice
4 oz/125 g cooked French beans, topped and tailed
½ yellow pepper, cored, deseeded and cut into strips
4 oz/125 g green grapes, halved, deseeded and peeled
4 radishes, thinly sliced
4 oz/125 g Brazil nuts, roughly chopped
6 oz/175 g lean cooked ham, finely chopped
Dressing:
4 tablespoons/60 ml vegetable oil
2 teaspoons/10 ml wine vinegar
1 tablespoon/15 ml lemon juice
1 teaspoon/5 ml Dijon mustard
To garnish: **radish roses**

Slice sweetcorn in half. Place all the salad ingredients in a bowl and mix well. Whisk together the dressing ingredients and season. Pour over the salad, toss well and garnish. **Serves 4**

LEEK AND TOMATO RISOTTO

2 tablespoons/30 ml oil
2 onions, chopped
8 oz/225 g risotto (arborio) rice
2 fl oz/60 ml dry white wine
pinch of saffron strands
1 pint/600 ml chicken stock
3 leeks, sliced
1 (14 oz/397 g) can chopped tomatoes
1 oz/25 g butter
1 oz/25 g freshly grated Parmesan
To garnish: **freshly grated Parmesan**

Heat half the oil in a large saucepan and fry the onions for 10 minutes until softened. Add the rice and fry for a further 5 minutes, stirring occasionally. Stir in the wine, saffron and stock and bring to the boil. Cover and simmer for 15-20 minutes until tender. Remove from heat. Heat the remaining oil in a frying pan and gently fry the leeks for 10 minutes. Add the tomatoes and freshly ground black pepper and heat through. Stir into the rice with the butter and Parmesan until well blended and creamy. Serve immediately with plenty of grated Parmesan and a green salad. **Serves 3-4**

NUTTY RICE PUDDING

1½ oz/40 g brown short grain rice
1½ oz/40 g white short grain or pudding rice
1 oz/25 g flaked almonds
2 oz/50 g dried dates, chopped
1¼ pints/750 ml fresh skimmed milk
¼ teaspoon/1.25 ml ground cardamom
1 tablespoon/15 ml honey
½ oz/15 g butter

Mix together the rice, almonds and dates and place in a lightly greased 2-pint/1-litre ovenproof dish. Bring the milk, cardamom and honey to the boil, stirring occasionally. Pour into the dish, dot with butter and bake at Mark 5 — 190°C — 375°F for 1 hour until golden. Then cover and cook for a further 20 minutes.

Serves 4

FIESTA RICE SALAD
LEEK AND TOMATO RISOTTO

COOKING PULSES

In hard-water areas beans generally take longer to cook because of naturally present dissolved minerals and salts. Cooking time depends also on the type and size of the beans and their age — the older and more dehydrated the longer they will take to cook. Soaking times vary according to size — split peas need only a couple of hours, and lentils don't need soaking at all. In general though, wash pulses under cold running water, put in a bowl or pan and cover with cold water, then leave to soak for about 8 hours or overnight. Discard water and replace with fresh — hot to speed up cooking time — but don't salt at this stage as it lengthens simmering time and can toughen the beans. Bring slowly to the boil, add an onion stuck with cloves, a carrot and a bouquet garni and simmer 1-2 hours. Salt after cooking.

LAMB PILAF

8 oz/225 g long-grain rice
2 tablespoons/30 ml olive oil
1 onion, peeled and chopped
2 garlic cloves, peeled and crushed
1 red pepper, cored, deseeded and sliced
2 tomatoes, skinned, deseeded, chopped
2 oz/50 g seedless raisins
1 oz/25 g cashew nuts
2 tablespoons/30 ml chopped parsley
½ teaspoon/2.5 ml ground cinnamon
¼ teaspoon/1.25 ml ground ginger
**8 oz/225 g cooked lamb, trimmed of all
    fat and cut into thin strips**

Cook the rice in boiling, salted water for 15 minutes or until tender.

Meanwhile heat the oil in a large frying pan and fry the onion and garlic for about 5 minutes, until softened. Add the pepper, tomatoes, raisins, nuts, parsley and spices and stir well to mix.

Drain the rice and add to the pan together with the lamb. Season with freshly ground black pepper and stir gently until heated through. Serve immediately with yogurt garnished with fresh coriander or parsley. **Serves 4**

MUSHROOM RISOTTO

1 onion, thinly sliced
2 celery sticks, chopped
2 tablespoons/30 ml oil
**12 oz/350 g open cap mushrooms, wiped
    and sliced**
1 lemon, finely grated rind and juice
6 oz/175 g risotto rice
10 fl oz/300 ml chicken stock
4 oz/125 g frozen peas, thawed
3 oz/75 g mature Cheddar cheese
**2 tablespoons/30 ml freshly grated
    Parmesan cheese**
**2 tablespoons/30 ml fresh chopped
    parsley**

Fry the onion and celery in the oil for 3 minutes. Add the mushrooms, lemon rind and juice and cook for a further 10 minutes. Add the rice and cook for 2 minutes, stirring, then add the stock and cook gently, covered, for about 15 minutes until the rice is tender. Stir in the remaining ingredients and heat through gently until the cheese has melted. Serve seasoned with plenty of freshly ground black pepper. **Serves 4**

FOUR-BEAN SALAD

For speed use canned beans drained of liquid and rinsed.

**4 asparagus spears or 1 (8 oz/225 g) can
    asparagus spears, drained**
2 oz/50 g cooked aduki beans
2 oz/50 g cooked pinto beans
2 oz/50 g cooked black-eyed beans
2 oz/50 g cooked flageolet beans
6 oz/175 g cooked ham, diced
Dressing:
4 tablespoons/60 ml olive oil
2 teaspoons/10 ml wine vinegar
2 teaspoons/10 ml chopped fresh mint
pinch of English mustard powder
To garnish: **mint sprigs**

Blanch the fresh asparagus spears in boiling salted water for 1 minute. Drain, rinse in cold water and slice. Combine all the salad ingredients. Mix together the dressing ingredients, season and pour over the salad. Toss to coat, chill. Serve garnished with mint sprigs. **Serves 3**

SPICED MIXED SPROUTS

2 tablespoons/30 ml oil
1 onion, peeled and very finely chopped
2 cloves garlic, peeled and crushed
1 teaspoon/5 ml garam masala
large pinch cumin seeds
½ teaspoon/2.5 ml cayenne pepper
1 tablespoon/15 ml lemon juice
5 fl oz/150 ml tomato juice
8 oz/225 g mixed sprouted beans
    (chick, mung, aduki)
1 oz/25 g flaked almonds, toasted
To serve: soft bread or chapattis

Heat oil in a pan. Add onion and garlic and cook gently for 5 minutes without colouring. Add the garam masala, cumin seeds, cayenne pepper and ground black pepper. Fry for another 4 minutes. Add the lemon juice, tomato juice and sprouted beans. Cook for 5 minutes. Stir in almonds and serve hot with soft bread or chapattis.   ***Serves 3-4***

TROPICAL SPROUTED SALAD

1 tablespoon/15 ml olive oil
3 oz/75 g cashew nuts
1 small pineapple, peeled, cored and
    chopped
1 cooked chicken, skinned, meat removed
    from the bone
6 oz/175 g sprouted chickpeas
6 oz/175 g sprouted mung beans
1 large avocado, peeled, stoned and
    thinly sliced
Dressing:
3 tablespoons/45 ml lemon juice
3 fl oz/90 ml olive oil
pinch of dry mustard
1 teaspoon/5 ml liquid honey
3 tablespoons/45 ml natural yogurt

Heat oil in a pan, add nuts and cook, stirring until browned. Drain on kitchen paper and place in a large bowl. Add pineapple, reserving the juice, and remaining salad ingredients.

Place the lemon juice, oil, mustard, honey and pineapple juice in a small screw-topped jar. Shake until blended. Blend in yogurt and pour over the salad. Toss gently. Serve immediately.   ***Serves 6***

FROM THE LEFT: ALFALFA SEAFOOD COCKTAIL, SUNFLOWER SEED SAMOSAS, TROPICAL SPROUTED SALAD

SUNFLOWER SEED SAMOSAS

2 tablespoons/30 ml olive oil
1 red pepper, cored, deseeded and
    sliced
1 green pepper, cored, deseeded and
    sliced
3 spring onions, sliced
4 oz/125 g sprouted sunflower seeds
2 tablespoons/30 ml fresh chopped mint
12 sheets filo pastry (strudel leaves)
3 oz/75 g polyunsaturated margarine,
    melted
Cucumber Raita:
2-inch/5-cm piece cucumber, grated
8 oz/225 g Greek yogurt
1 teaspoon/5 ml lemon juice
large pinch ground coriander

Heat the oil in a pan. Add peppers and spring onions. Stir-fry for 2 minutes. Season with black pepper and add sunflower sprouts and mint.

Work with one sheet of pastry at a time, keeping the rest under a damp tea towel. Lay a sheet of pastry out. Brush all over with margarine. Fold the top third, lengthways, down over the centre third and the bottom third lengthways up over the centre. Brush the strip with margarine. Place a spoonful of filling in the centre, 1-inch/2.5-cm in from the end of the strip. Fold the same end diagonally over the filling to make a triangle. Continue folding the pastry over the filling to finish with a neat triangle. Brush again with margarine and place the parcel on a greased baking sheet. Repeat process to make 12. Bake at Mark 7 — 220°C — 425°F for 15-20 minutes until golden.

For the raita: squeeze excess liquid from the cucumber and stir into the remaining ingredients. Serve with the hot samosas.   ***Makes 12***

ALFALFA SEAFOOD COCKTAIL

4 oz/125 g peeled prawns
3 oz/75 g cooked mussels
2 tablespoons/30 ml lemon juice
8 fl oz/250 ml low calorie mayonnaise
2 tablespoons/30 ml tomato purée
few drops Tabasco sauce
½ teaspoon/2.5 ml Worcestershire sauce
4 oz/125 g alfalfa sprouts
To garnish: **paprika, prawns, and lemon**
slices

Place the shellfish in a bowl and sprinkle with 1 tablespoon/15 ml lemon juice and freshly ground white pepper. Blend the mayonnaise, purée and sauces. Add the remaining lemon juice. Arrange alfalfa round the edge of four serving plates. Spoon the shellfish in the centre and top with mayonnaise and garnish.   *Serves 4*

LENTIL SPROUT SALAD

6 oz/175 g sprouted lentils
1 bunch watercress, trimmed, chopped
2 oranges, peeled, segmented, all with
pith removed
2 tomatoes, deseeded and diced
¼ head Chinese leaves, shredded
Dressing:
1 tablespoon/15 ml olive oil
1 clove garlic, peeled and crushed
large pinch turmeric
1 teaspoon/5 ml fresh grated root ginger
grated rind and juice of 1 lemon
10 black olives, stoned

Place the lentils, watercress, orange segments, tomatoes and Chinese leaves in a large bowl and mix well. For the dressing heat the oil in a pan and fry the garlic and turmeric for 3 minutes. Add the ginger and lemon rind and juice and simmer for 30 seconds. Pour over the salad with the olives and toss to coat. Serve immediately.   *Serves 4*

STIR-FRY SPROUTS WITH MONKFISH

2 tablespoons/30 ml oil
½-inch/1-cm fresh root ginger, peeled
and grated
3 spring onions, sliced
1¼ lb/575 g monkfish, boned, skinned
and cut into thin strips
3 oz/75 g sprouted aduki beans
2 tablespoons/30 ml dry sherry
2 tablespoons/30 ml light soy sauce
1 tablespoon/15 ml chilli sauce
2 tablespoons/30 ml tomato purée
1 tablespoon/15 ml set honey
1 tablespoon/15 ml walnut oil
To garnish: **spring onion tassels**

Heat the oil in a large pan or wok until very hot. Add the ginger and onions and stir-fry for 1 minute. Add the monkfish and fry for 2 to 3 minutes. Stir in the beansprouts, sherry, soy sauce, chilli sauce, tomato purée, ground black pepper and honey. Continue to stir-fry for 2 minutes. Add the walnut oil and cook for 30 seconds more. Serve immediately, garnished with spring onion tassels.
     Serves 4

CASSOULET

12 oz/350 g belly pork
1 carrot
2 onions
3 or 4 cloves
2 garlic cloves
bouquet garni: 3 sprigs parsley,
small sprig thyme, 1 bay leaf
1 (2-inch/5-cm) piece of orange peel
1 lb/450 g soaked haricot beans
1 oz/25 g lard or goose fat
1½ lb/700 g boned breast or shoulder
of lamb
2 (10-12 oz/300-350 g) portions fresh or
frozen duck
1 lb/450 g Toulouse or garlic boiling
sausage
1 (14 oz/397 g) can tomatoes
2 tablespoons/30 ml tomato purée
5 fl oz/150 ml red wine
4 oz/125 g fresh white breadcrumbs

Stage 1. Cut belly pork into 1-inch/2.5-cm pieces. Peel carrot and one onion and stick with cloves. Lightly crush unpeeled clove of garlic and tie parsley, thyme, bay leaf and orange peel into bouquet. Place ingredients in saucepan with soaked haricot beans. Cover with cold water, bring to the boil. Reduce heat, cover and cook slowly for 1½ hours. Salt when cooked. Strain, reserving liquid, beans, carrot and pork.

Stage 2. Melt lard in flameproof casserole and lightly fry the other peeled and sliced onion for 2 minutes. Add lamb, cut into chunks, duck portions and sliced sausage. Brown evenly, add tomatoes, purée and wine. Bring to the boil, season and simmer for 30 minutes. Drain, reserving liquid.

Stage 3. Wipe inside of an earthenware pot with a cut clove of garlic. Cut duck into pieces, discarding bones, and cut carrot into thick chunks. Place a layer of beans in the pot. Cover with a layer of pork, lamb, duck, sausage and carrot and continue in layers, finishing with a layer of beans. Add casserole stock until liquid has risen just to the surface of the beans. Dust with about three-quarters of the breadcrumbs and cook in a slow oven (Mark 2 — 150°C — 300°F) for at least 2½ hours. Check cassoulet regularly. When crust forms, press in with back of spoon and baste with bean stock. Sprinkle with more of the breadcrumbs, and then return to the oven.   *Serves 6*

Meat, Poultry and Game

It's the British meat and two veg habit that has forced us into a rut in our treatment of meat, and now that we're being told to eat less meat it's no wonder we're worried. No one is insisting that we should give up meat altogether, only that we reduce our intake of red meats — beef, lamb and pork, which are all high in saturated animal fat — and eat more chicken and turkey instead.

● This healthier approach means changing your cooking repertoire slightly: instead of chops with potatoes and peas, you incorporate smaller quantities of meat into recipes with vegetables, pasta, rice and pulses in such dishes as curries, risottos and spaghetti Bolognese. A stir-fry, in which 4-8 oz/125-225 g meat can feed four, is the perfect example of the new approach. Cut wafer-thin, the meat is quickly cooked with plenty of vegetables. It is colourful, crunchy and vitamin-packed; and since you'll be buying less meat, you'll be able to afford to choose the more expensive, leaner cuts.

● Heart-warming roasts and stews needn't be banished altogether, just eaten less often; trim away all visible fat before cooking, and grill or roast on a rack. Try, if possible, to make stews and meat sauces the day before, then chill and remove solidified fat before re-heating — the flavour benefits from standing. You'll also find some game recipes in this chapter as game is generally lower in fat than farmed meat, and although it's expensive, particularly in August at the beginning of the game season, it does drop in price towards February, when the end-of-season birds are older and perfect for gentle cooking methods.

● Sausages are a favourite convenience food, but is the great British banger, often high in rusk and fat and pretty low in taste, all it's supposed to be? Much better to make your own, and then you can add just as much or as little fat as you wish, and you can create endless flavours with different combinations of meat, herbs and spices. Ours were devised by Malvern Hostick, a friend and passionate amateur sausage-maker from Lincolnshire, home of one of our favourite sausages.

SPRING LAMB WITH APPLE AND HERB SAUCE

For extra tenderness and flavour marinate the lamb overnight in 1 tablespoon/15 ml olive oil and 4 tablespoons/60 ml red or white wine. Pat dry lamb and reserve marinade.

4 lb/1.75 kg leg of lamb
3 garlic cloves, peeled and cut into thin slivers
1 tablespoon/15 ml chopped fresh rosemary, or 1 teaspoon/5 ml dried rosemary
1 tablespoon/15 ml olive oil

With a small sharp knife, make slits all over the surface of the lamb and insert slivers of garlic. Mix the rosemary with the olive oil and season with black pepper. Brush all over the lamb. Roast for 20 minutes at Mark 8 — 230°C — 450°F then reduce the heat to Mark 4 — 180°C — 350°F and roast for a further 17 to 20 minutes per lb, depending on how you like your lamb cooked. Baste from time to time with the reserved marinade or roasting juices. Allow to rest in a warm place for 20 to 30 minutes before carving.

Serves 6-8

APPLE AND HERB SAUCE

1½ lb/700 g Bramley apples
2 to 3 sprigs fresh rosemary

Peel, core and slice apples. Place in a saucepan with a tablespoon/15 ml water and rosemary. Cover and stew for 5 to 10 minutes until soft. Add a pinch of sugar to taste, remove rosemary and serve with the lamb.

SPRING LAMB WITH APPLE AND HERB SAUCE

CHICKEN KIEV

Ask your butcher for breast/wing fillets; or if you can't buy them use chicken breasts.

3 oz/75 g unsalted butter, softened
1½ tablespoons/20 ml chopped parsley
2 cloves of garlic, peeled and crushed
squeeze of lemon juice
4 breast/wing chicken fillets, skinned
2 oz/50 g seasoned flour
2 eggs, beaten
4 oz/125 g breadcrumbs
vegetable oil

Beat the butter, parsley, garlic, lemon juice and freshly ground black pepper together until well blended. Shape into a cylinder about ½-inch/1-cm in diameter and cut into four lengths. Wrap and freeze until hard.

Place chicken breasts, boned side uppermost, between cling film and beat with mallet until flat and about ¼-inch/5 mm thick.

Place a roll of butter in the centre and roll up to form a long sausage shape with a tapering end. The edges seal together quite naturally — but make sure that there are no holes for the filling to escape.

Place seasoned flour, beaten eggs and breadcrumbs in three separate dishes. Coat the rolled breasts first in the flour, shaking off the excess, then in beaten egg and breadcrumbs. Recoat with egg and breadcrumbs for an extra crisp coating. Chill for 1 hour for the coating to set.

Heat vegetable oil to 160°C (325°F), gently lower the chicken breasts one at a time into the pan and deep fry for 6 to 7 minutes until golden. Drain on absorbent paper and serve. **Serves 4**

WATCHPOINTS

● Ensure butter is very hard so it doesn't melt too quickly.
● When beating out the chicken, don't break the flesh.
● If deep frying, make sure that the oil is not too hot (use a thermometer) so the coating doesn't burn before the inside is cooked.
● At the table, when cutting into the chicken, beware. The melted butter may squirt at you!

OVEN BAKE

For the health conscious, you can bake Chicken Kiev. For an especially golden finish, mix 1 oz/25 g grated Parmesan cheese in with the breadcrumbs. Bake on a rack over a roasting tin in a hot oven (Mark 6 — 200°C — 400°F) for 25 minutes.

CHICKEN ROMA

Lay 1 slice of cooked ham on each of 4 beaten chicken breasts. Top each with three thin slices Mozzarella cheese. Sprinkle with a pinch of chopped fresh basil or sage and seasoning. Continue as for Chicken Kiev.

CHICKEN MARTINIQUE

Peel and slice 1 small fresh mango or nectarine, lay a few slices on each of 4 beaten chicken breasts. Squeeze juice from ½ lime or lemon, sprinkle over chicken, season. Continue as for Chicken Kiev.

CHICKEN LUCERNE

Mix together 4 oz/125 g defrosted frozen spinach, 1 rounded tablespoon/15 ml Parmesan cheese, 1 tablespoon/15 ml lemon juice, 2 oz/50 g melted butter, pinch of grated nutmeg, seasoning. Place a spoonful of filling on each of 4 beaten chicken breasts and roll up. Continue as for Chicken Kiev.

CHICKEN PARISIENNE

Beat 2 oz/50 g softened butter, 1 peeled and crushed clove of garlic and seasoning until smooth. Chill slightly. Dot 4 beaten chicken breasts with the butter. Divide 1 (12 oz/350 g) can asparagus between the breasts, roll up. Continue as for Chicken Kiev.

CHICKEN KIEV

WINTER BEEF STEW WITH RED CABBAGE

WINTER BEEF STEW

2 lb/900 g lean stewing steak
1 oz/25 g butter
2 tablespoons/30 ml vegetable oil
12 pickling onions, peeled
8 oz/225 g carrots, cut in 1-inch/
     2.5-cm pieces
1 lb/450 g baby turnips, peeled and
     quartered
5 fl oz/150 ml red wine
15 fl oz/450 ml beef stock
1 bouquet garni
12 oz/350 g flat mushrooms, washed and
     sliced

Cut the beef into 1½-inch/3.5-cm cubes. Heat the oil and butter in a flame-proof casserole and fry the beef for 2 to 3 minutes, until browned on all sides. Remove. Add the onions, carrots and turnips and fry for 5 minutes. Add the wine, stock, beef, bouquet garni and seasoning. Bring to the boil. Cook at Mark 3 — 160°C — 325°F for 2 hours. Add the mushrooms and cook, uncovered, for a further 30 minutes. Serve with red cabbage.   **Serves 4**

CARBONADE OF BEEF

2 lb/900 g braising or chuck steak
1 oz/25 g lard
2 onions, peeled and sliced
1 garlic clove, peeled and crushed
4 oz/125 g streaky bacon, derinded and
     sliced into ½-inch/1-cm pieces
2 tablespoons/30 ml flour
15 fl oz/450 ml pale ale
1 teaspoon/5 ml sugar
bay leaf
1 tablespoon/15 ml red wine vinegar

Trim meat and cut into 1-inch/2.5-cm cubes. Melt lard in a flameproof casserole and fry meat a little at a time until browned, set aside. Gently fry onion, garlic and bacon for about 10 minutes until beginning to brown, then stir in flour and cook for 2 minutes. Gradually add beer, stirring constantly to make a smooth sauce. Bring to boil and add meat, sugar, bay leaf, vinegar and seasoning. Cover and cook in a slow oven (Mark 2 — 150°C — 300°F) for 2 hours. Serve the carbonade with fresh noodles and salad.
Serves 6

GIGOT D'AGNEAU A LA BOULANGERE

1 leg of lamb (about 3 lb/1.4 kg)
3 lb/1.4 kg potatoes, peeled, thinly sliced
2 onions, peeled and thinly sliced
5 fl oz/150 ml chicken stock
2 garlic cloves, peeled and cut into slivers
sprig of rosemary

Preheat oven, weigh meat and calculate cooking time (see charts, page 55). Wipe with damp kitchen paper. Layer potatoes, onions and seasoning in roasting tin, ending with layer of overlapping potatoes. Pour over stock, make slits in skin of meat and insert slivers of garlic and the rosemary. Place meat on potatoes and sprinkle over salt. Roast for calculated time. If potatoes become dry, top up with a little stock — by the end of cooking time potatoes should have absorbed it all.   **Serves 6**

LEMON ROAST PORK

4 lb/1.8 kg loin of pork, boned and rolled
1 teaspoon/5 ml salt
grated rind of 2 lemons
sprig of fresh sage, chopped
To garnish: fresh sage, lemon slices

With a sharp knife, score rind at ¼-inch/ 5-mm intervals without cutting the flesh. Rub in salt, lemon rind and sage and roast

at Mark 7 — 220°C — 425°F for 20 minutes. Reduce oven temperature to Mark 4 — 180°C — 350°F and cook for a further 2 to 2½ hours. To make sure the pork is thoroughly cooked, pierce meat with a skewer — the juices should run clear. Allow to rest in a warm place for 15 to 20 minutes before carving. Garnish.
Serves 8-10

LOIN OF PORK WITH APRICOT AND APPLE STUFFING

3 oz/75 g dried apricots
loin of pork (about 3 lb/1.4 kg), boned
1 small eating apple
1 small onion, peeled and finely chopped
1 stick celery, finely chopped
1 oz/25 g fresh breadcrumbs
1 oz/25 g butter, melted

Soak apricots overnight in cold water. Drain and chop. Heat oven to moderate (Mark 4 — 180°C — 350°F). Weigh meat and calculate cooking time (see roasting chart, page 55). Wipe meat with damp kitchen paper. Score the skin. Peel, core and finely chop apple and mix with apricots, onion, celery, breadcrumbs and butter. Spread stuffing over meat, roll up and tie securely with string. Rub salt over skin. Place in a roasting tin and roast for calculated time. Transfer to a warmed carving dish.   **Serves 4-6**

LAMB AND LEEK STIR-FRY

Here's a good way of making a tender cut of lamb go further.

8 oz/225 g lamb leg steak, cut into thin strips
2 tablespoons/30 ml light soy sauce
1 tablespoon/15 ml dry sherry
2 teaspoons/10 ml wine vinegar
½ teaspoon/2.5 ml freshly ground black pepper
2 tablespoons/30 ml vegetable oil
1 clove of garlic, peeled and crushed
2 carrots, sliced
8 oz/225 g leeks, trimmed and sliced diagonally
1 small green pepper, cored and deseeded and cut into matchsticks

Place the lamb in a shallow dish. Combine the soy sauce, sherry, vinegar and black pepper and pour over the lamb. Leave to marinate for 30 minutes.

Drain the lamb, reserving marinade, and heat a wok or large frying pan. Add the oil and heat through. Fry the garlic for 10 seconds, then add the lamb and stir-fry for 1 minute until browned. Remove.

Add the carrots and marinade and stir-fry for 1 minute, add remaining vegetables and cook for 2 minutes. Return lamb, toss together for 30 seconds.

Serves 2-3

CITRUS ROAST DUCK

1 5 lb/2.3 kg duck
1 lime, halved
2 tablespoons/30 ml brandy or Grand Marnier
1 orange
***To garnish:* orange and lime rind and slices, watercress sprigs**

Prick duck all over with a fork. Place one half of lime inside the duck. Roast the duck on a wire rack over a roasting tin at Mark 4 — 180°C — 350°F for 20 minutes per lb plus 20 minutes. Remove duck and leave to rest in a warm place for 20 minutes. To make gravy, pour away all but 1 tablespoon/15 ml of the fat from the roasting tin and scrape juices into a saucepan. Pour brandy into tin to remove any deposits. Add to saucepan with squeezed lime and orange juices. Simmer for 5 minutes. Serve gravy separately. Garnish duck and serve. **Serves 4**

LEMON CHICKEN WITH MIXED PEPPERS

Tender pieces of chicken, cooked with aromatic vegetables and the fresh taste of lemon.

4 chicken breasts, skinned and boned
juice of 1 lemon
few sprigs fresh thyme
2 tablespoons/30 ml white wine
½ each red, green and yellow pepper, cored and deseeded
8 oz/225 g button mushrooms, sliced
***To garnish:* lemon slices**

Cut the chicken into 4-inch/10-cm by 1-inch/2.5-cm strips. Mix together the lemon juice, thyme, wine and seasoning. Add the chicken and marinate for 1 hour. Cut the peppers into small diamonds. Arrange the peppers, chicken and a few sprigs of thyme on a dish and steam for 5 minutes. Add the mushrooms and gently steam for a further 4 minutes.

Garnish with lemon slices and serve hot with rice. **Serves 4**

LEMON CHICKEN WITH MIXED PEPPERS

FROM THE LEFT: PIGEON PIE, PHEASANT WITH APPLES, GAME PÂTÉ, BLANQUETTE OF RABBIT, VENISON STEAKS WITH CRANBERRY SAUCE, GUINEA FOWL WITH SWEET PEPPERS, HARE ITALIENNE

HARE ITALIENNE

1 hare, about 1¼ lb/575 g
1 oz/25 g butter
1 tablespoon/15 ml olive oil
1 garlic clove, peeled and crushed
2 rashers back bacon, rinds removed, chopped
1 stick of celery, chopped
1 small carrot, chopped
1 small onion, chopped
1 (14 oz/397 g) can tomatoes, sieved
4 oz/125 g mushrooms
5 fl oz/150 ml red wine
sprig of fresh basil

Remove the meat from the front and back legs of the hare and finely chop. Reserve the saddle for roasting. Heat the butter and oil in a saucepan. Add the garlic, bacon, celery, carrot and onion. Fry gently for 5 minutes until softened. Add the hare and stir until sealed on all sides. Add remaining ingredients, partially cover and simmer gently for 1 hour. If necessary, uncover the pan 10 minutes before the end of the cooking time to reduce the sauce. Serve with fresh tagliatelle and sprinkle over grated Parmesan cheese. **Serves 4**

VENISON STEAKS WITH CRANBERRY SAUCE

5 fl oz/150 ml red wine
2 tablespoons/30 ml port
6 juniper berries, crushed
2 tablespoons/30 ml vegetable oil
freshly ground black pepper
6 venison steaks
2 oz/50 g butter
4 oz/125 g fresh or frozen cranberries
5 fl oz/150 ml half fat cream

Mix together wine, port, juniper berries and oil for the marinade. Season with black pepper. Pour over the venison, cover and leave overnight in the fridge. Remove and pat dry. Reserve the marinade. Melt the butter in a large frying pan until foaming and quickly seal the steaks until browned on both sides. Lower the heat slightly and cook for 3 minutes each side. Remove and keep warm. Add the marinade and cranberries to the pan and simmer rapidly until the cranberries have softened. Sieve. Return to the pan. Season, add the cream and heat gently without boiling. Serve with the steaks. **Serves 6**

PHEASANT WITH APPLES

1 cooking apple, peeled and cored
2 hen pheasants
pork fat or 6 rashers streaky bacon, rinded
few sprigs of thyme
1 onion
2 tablespoons/30 ml Calvados (apple brandy) or brandy
1½ oz/40 g unsalted butter
4 eating apples, peeled and cored
5 fl oz/150 ml single cream

Place ½ cooking apple inside each pheasant. Cover birds with a thin layer of pork fat or bacon rashers and secure with string. Place pheasant on a rack in a roasting tin and pour a little boiling water into the tin. Add a few sprigs of thyme and an unpeeled and halved onion to the water. Cover the whole tin with foil and bake at Mark 3 — 160°C — 325°F for 30 minutes. Remove the foil and fat. Increase the oven temperature to Mark 5 — 190°C — 375°F for 35 minutes to brown the breast. Remove birds and keep warm. Spoon off fat from roasting juices, add Calvados to deglaze.

Melt the butter in a frying pan, add the apples and sauté gently for 5 to 10 minutes until softened. Add the roasting juices and the Calvados. Stir in the cream and warm gently. Pour over pheasant and serve immediately. **Serves 4**

BLANQUETTE OF RABBIT

1 rabbit, jointed
thinly pared rind of ½ lemon
1 tablespoon/15 ml lemon juice
pinch of mace
1 sprig of thyme
few sprigs of parsley
2 oz/50 g butter
8 oz/225 g pickling onions, peeled
4 oz/125 g button mushrooms
1 tablespoon/15 ml flour
2 egg yolks
To garnish: fresh chopped parsley

Put the rabbit joints into a large saucepan and just cover with cold water. Add the lemon rind and juice, mace, thyme, parsley and seasoning. Bring to the boil, remove any scum. Reduce the heat, cover and simmer gently for 15 minutes.

Melt half the butter in a small pan. Sauté the onions for about 5 minutes until golden, remove and set aside. Add the mushrooms and cook for 2 to 3 minutes. Add the onions and mushrooms to the rabbit and simmer for 5 minutes. Strain the cooking liquid and reserve. Keep the rabbit and vegetables warm.

Melt the remaining butter in a saucepan until foaming. Add the flour and cook, stirring for 2 minutes. Do not brown. Add a little of the cooking liquid and whisk well to blend. Add about 15 fl oz/450 ml of the remaining liquid and cook, stirring, for 10 minutes. Remove from the heat and stir in the egg yolks. Stir over a very low heat for 1 minute. Add the rabbit and vegetables and cook very gently until heated through. Garnish and serve with boiled rice. **Serves 4**

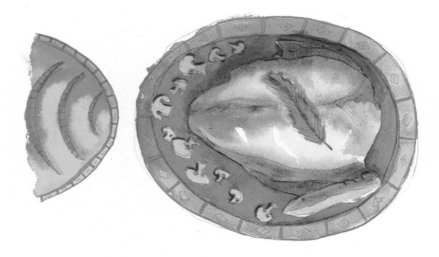

GAME PATE

5 fl oz/150 ml red wine
1 bouquet garni
10 black peppercorns
1 carrot, sliced
1 celery stalk, sliced
12 oz/350 g casserole venison
1 lb/450 g belly pork
8 oz/225 g pig's liver
1 onion, roughly chopped
1 garlic clove, peeled and chopped
4 oz/125 g mushrooms, chopped
1 teaspoon/5 ml fresh thyme
6 juniper berries, crushed
pinch of ground cloves
2 tablespoons/30 ml brandy (optional)
pork back fat

Mix together wine, bouquet garni, peppercorns, carrot and celery for the marinade. Roughly chop the venison and put into a shallow non-metallic dish. Pour over the marinade. Cover and leave to marinate in the fridge for 24 hours.

Drain and mince coarsely with remaining ingredients except pork fat. Season. Line a 2-pint/1.25-litre terrine dish with pork back fat. Spoon in the mixture. Press down firmly and cover the top with another layer of fat. Cover with foil and cook, in a roasting tin half-filled with boiling water, at Mark 3 — 160°C — 325°F for 2 hours. Cover with a board and weight. Chill overnight.

Makes a 2 lb/1 kg pâté

GUINEA FOWL WITH SWEET PEPPERS

2 tablespoons/30 ml olive oil
2 garlic cloves, peeled and crushed
1 guinea fowl
1 large onion, chopped
1 red, 1 green, 1 yellow pepper, cored, deseeded and roughly chopped
1 lb/450 g courgettes, cut into ½-inch/ 1-cm pieces
2 (14 oz/397 g) cans tomatoes, sieved
1 teaspoon/5 ml dried oregano

Heat the oil in a large casserole dish and gently fry the garlic for 2 minutes without browning. Add the guinea fowl and brown on all sides. Remove. Add the onion, peppers and courgettes and fry gently for 2 to 3 minutes. Add the

tomatoes, herbs and seasoning and the guinea fowl. Cover and bake at Mark 2 — 150°C — 300°F for 45 minutes. Remove the lid and cook for a further 30 minutes. Transfer the guinea fowl to a warmed serving platter. Skim off excess fat from the sauce and pour over the bird. Serve with boiled rice or potatoes. **Serves 4**

LAMB VENISON-STYLE

4-5 lb/1.8-2.25 kg leg of lamb
½ oz/15 g salt
For marinade:
2 onions, peeled and sliced
2 carrots, sliced
3 tablespoons/45 ml olive oil
10 fl oz/300 ml red wine vinegar
sprig of parsley
4 sprigs of thyme
bay leaf
2 sprigs of sage
10 peppercorns, crushed
2 sprigs of rosemary
4 garlic cloves, peeled and sliced
12 juniper berries, bruised
2½ pints/1.5 litres red wine
For sauce:
7 fl oz/200 ml double cream
2 tablespoons/30 ml redcurrant jelly

Remove any loose skin from the lamb, pierce meat with a larding needle or sharp knife in about 20 places. Rub all over with salt. Place in a deep non-metallic dish. Fry onions and carrots in 2 tablespoons/30 ml olive oil for 2 minutes until soft. Add remaining marinade ingredients and bring to the boil. Simmer for 5 minutes. Allow to cool. Pour marinade over lamb. Cover and leave for 2 to 3 days, turning lamb every morning and evening and basting occasionally. Remove lamb from marinade and dry. Strain marinade and set liquid aside. Place lamb in a roasting pan. Rub meat all over with remaining olive oil and then sear in a very hot oven (Mark 8 — 230°C — 450°F) for 20 minutes. Reduce heat to Mark 4 — 180°C — 350°F and cook joint for 20 minutes per pound/450 g, basting with heated reserved liquid until all marinade is used and turning joint occasionally. Remove joint from pan, place on a warm serving plate and leave to rest in a warm place for 20 minutes. For sauce, deglaze roasting pan by scraping the solidified cooking juices off the bottom

of the pan and stirring with the rest of the cooking liquid, bring to the boil. Continue boiling until reduced by half, add double cream and redcurrant jelly. Heat gently, strain and pour into sauce boat. Carve the meat and serve with the sauce.

Serves 6-8

PIGEON PIE

5 fl oz/150 ml red wine
2 tablespoons/30 ml port
6 juniper berries, crushed
2 tablespoons/30 ml vegetable oil
4 pigeons
1 oz/25 g butter
1 tablespoon/15 ml vegetable oil
1 onion, finely chopped
4 rashers streaky bacon, rinds removed, chopped
12 oz/350 g chuck steak, trimmed and cut into 1-inch/2.5-cm cubes
6 oz/175 g flat mushrooms, thickly sliced
few sprigs of parsley, chopped
½ teaspoon/2.5 ml dried thyme
12 oz/350 g shortcrust pastry

Mix together wine, port, juniper berries and oil for the marinade and season with freshly ground black pepper. Remove breasts from the pigeons and cut into large pieces. Put into a non-metallic dish, pour over the marinade, cover. Leave in fridge overnight.

Melt the butter and oil in a frying pan, add the onion and bacon and fry gently for 5 minutes. Remove with a slotted spoon, reserve.

Remove pigeon from the marinade, drain. Reserve marinade. Increase heat and fry the pigeon and the steak in batches, sealing on all sides.

Put the pigeon, steak, onion and bacon into a 2-pint/1.25-litre pie dish and top with the mushrooms. Sprinkle with herbs, pour over the reserved marinade.

Roll out the pastry to ¼-inch/5-mm thick, put a pie funnel into the dish. Cut a ½-inch/1-cm strip of pastry and place around the edge of the dish. Brush with water and top with the remaining pastry. Use the pastry trimmings to decorate the top of the pie. Bake at Mark 4 — 180°C — 350°F for 20 minutes, then reduce the heat to Mark 2 — 150°C — 300°F and cook for a further 1½ hours. Cover the pastry with foil if it browns too much during cooking.

Serves 5-6

MAKING SAUSAGES

To make your own sausages, you will need a hand mincer or food mixer with a sausage attachment. You also need to buy pig's or sheep's sausage casings, available from good butchers or by mail order from Gysin & Hanson, 96 Trundleys Road, London SE8 5JG. One yard of casing will make about 1 lb/450 g sausages. Casings freeze well. For pork sausages use shoulder or the hand and spring, for beef, stewing steak and for lamb, shoulder.

Method: Cut the meat into chunks, reserve a quarter and mince the rest. Put the minced meat into a bowl. Handflake the bread and add to the minced meat with the reserved meat and remaining ingredients. To test for seasoning, fry a spoonful of the mixture and season to taste. Sausages mellow during hanging so err on the over-spiced side. To prepare the casings, plunge into a large bowl of cold water to wash away the salt. Slip one end of the casing over a clean tap and run cold water through to rinse the inside. Gather the casing over the sausage attachment and tie a knot in the loose end. Force the mixture into the skin and, when filled, knot the end. Plait the sausage length into twos or threes. Hang in a cold dry place for 3 to 4 days.

Do not prick sausages before cooking as this releases their juices and makes the meat dry and tough.

BEEF, MUSHROOM AND HORSERADISH SAUSAGE

5 lb/2.25 kg minced stewing steak
1 lb/450 g bread
3 teaspoons/15 ml salt (or to taste)
4 teaspoons/20 ml ground black pepper
1 dessertspoon/10 ml fresh horseradish
8 oz/225 g mushrooms

Wash the mushrooms and cut into pieces no larger than a 1-inch/2.5-cm cube. Add to the other prepared ingredients. The mushrooms ensure that the result is splendidly succulent. ***Makes 6½ lb/2.9 kg***

LIVER SAUSAGE

5 lb/2.25 kg pork
1 lb/450 g bread
2 lb/900 g (at least) pig's or lamb's liver
4 teaspoons/20 ml salt
2 onions, finely chopped
4 teaspoons/20 ml ground white pepper
1 teaspoon/5 ml mace
1 teaspoon/5 ml marjoram or sage
1 pint/600 ml orange juice

A richly flavoured sausage. The orange juice sweetens the mixture and lightens the taste of the liver. The pork should be half lean, half fat, as the liver, which must be finely chopped, tends to harden as it cooks. ***Makes 8 lb/3.6 kg***

LAMB AND CUMIN SAUSAGE

5 lb/2.25 kg minced lamb, two-thirds lean, one-third fat
1 lb/450 g bread
4 teaspoons/20 ml salt
5 teaspoons/25 ml ground cumin
2 teaspoons/10 ml dried parsley or 3 sprigs finely chopped fresh parsley
3 teaspoons/15 ml ground black pepper
a squeeze of lemon

The flavours of cumin and parsley make a perfect foil to the subtle taste of lamb. ***Makes 6 lb/2.7 kg***

BEEF AND WINE SAUSAGE

5 lb/2.25 kg minced stewing steak
1 lb/450 g bread
3 oz/75 g tomato purée
1½ glasses of full bodied red wine (Rioja is especially good)
3 teaspoons/15 ml salt
2 teaspoons/10 ml ground black pepper
2 teaspoons/10 ml paprika
1 teaspoon/5 ml mace or cinnamon

Like all strong-tasting sausages this one is a favourite at parties and barbecues. The wine will make the sausage meat rather wet, so remember to allow more time for hanging in a cool dry place. ***Makes 6½ lb/2.9 kg***

RINSING SALTED SAUSAGE CASINGS IN COLD WATER

of lemon to most recipes is very pleasing, giving the sausage a slight tang and lightening the taste. It may also act as a natural preservative.

My grandfather's Lincolnshire sausage mix was 2 lb/900 g lean pork, 1¾ lb/800 g of fat and 1¾ lb/800 g breadcrumbs. I use less bread than he did but obviously the more bulking agent there is, the cheaper the sausage. **Makes 6 lb/2.7 kg**

ONION SAUSAGE

5 lb/2.25 kg pork
1 lb/450 g bread
1½ lb/700 g onions, finely chopped
3 teaspoons/15 ml salt
2 teaspoons/10 ml ground black pepper
1 teaspoon/5 ml dried marjoram
½ teaspoon/2.5 ml mace
a squeeze of lemon

This is perhaps the most succulent sausage you can make. As it cooks, moisture is released from the onions. If the sausage is not overcooked, it reaches the plate in a highly juicy condition.
Makes 7½ lb/3.3 kg

LINCOLNSHIRE SAUSAGE

5 lb/2.25 kg pork
1 lb/450 g bread
2 heaped teaspoons/10 ml dried sage
3 teaspoons/15 ml salt (or to taste)
4 teaspoons/20 ml ground white pepper
juice of ½ lemon

This is undisputedly the king of English sausage. Fresh dried sage is far preferable to the packaged variety. It has a much sweeter taste. A useful policy is to raid friends' herb gardens. The addition

CUMBERLAND SAUSAGE

5 lb/2.25 kg pork (preferably chopped, not minced)
3 teaspoons/15 ml salt (or to taste)
3 teaspoons/15 ml ground white pepper
1 teaspoon/5 ml cayenne pepper
1 teaspoon/5 ml mace

The Cumberland is a meal in itself. Traditionally it was sold unlinked though I find a linked sausage more convenient.
Makes 5 lb/2.25 kg

GARLIC SAUSAGE

5 lb/2.25 kg pork
1 lb/450 g bread
3 medium garlic cloves (or more if preferred), finely chopped
3 teaspoons/15 ml salt
4-5 teaspoons/20-25 ml ground black pepper
2 sprigs of finely chopped fresh mint

A great attraction at parties. The mint takes the somewhat cloying edge off a large amount of garlic. **Makes 6 lb/2.7 kg**

CUMBERLAND, LIVER, AND BEEF AND RED WINE SAUSAGES

CHICKEN AND BROCCOLI PASTRY

8 oz/225 g broccoli, broken into small
    florets
½ bunch spring onions, trimmed and
    chopped
4 oz/125 g cooked chicken, roughly
    chopped
1 (14 oz/397 g) can baby sweetcorn,
    thickly sliced
grated rind of ½ lemon
12 oz/350 g filo pastry (about 10 sheets)
2 oz/50 g polyunsaturated margarine,
    melted
2 oz/50 g flaked almonds

Blanch the broccoli and onions in boiling
water for 1 minute. Plunge into cold water
and drain well. Mix with the chicken,
baby sweetcorn and lemon rind. Take 10
sheets filo pastry and fold in half to form
a book, brush pastry with melted
margarine, unfolding the "leaves" until
both sides of the pastry are coated.

Spoon the filling along one edge about
2-inches/5-cm in and leaving 2-inches/5-
cm of pastry at either end. Fold the ends
over the filling and carefully roll up so
that the seam is underneath. Brush with
remaining margarine and sprinkle with
flaked almonds. Transfer to a baking
sheet and cook at Mark 6 — 200°C —
400°F for 20-25 minutes until golden
brown. Allow to rest for 5 minutes. Serve
in slices. **Serves 4-6**

BARBECUED PORK

2 tablespoons/30 ml clear honey
2 tablespoons/30 ml hoisin sauce
2 teaspoons/10 ml tomato purée
½-inch/1-cm piece fresh root ginger,
    peeled and shredded
1 small pork fillet, trimmed of fat
6 oz/175 g brown rice
1 red and 1 yellow pepper, sliced
4 oz/125 g broad beans, shelled
2 oz/50 g hazelnuts, toasted and halved

Mix the honey, hoisin sauce and tomato
purée together until smooth. Stir in the
root ginger. Put pork in a shallow non-
metallic dish and pour over the
marinade. Cover and leave for 2-3 hours,
turning occasionally. Remove from the
marinade, place on a rack in a roasting

tin and cook at Mark 6 — 200°C — 400°F for 20 minutes, basting with the reserved marinade.

Meanwhile, cook the rice in boiling water for 25-30 minutes. Stir-fry the peppers in a little oil for 10 minutes and add broad beans. Cook for 2 minutes. Drain rice, stir in vegetables and nuts. Thinly slice the pork and arrange on top of the rice. **Serves 4**

CABBAGE PARCELS WITH TOMATO SAUCE

For the sauce:
1 tablespoon/15 ml oil
1 medium onion, finely chopped
1 (14 oz/397g) can tomatoes, sieved
½ teaspoon/2.5 ml dried oregano or marjoram
Cabbage parcels:
8 large green cabbage leaves
1 tablespoon/15 ml oil
2 sticks celery, finely chopped
1 carrot, finely chopped
4 oz/125 g pork steak, finely chopped
2 oz/50 g button mushrooms, wiped and sliced
4 oz/125 g cooked brown rice
grated rind of 1 lemon
2 teaspoons/10 ml soy sauce
5 fl oz/150 ml chicken stock

To make the sauce, heat the oil and fry the onion over a low heat until transparent and softened, about 10-15 minutes, stirring occasionally. Add the tomatoes and herbs and simmer gently, for 20-25 minutes, until reduced and thickened. Season with freshly ground black pepper.

For the cabbage parcels, blanch the leaves in boiling water for 2 minutes. Plunge into cold water and drain. Cut away the thick stalk. Heat the oil in a small pan and fry the celery, carrot and pork for 1 minute. Add the mushrooms and cook gently for 2 minutes. Stir in the rice, lemon rind and soy sauce. Remove from the heat. Put a heaped tablespoon of the filling in the centre of each leaf. Fold over the base, then each side and roll up tightly. Pack the parcels in an ovenproof dish so that they can't move around. Pour over the stock, cover and bake at Mark 4 — 180°C — 350°F for 30 minutes. Meanwhile heat through the tomato sauce and serve hot with parcels.

Serves 4

CLOCKWISE FROM THE LEFT: CHICKEN AND BROCCOLI PASTRY, CRISPY DUCK SALAD, CABBAGE PARCELS, BEEF AND VEGETABLE STIR-FRY, BARBECUED PORK

BEEF AND VEGETABLE STIR-FRY

4 oz/125 g rump steak, trimmed
1 tablespoon/15 ml soy sauce
1 tablespoon/15 ml sherry
2 tablespoons/30 ml vegetable oil
1 clove garlic, peeled and bruised
½-inch/1-cm piece fresh root ginger, peeled and shredded
2 carrots, cut into thin sticks
2 small onions, quartered
8 oz/225 g courgettes, cut into sticks
8 oz/225 g bean sprouts

Freeze the steak until firm but not solid. Cut across the grain into paper thin slices. Mix the soy sauce and sherry and add beef. Marinate for 30 minutes. Heat the oil in a wok or large frying pan until almost smoking and add the garlic and ginger. Stir-fry for 1 minute. Add the carrots and cook for 2 minutes, followed by the onions and courgettes — stir-fry for 2 minutes. Add the bean sprouts and toss well for 1 minute. Transfer to a hot serving dish. Remove the beef from the marinade and cook for 30 seconds. Add the marinade, toss well, spoon beef over vegetables. **Serves 2**

CRISPY DUCK SALAD

1 duck breast, boned
2 oranges
4 oz/125 g mange-tout, topped and tailed
juice of 1 orange
1 teaspoon/5 ml lemon juice
1 teaspoon/5 ml wholegrain mustard
3 tablespoons/45 ml olive oil
1 small head Chinese leaves, sliced
10 radishes, trimmed and quartered

Prick the duck skin thoroughly and roast on a rack in a roasting tin at Mark 6 — 200°C — 400°F for 20 minutes, until golden brown. Allow to cool. Remove the skin and crisp under a grill. Slice skin and duck breast.

Cut peel and bitter white pith from oranges and segment over a bowl to catch any juice. Blanch the mange-tout in

ORCHARD PORK

boiling water for 1 minute, drain and plunge into cold water. For the dressing, blend orange and lemon juices and any reserved orange juice, mustard and oil and season with freshly ground black pepper.

Arrange all the salad ingredients in a bowl, top with the duck meat, pour over the dressing and toss well. Sprinkle over the crispy duck skin and serve immediately. **Serves 4**

ORCHARD PORK

3 Cox's apples
1 lb/450 g pears
lemon juice
2 lb/900 g spare-rib pork chops, trimmed of fat
1 oz/25g butter
2 tablespoons/30 ml vegetable oil
1 onion, peeled and sliced
2 tablespoons/30 ml quince or redcurrant jelly
10 fl oz/300 ml chicken stock
10 fl oz/300 ml cider
1 bay leaf

Peel, core and thickly slice apples and pears. Toss in lemon juice. Cut the pork into 3-inch/7.5-cm pieces. Heat butter and oil in a flame-proof casserole and fry the pork for 5 minutes until golden brown. Remove and fry the onion until soft. Return pork to pan along with the quince jelly, chicken stock, cider and bay leaf. Bring to the boil, cover and simmer for 45 minutes. Add the apples and pears and cook for 30 minutes.

Strain off the liquid and reduce to half by rapid boiling. Pour over meat. Garnish with fresh bay leaf. **Serves 4-6**

CHICKEN WITH FORTY CLOVES OF GARLIC

This dish is not as fiery as it sounds. The garlic mellows, giving the meat a delicious sweet succulence.

2 tablespoons/30 ml olive oil
1 oz/25 g butter
3 lb/1.4 kg chicken, quartered
40 garlic cloves, unpeeled
1 bouquet garni
sprig of thyme
1 bay leaf
To garnish: 1 teaspoon/5 ml fresh chopped parsley, croûtons of fried bread

Place the oil and butter in a flameproof casserole. Heat gently and fry the chicken pieces until golden. Add the garlic, bouquet garni, thyme and bay leaf. Reduce the heat to very low. Cover tightly and cook for 45 minutes. Remove the bouquet garni and herbs and place the chicken, garlic and juices on a hot serving platter. Sprinkle with chopped parsley. The cooked garlic becomes very soft. Squeeze the garlic from its skin and spread on the croûtons to eat. **Serves 4**

ROASTING TIMES*

POULTRY

BIRD	QUICK ROASTING	SLOW ROASTING
Chicken	Mark 7, 220°C, 425°F for 15 mins per lb + 20 mins	Mark 3, 160°C, 325°F for 25 mins per lb + 25 mins
Turkey (under 12 lb)*	Mark 6, 200°C 400°F for 12 mins per lb + 20 mins	Mark 3, 160°C 325°F for 25 mins per lb
Turkey (over 12 lb)	not recommended.	Mark 3, 160°C 325°F for 22 mins per lb
Duck	Mark 4, 180°C, 350°F for 20 mins per lb + 20 mins	not recommended

* for specially prepared roasts follow manufacturer's instructions on packet

MICROWAVE TIMES
600 watt output at full power/high

	MICRO-WAVE	STANDING TIME
Chicken (whole roast)	6-8 mins per lb	15-30 mins
Duck (whole roast)	8-9 mins per lb	15 mins

To stand: wrap tightly in foil.
To brown: birds under 3 lb, flash under grill.
Place large joints in hot oven for about 10 mins.

BACON COOKING TIMES

Cooking Times	Oven Temperature
Joints up to 10 lb, 20-25 mins per lb + 20 mins*	Mark 4, 180°C, 350°F
Joints over 10 lb, 15-20 mins per lb + 15 mins	Mark 7, 220°C, 425°F

BRAISE at low temperature.
For last 30 mins, strip off skin, cook at high temperature.

Bacon Cookery Times continued
BAKE wrapped in foil at low temperature. For last 30 minutes, remove foil, strip off skin, glaze and cook at high temperature.

ROAST at low temperature. For last 15 mins, strip off skin, glaze, cook at high temperature.

* Whether braising, baking or roasting, calculate total cooking time. Place joint in fresh cold water, bring to the boil, simmer for first half of cooking time. For second half of cooking time cook in oven as above.

MICROWAVE TIMES
600 watt output at full power/high

Cook prime joints, like collar, for 7½ mins per lb. and then stand for 10-15 mins.

To stand: wrap tightly in foil.
To brown: place in hot oven for about 10 mins.

BEEF

	HIGH HEAT Mark 5, 190°C, 375°F	LOW HEAT Mark 3, 160°C, 325°F
Rare	15 mins per lb	—
Medium	20 mins per lb	30 mins per lb
Well done	25 mins per lb	35 mins per lb

For both methods: sear at Mark 8, 230°C, 450°F, for first 15 minutes, then roast for required time

MICROWAVE TIMES
600 watt output at full power/high

	Topside or sirloin joint	Boned or rolled rib
Rare	5 mins per lb	6 mins per lb
Medium	6-7 mins per lb	7-8 mins per lb
Well done	8-10 mins per lb	8-10 mins per lb
Standing times	15-20 mins	15-30 mins

To stand: wrap tightly in foil.
To brown: joints under 3 lb flash under grill.
Place large joints in hot oven for about 10 minutes.

PORK

Roast in a hot oven
(Mark 6 — 200°C — 400°F), 30 minutes per lb

MICROWAVE TIMES
600 watt output at full power/high

	Fillet end of leg or knuckle	Loin
Cooking time	10 mins per lb	10-13 mins per lb
Standing time	20 mins	20-25 mins

To stand: wrap tightly in foil.
To brown: joints under 3 lb, flash under grill.
Place larger joints in hot oven for about 10 minutes.

LAMB

Rare	Mark 5 190°C, 375°F
	15-17 mins per lb
Medium	20 mins per lb
Well done	25 mins per lb

For both methods: sear at Mark 8, 230°C, 450°F, for first 15 minutes, then roast for required time

After roasting, rest joint for 20 mins in a warm place to further tenderise the meat, help retain juices and make carving easier.

MICROWAVE TIMES
600 watt output at full power/high

	MICRO-WAVE	STANDING TIME
Medium	7 mins per lb	25-30 mins
Well done	8 mins per lb	30 mins
Stuffed rolled breast	12 mins per lb	30 mins

To stand: wrap tightly in foil.
To brown: joints under 3 lb, flash under hot grill.
Place larger joints in hot oven for about 10 minutes.

*450g = 1lb

Fish and Shellfish

Fish is the ultimate healthy convenience food. It's quick and easy to cook, low in fat and calories but packed with vitamins and minerals — and speed and simplicity in cooking are the keys to success. If you can't cope with skinning and filleting, your fishmonger will take over, but you must always buy the very freshest fish you can find: look for bright eyes, red gills and firm flesh. It should smell of the sea and not in the least fishy.

● Fish can be steamed, poached, baked, pan-fried, or tossed in a protective coat of seasoned flour, breadcrumbs or batter and deep-fried to golden crispness. However you cook it, keep it brief. Cook your fish just till the flesh becomes opaque and starts to come away from the bone — any longer and the flesh will become dry and tasteless. Once cooked, you can serve it in perfect simplicity, with just a squeeze of lemon or a pat of savoury butter for those cooked without fat.

● We shouldn't forget that our smoked fish, particularly kippers, have gained us a great reputation abroad. Do insist on the highest standards at home too and buy naturally-smoked fish, checking ingredients' labels to avoid artificial flavours or colours such as Brown FK or Tartrazine.

● Fish and shellfish mixtures can be assembled into spectacular fish soups and stews, readily accepting aromatic flavours such as tomato, herbs and sweet spices (see page 66) but, while many fish are seasonal, shellfish are more so. September to April are the shellfish months, with crab and lobster around from April (or May for crab) until October. Shop carefully: shellfish should feel heavy for their size and crab and lobster should be freshly boiled. Lobsters sold alive from tanks are often in poor condition; frozen crab tends to be watery and tasteless, and crabsticks, which are white fish mixed with a little crabmeat, dyed and flavoured, are a poor substitute. Better to look, in the winter months, for mussels, which are cheap and sold by the huge bagful, often now ready-cleaned to save you the job of scraping the shells and pulling away their fibrous beards.

BUYING MUSSELS

Buy mussels from a good fishmonger and make sure shells are black, shiny and closed. Buy more than the recipe requires to be sure of having enough after rejecting any damaged ones.

PREPARING MUSSELS

Place mussels in a bucket of water to keep fresh. If you're keeping mussels overnight you can feed them a handful of porridge oats which helps to clean them, but as a rule they should be cooked on the day of purchase. It is important to clean mussels thoroughly. Rinse in running water then scrub with a clean stiff brush or scouring pad. Pull away the beard that clings round the edge of the shell and scrape away barnacles. Discard any mussels that have damaged shells and any that do not tightly close when tapped sharply with a knife.

MUSSELS ON A BED OF LEEKS

Mussels can quickly dry out during cooking — but if steamed they are kept beautifully succulent.

1½ lb/700 g leeks, washed and trimmed
3 lb/1.5 kg mussels, washed
3 fl oz/90 ml white wine or Pernod
fresh chopped parsley

Slice the leeks ½-inch/1-cm thick. Place in a steamer and steam for 5 minutes. Add the mussels and cook for a further 1½ minutes until just beginning to open. Sprinkle over the wine or Pernod and continue to steam for a further 1 to 2 minutes. Serve sprinkled with a little chopped parsley. ***Serves 3-4***

MUSSELS ON A BED OF LEEKS

MOULES MARINIERE

4 small shallots, finely chopped
5 stalks parsley
5 fl oz/150 ml dry white wine
4½ lb/2 kg fresh mussels
To garnish: fresh chopped parsley

Put the shallots, the parsley stalks and the white wine into a large pan. Cover with a tight-fitting lid and cook over a high heat for 5 minutes. Add the mussels, cover tightly and cook over a high heat until the mussels open – about 4 minutes. Pour contents into a colander, reserving liquid and discarding any unopened mussels. Put mussels in a warm serving dish.

Strain the juices into a saucepan and bring to the boil. Boil for about 3 minutes. Pour over mussels and sprinkle with chopped parsley. Serve with fresh crusty bread to mop up the juices. **Serves 6**

VARIATIONS

Learn the principles, then cook mussels in different ways for delicious starters or main courses.

Mussels with Pernod

Prepare and cook mussels as for Moules Marinière, but add 2 tablespoons/30 ml Pernod along with the wine.

Mussels with Cider

Prepare mussels. Melt 1 oz/25 g butter in a saucepan and lightly fry 1 small chopped onion until soft. Add bay leaf, sprig of thyme or a pinch of dried thyme and 1 pint/600 ml cider and the mussels. Cover and cook for 5 minutes. Strain, discarding bay leaf and fresh thyme. Bring liquid to the boil and pour over mussels.

SMOKED TROUT PANCAKES

4 oz/125 g plain flour
pinch of salt
1 egg, beaten
10 fl oz/300 ml milk
1 oz/25 g butter, melted
½-inch/1-cm piece root ginger, peeled and cut into matchsticks
1 bunch spring onions, trimmed and cut into matchsticks
1 medium carrot, cut into matchsticks
1 tablespoon/15 ml oil
2 tablespoons/30 ml soy sauce
2 smoked trout fillets, skinned, boned and flaked
2 tablespoons/30 ml soured cream

Sieve flour and salt into a bowl. Make a well in the centre and pour in the egg. Beat in the milk with a wooden spoon until smooth. Heat a 6-inch/15-cm frying pan and brush with a little melted butter. Pour in just enough batter to cover the bottom and swirl to coat evenly. Cook for 2 minutes, turning once. Keep warm. Repeat to make 12 pancakes.

Fry the root ginger, spring onions and carrot in the oil for 5 minutes until softened. Add soy sauce and trout and simmer for 2 minutes. Gently stir in the soured cream, season with black pepper and heat through. Fold each pancake into four to make a pocket and divide the filling between them. Serve with sliced, steamed courgettes. **Serves 4**

CEVICHE

A summer dish with a Mexican flavour.

1 lb/450 g firm white fish fillets, sliced into thin strips
juice of 4 limes
mange-tout, blanched
onions, cut into rings
chillies, deseeded and chopped
vinaigrette dressing
To garnish: lime slices, fresh dill

Marinate the fish for 5 hours in the lime juice. Drain, toss with the mange-tout, onion rings, chillies and vinaigrette dressing. Garnish and serve. **Serves 4**

LEFT: MOULES MARINIERE, RIGHT: CEVICHE

MARINER'S PIE

1½ lb/700 g cod or coley
8 oz/225 g smoked haddock
1 onion, coarsely chopped
1 pint/600 ml milk
1 oz/25 g butter
1 oz/25 g flour
4 oz/125 g peeled prawns
2 tablespoons/30 ml fresh chopped
   parsley
4 oz/125 g grated Cheddar cheese
12 oz/350 g puff pastry
1 egg, beaten, to glaze

Poach fish and onion in milk for 10
minutes. Drain, reserve milk. Remove
skin and bone from fish, set aside fish.
Melt butter in a pan, remove from heat
and stir in flour. Cook, stirring for 1
minute. Gradually stir in the milk off the
heat. Cook, stirring, until thick. Fold in the
fish, prawns, parsley, cheese, and
season. Spoon into a 2-pint/1½-litre pie
dish. Roll out the pastry and cut a strip to
fit the rim. Dampen the rim and top with
remaining pastry. Seal edges. Re-roll
pastry trimmings, cut out 2 fish shapes.
Glaze with beaten egg and bake at Mark
7 — 220°C — 425°F for 30 to 35 minutes
until puffed and golden.   ***Serves 6-8***

MONKFISH KEBABS

1 lb/450 g monkfish, cut into 1-inch/
   2.5-cm cubes
juice of 1 lemon
1 tablespoon/15 ml vegetable oil
1 small red pepper
1 small green pepper
4 rashers streaky bacon, rinds removed
2 oz/50 g button mushrooms
a little melted butter

Marinate monkfish in lemon juice and oil
for 20 minutes. Core and deseed peppers
and cut into 1-inch/2.5-cm squares.
Blanch and drain. Cut bacon rashers into
2-inch/5-cm pieces, make small rolls.
Remove fish from marinade. Place a
mushroom on the end, then thread fish
alternately with the peppers and bacon,
on to eight small skewers. Brush with
butter. Grill for 4 to 5 minutes each side.
                                    Serves 4

**FROM THE LEFT: PLAICE STUFFED WITH PRAWNS,
MARINER'S PIE, SMOKED MACKEREL SOUFFLÉS,
MONKFISH KEBABS, BOUILLABAISSE, SWEET AND
SOUR COD**

SWEET AND SOUR COD

3 spring onions, trimmed
4 cod steaks
a little vegetable oil
1 tablespoon/15 ml tomato purée
1 tablespoon/15 ml soy sauce
1 tablespoon/15 ml honey
1 tablespoon/15 ml dry sherry
juice of 1 orange
pinch of cayenne pepper
1 carrot, cut into matchsticks

Cut spring onions into very fine strips and put into iced water to curl. Brush cod steaks with oil, season and grill for 4 to 5 minutes each side. Mix all remaining ingredients, simmer until thickened slightly. Put steaks on a platter, pour over sauce and top with the curled spring onion shreds. **Serves 4**

BOUILLABAISSE

2 garlic cloves, peeled and crushed
2 large onions, coarsely chopped
3 fl oz/90 ml olive oil
4 large tomatoes, skinned, deseeded and chopped
6 tablespoons/90ml fresh chopped parsley
4 fresh bay leaves
½ teaspoon/2.5 ml fennel seeds, crushed
pinch of saffron strands or powder
1 tablespoon/15 ml paprika
pared rind of ½ orange
1½ lb/700 g mixed firm-fleshed fish: fillets or steaks of cod, haddock, monkfish or hake
2 pints/1.2 litres fish stock
5 fl oz/150 ml white wine
1½ lb/700 g mixed soft-fleshed fillets of whiting, sole or plaice
12 mussels, scrubbed
1 squid, prepared
4-6 fresh anchovies (optional)
3 leeks, cut into 1-inch/2.5-cm pieces
To serve: toasted slices French bread

Fry garlic and onion in oil until soft. Add tomatoes, cook for 3 minutes. Add 4 tablespoons/60 ml of parsley, and the herbs, spices and orange rind. Season, then lay the firm-fleshed fish on top. Pour over the stock and wine, bring to the boil, cover and simmer for 5 minutes. Add the soft-fleshed fish, mussels, squid, anchovies (if using) and leeks. Cover and simmer for 10 minutes. Discard orange rind and bay leaf. Sprinkle with remaining parsley. Using a slotted spoon transfer the fish to a heated serving platter. Remove skin and bones and cut into pieces. Serve the broth separately with toasted French bread. **Serves 8**

HOT KIPPER SALAD

1 tablespoon/15 ml oil
6 oz/175 g streaky bacon, derinded and chopped
1 orange, pared rind and juice
2 smoked boneless kippers, skinned and flaked
1 lettuce
1 head chicory
1 teaspoon/5 ml wholegrain mustard

Fry the bacon in a non-stick frying pan for 5 minutes until golden. Add the orange juice and kippers and simmer gently for 3 minutes. Place the lettuce and chicory in a salad bowl. Cut orange rind into matchsticks and stir into the kipper mixture. Add the mustard and freshly ground black pepper and heat. Pour over salad and toss. Serve with hot crusty bread. **Serves 4**

SMOKED MACKEREL SOUFFLES

5 fl oz/150 ml milk
½ onion
1 celery stick, trimmed
1 small carrot, peeled
1 (8 oz/225 g) smoked mackerel, filleted
juice of 1 lemon
freshly ground black pepper
1 oz/25 g butter
1 oz/25 g flour
3 eggs, separated
1 tablespoon/15 ml grated Parmesan

Infuse the milk with the onion, celery and carrot for 15 minutes. Remove any skin and bones from the mackerel and mash the flesh with the lemon juice and pepper. Spoon into 6 greased ramekin dishes. Strain the milk. Melt butter in a pan. Remove from heat, stir in flour and cook for 1 minute. Gradually stir in the milk until smooth. Then cook, stirring for 1 minute. Beat in the egg yolks. Stiffly beat the egg whites and stir a little into the egg yolk mixture. Gently fold in the remaining egg whites. Spoon on top of the mackerel and bake at Mark 6 — 220°C — 400°F for 15 to 20 minutes, until puffed and golden. Sprinkle with Parmesan. **Serves 6**

PLAICE STUFFED WITH PRAWNS

6 fillets white plaice, skinned
4 oz/125 g peeled prawns
1 tablespoon/15 ml tomato purée
5 fl oz/150 ml white wine
1 oz/25 g butter
1 oz/25 g flour
5 fl oz/150 ml fish stock
1 tablespoon/15 ml lemon juice
2 tablespoons/30 ml single cream
To garnish: fresh chopped parsley

Roughly chop 2 plaice fillets and half the prawns. Process or pound to a paste with tomato purée. Season. Lightly score remaining fillets on skinned side and spread with fish paste. Sprinkle with remaining prawns. Roll up and pack closely in a buttered ovenproof dish. Pour wine around the fish. Cover and bake at Mark 4 — 180°C — 350°F for 30 minutes. Remove fish, keep warm. Reserve liquid. Melt the butter in a pan, add the flour and cook, stirring, for 2 minutes. Add stock and simmer for 5 minutes. Strain cooking liquid into sauce. Add lemon juice and cream. Heat and serve with garnished fish. **Serves 4**

FRESH SALMON WITH WATERCRESS SAUCE

4 (4 oz/125 g) salmon cutlets
5 oz/150 g Greek yogurt
1 bunch watercress, washed
juice ½ lemon
To serve: mange-tout

Brush the salmon cutlets with a little melted butter and grill for 5 minutes each side. Keep hot. Blend the yogurt, watercress and lemon juice until smooth, serve with the salmon and mange-tout. **Serves 4**

FRESH SALMON WITH WATERCRESS SAUCE

CITRUS-STEAMED RED MULLET WITH FENNEL

Steaming really emphasises the beautiful vibrant colour of red mullet or snapper.

4 small red mullet or red snapper, cleaned
1 tablespoon/15 ml soy sauce
1-inch/2.5-cm piece fresh root ginger, peeled and shredded
4 spring onions, trimmed and shredded
1 lime, thinly sliced
½ lemon, thinly sliced
2 sprigs fresh fennel or dill
½ green chilli, deseeded and thinly sliced (optional)

Make 3 slashes in each side of the fish and rub with the soy sauce. Put a little ginger and spring onion in each cavity and place on a plate. Cover the fish with the lime and lemon slices, fennel and chilli. Scatter over the remaining ginger and spring onion. Cover and steam for 7 minutes. **Serves 4**

SMOKED HADDOCK KEDGEREE

6 oz/175 g long grain brown rice
1½ pints/900 ml cold water
12 oz/350 g smoked haddock fillet
1 bay leaf
2 black peppercorns
1 oz/25 g butter
2 hard-boiled eggs, quartered
2 tablespoons/30 ml fresh chopped parsley
1 lemon, juice only
To garnish: bay leaves

Cook the rice in boiling salted water until tender. Place the haddock fillet, bay leaf and peppercorns in a large frying pan, cover with water and poach, with lid on, for 15-20 minutes until fish flakes. Drain and reserve 2 fl oz/60 ml of the liquor. Flake the fish, discard skin and bones and drain the rice.

Melt the butter in a frying pan and add the rice, eggs, fish, reserved liquor and parsley, stirring until heated through.

Add lemon juice, freshly ground black pepper and spoon into a warmed serving dish. Garnish with the bay leaves.

Serves 2-3

CITRUS-STEAMED RED MULLET WITH FENNEL

SCALLOPS WITH WINTER VEGETABLE STIR-FRY

SCALLOPS WITH WINTER VEGETABLE STIR-FRY

1 tablespoon/15 ml soy sauce
3 tablespoons/45 ml vegetable oil
½-inch/1-cm piece root ginger,
   peeled and grated
10 scallops, sliced in half widthways
3 carrots, peeled and cut into matchsticks
8 oz/225 g Savoy cabbage
4 spring onions, trimmed, cut into strips

Mix together the soy sauce, 1 tablespoon/
15 ml of the oil and the root ginger, add
the scallops and leave to marinate for 1
hour. Heat rest of oil in a wok or frying
pan, until almost smoking. Add the
carrots and stir-fry over a high heat for 1
minute. Add the scallops with marinade
and cook for a further 2 minutes. Then
add cabbage and onions and fry for a
minute. Serve immediately with boiled
rice. **Serves 4**

MACKEREL WITH RHUBARB SAUCE

4 medium mackerel, cleaned
juice of 2 large oranges
2 large spring onions, finely chopped
1 lb/450 g rhubarb, trimmed and
   chopped
2 tablespoons/30 ml soft light brown
   sugar
1 teaspoon/5 ml grated orange rind
2 tablespoons/30 ml white wine or 1
   tablespoon/15 ml Pernod
1 oz/25 g butter
To garnish: orange slices

Make three diagonal cuts on each side of
the mackerel and marinate in orange
juice and onion. To make the sauce, place
rhubarb, sugar, orange rind and wine in
a pan. Cook gently, stirring occasionally,
until rhubarb is soft. Season to taste, then
blend until smooth. Remove mackerel
from marinade. Season. Remove onion
with a slotted spoon and fry in butter until
softened, then place inside mackerel.
Grill fish under a moderate heat for about
8 minutes on each side, until cooked
through. Gently reheat sauce, serve with
garnished mackerel. **Serves 4**

SPICY COCONUT COD

1 (7-oz/200-g) packet creamed coconut
12 fl oz/350 ml boiling water
2 tablespoons/30 ml olive oil
1 large onion, thinly sliced
1 garlic clove, peeled and crushed
3 fresh green chillies, deseeded and
   finely chopped
1-inch/2.5-cm piece root ginger, peeled
   and grated
1½ teaspoons/7.5 ml ground cumin
grated rind and juice of 1 lime
1½ lb/700 g cod fillets, skinned and cut
   into 4 equal pieces
To garnish: 1 sliced lime

Dissolve the coconut in the water and set
aside. In a flameproof casserole heat the
oil and fry the onion, garlic, chillies, and
ginger until softened. Add the cumin and
lime rind and juice and cook for a further
2 minutes. Add the cod pieces to the
casserole and pour over the coconut
cream. Season. Cover and simmer gently
for about 10 minutes, or until the cod is
cooked and just flakes when pierced.
Garnish with lime slices and serve with
plain boiled rice. **Serves 4**

SPICED MIXED SHELLFISH

1 tablespoon/15 ml oil
1 onion, finely chopped
1-inch/2.5-cm piece root ginger, peeled
   and grated
2 teaspoons/10 ml ground cumin
1 teaspoon/5 ml paprika
2 teaspoons/10 ml coriander seeds,
   crushed
½ lemon, juice only
2 tablespoons/30 ml dry sherry
1 pint/600 ml fish stock
2 fl oz/60 ml double cream
8 oz/225 g peeled prawns
8 oz/225 g cockles
8 oz/225 g cooked mussels, shelled

Heat the oil in a large saucepan and fry
the onion and ginger for 5 minutes until
softened. Stir in the cumin, paprika and
coriander and fry for a further 2 minutes,
stirring constantly. Pour in the lemon
juice, sherry and fish stock, stir until well
blended. Bring to the boil and boil rapidly
until reduced by two-thirds. Stir in the
cream, shellfish and simmer gently for 2
minutes until heated through. Serve with
noodles. **Serves 4**

CREAMY SCALLOPS

1 oz/25 g butter, softened
1 clove garlic, crushed
½ bunch spring onions, thinly sliced
2 carrots, peeled and cut into matchsticks
4 fl oz/120 ml vermouth
2 fl oz/60 ml fish stock
8 oz/225 g queen scallops
½ lemon, pared rind cut into matchsticks, and juice
2 tablespoons/30 ml natural yogurt
***To serve:* creamed potatoes, sliced lime or lemon and fresh dill**

Melt the butter in a saucepan and fry the garlic, spring onions, and carrots for 5 minutes until softened. Stir in the vermouth, fish stock, shellfish, lemon rind and juice. Bring to the boil and simmer for 4-5 minutes. Remove scallops and reduce liquid. Stir in the natural yogurt and seasoning and heat through. Serve immediately with creamed potato. Garnish with lime or lemon. **Serves 2-3**

SMOKED COD FISHCAKES

1 tablespoon/15 ml oil
1 onion, grated
1 red pepper, cored, deseeded and finely chopped
8 oz/225 g smoked cod fillet, skinned
1½ lb/700 g cooked potato, mashed
4 oz/125 g cooked parsnip, mashed
2 tablespoons/30 ml fresh chopped herbs
1 teaspoon/5 ml anchovy essence
seasoned flour
2 eggs, beaten
2 oz/50 g wholemeal breadcrumbs
1 tablespoon/15 ml oil

Heat the oil in a frying pan and fry onion and pepper for 10 minutes until softened. Mix the onion, pepper, cod, potato, parsnip, herbs, anchovy essence and freshly ground black pepper together.

Mould the mixture into fish cake shapes. Gently dip each one in seasoned flour, egg and then breadcrumbs. Place on a lightly oiled baking sheet, cover and chill for 30 minutes. Brush with a little oil and bake at Mark 6 — 200°C — 400°F for 35 minutes until golden. Serve with a twist of lemon or lime. **Serves 6**

FISH STEAKS WITH ORANGE AND GIN

4 cod steaks, about 1-inch/2.5-cm thick
½-inch/1-cm fresh ginger root, peeled and shredded
2 oz/50 g button mushrooms, halved
2 tablespoons/30 ml gin
pared rind and juice of ½ orange

Arrange the fish in a single layer on a plate, sprinkle over the ginger and mushrooms. Mix the gin with the orange rind and juice and pour over the mushrooms. Cover and steam for 10-15 minutes or until the flesh just flakes. Remove immediately and serve with rice or noodles and green vegetables. **Serves 4**

CREAMY SCALLOPS

Vegetables and Salads

The exotic imported vegetables that have reached our shores in such abundance may be more expensive, but at least they have taught us to treat vegetables with the respect they deserve and to cook them in such a way that colour, texture and taste will be preserved. Steaming is gentler than boiling, which can reduce vegetables to a tasteless, watery pulp.

● Experiment with the new vegetable varieties but try different cooking methods for familiar ones, too — carrots cooked with orange juice are sweet, fruity and delicious. Experiment with different combinations of vegetables in puréed mixtures. Choose potatoes as your base and add celeriac, parsnip and leek, or even fruits like apple and pear.

● Stir-frying is the perfect method for quick cooking either a single vegetable or a selection. Use only enough oil to stop them from sticking and burning; start with those needing longer cooking, then toss in leafy varieties at the end.

● Late additions can brighten up any vegetable: add caramelised onions or crispy bacon; sharpen with a squeeze of lemon; top with a sprinkling of toasted wholewheat breadcrumbs, nuts or sesame seeds or a handful of fresh chopped herbs.

● Curly endive, oak leaf lettuce and radicchio have come to join the stalwarts of our salad leaves — round, cos, Webb's wonder or iceberg. Sometimes there's lamb's tongue, also called corn salad, their small and tender leaves elongated like petals, spinach, dandelion leaves, and chicory. We're also taking notice of the French and the American way with salad, and the days of the limp leaf with three slices of cucumber and a tomato are, thank goodness, over. You can get edible flowers such as nasturtiums from Sainsbury's; they taste peppery and look wonderfully fiery tossed into a salad. See page 94 about perfect dressings.

● Salads needn't be all cold ingredients either: hot bacon and crisp croûtons, cooked chicken livers and cheese grilled just to melting point can all be incorporated. These "wilted" salads, their dressing added hot deliberately to soften the leaves, are good with tougher spinach, radicchio and curly endive.

BRUSSELS SPROUTS WITH WATER CHESTNUTS

A classic combination of sprouts and chestnuts with a truly Chinese feel. As is the intention with all stir-fried vegetables, the sprouts should stay crunchy. Serve with pork, gammon or turkey.

1 lb/450 g Brussels sprouts, trimmed
1 tablespoon/15 ml vegetable oil
1 small onion, finely chopped
2 tablespoons/30 ml sherry
2 teaspoons/10 ml soy sauce
1 (10-oz/300-g) can water chestnuts, drained and sliced
1 tablespoon/15 ml sesame seeds

Thinly slice the sprouts lengthways. Heat the oil in a frying pan, add the onion and fry gently until softened. Add the sprouts, sherry and soy sauce and stir-fry for 1-2 minutes. Add the chestnuts and toss until heated through. Sprinkle with sesame seeds and serve immediately. **Serves 4**

ORIENTAL AUBERGINE

1 large aubergine
2 tablespoons/30 ml olive oil
4 celery sticks, chopped
1 (7½-oz/210-g) can peeled, chopped tomatoes
2 tablespoons/30 ml chopped fresh mint or 1 tablespoon/15 ml dried mint
a squeeze of lemon
To garnish: **fresh mint**

Chop aubergine into 1-inch/2.5-cm cubes. Place in a colander over a plate, sprinkle with salt and leave for 30 minutes to draw out the bitter juices. Rinse and pat dry.

Heat the oil in a large frying pan, add the celery and fry, stirring, for 3 minutes. Add the tomatoes with their juice, the aubergine and the mint. Season, cover and cook for about 20 minutes or until the aubergine is tender. Add the lemon juice and serve hot or cold garnished with fresh mint. **Serves 4**

SWEET AND SOUR RED CABBAGE

½ red cabbage, trimmed
½ teaspoon/2.5 ml ground caraway
juice 2 lemons
3 oranges
2 pieces stem ginger, sliced

Shred the cabbage ½ inch/1 cm thick, then add the caraway and lemon juice and toss. Steam for 8 minutes. Meanwhile, pare the rind from oranges and cut into thin strips. Trim away the remaining pith and slice the flesh ¼ inch/5 mm thick. Add oranges and steam for 2 minutes.   **Serves 4**

VEGETABLES IN ORANGE JUICE

1 lb/450 g carrots
1 lb/450 g turnips
1 lb/450 g sweet potatoes
1 lb/450 g parsnips
1 lb/450 g baby onions
2½ pints/1.5 litres orange juice
2 teaspoons/10 ml cornflour

Peel and chop vegetables. Simmer in orange juice until tender. Drain and place them in a dish. Dissolve the cornflour in a little of the cooking liquid, then stir into remainder. Cook until thickened slightly. Pour over the vegetables and serve.
Serves 8-10

LEAF SPINACH WITH ALMONDS

3 lb/1.4 kg fresh spinach
2 oz/50 g butter
1 oz/25 g toasted flaked almonds

Trim and remove coarse stalks from the spinach and wash in several changes of cold water. Shake off excess water. Melt 1 oz/25 g of the butter in a large frying pan and stir-fry half of the spinach leaves for about 2 minutes, until just wilted. Fry remaining spinach in remaining butter. Toss together. Sprinkle with almonds.
Serves 6

SWEET AND SOUR RED CABBAGE

POTATO PANCAKES

1 lb/450 g potatoes
2 oz/50 g flour
1 egg, beaten
1 teaspoon/5 ml fresh chopped dill
oil for shallow frying
**To serve: fromage frais, lumpfish roe,
fresh dill**

Parboil the potatoes for 5 minutes. Cool and grate them coarsely into a bowl. Turn the potato into a clean tea towel and squeeze hard to remove excess liquid. Stir in the flour, egg and dill. Heat a little oil in a heavy based frying pan and drop in 1 tablespoon/15 ml of the mixture at a time. Cook for 3 minutes each side until golden brown and serve hot, topped with *fromage frais*, lumpfish roe and a sprinkle of fresh dill. **Makes 6**

MEXICAN POTATOES

**½-inch/1 cm thick rasher smoked streaky
bacon, derinded and chopped**
1 lb/450 g potatoes, sliced
**1 (14 oz/397 g) can red kidney, pinto,
or borlotti beans**
**1 (7 oz/200 g) can red pimientos,
drained and sliced**
5 fl oz/150 ml chicken stock
**½ teaspoon/2.5 ml dried marjoram or
oregano**
To garnish: sprig fresh parsley

Mix all the ingredients together in a casserole, cover and bake at Mark 3 — 160°C — 325°F for 1 hour. Garnish and serve hot. **Serves 4**

LEMON HERB POTATOES

5 tablespoons/75 ml olive oil
1 lb/450 g Spanish onions, thinly sliced
2 cloves garlic, peeled and sliced
2 lb/900 g potatoes, thinly sliced
½ lemon, grated zest and juice
**2 tablespoons/30 ml grated Parmesan
cheese**

Heat 2 tablespoons/30 ml of the oil in a frying pan and gently fry the onions and garlic until softened. Pour 1 tablespoon/15 ml of oil into an ovenproof dish and stack the potatoes and onions standing upright in layers. Sprinkle over the lemon zest and juice, Parmesan, salt, freshly ground black pepper and remaining olive oil. Cover and bake at Mark 4 — 180°C — 350°F for 45 minutes. Uncover, increase heat to Mark 6 — 200°C — 400°F and cook for a further 40 minutes until golden brown. **Serves 4-6**

SPICED POTATO

2 tablespoons/30 ml oil
**½-inch/1-cm piece fresh root
ginger, peeled and shredded**
2 teaspoons/10 ml medium curry powder
1 lb/450 g potatoes, roughly chopped
5 fl oz/150 ml chicken stock

Heat the oil in a saucepan and fry the ginger and curry powder, stirring constantly until the spices release their aroma — about 5 minutes. Add potatoes and toss until coated. Add stock and cook for 40 minutes until the potatoes are tender. **Serves 4**

POTATOES WITH TOMATO SAUCE

2 tablespoons/30 ml olive oil
1 clove garlic, peeled and crushed
1 small onion, finely chopped
1 (14 oz/397 g) can tomatoes, sieved
10 fl oz/300 ml water
pinch of chilli powder
½ teaspoon/2.5 ml dried oregano
**3 tablespoons/45 ml fresh chopped
parsley**
2 lb/900 g small potatoes, quartered

Heat the oil in a pan and fry the garlic and onion for 10 minutes. Add remaining ingredients except the potatoes, bring to boil and simmer for 15 minutes. Add the potatoes and simmer gently for 40 minutes until tender. Serve hot. **Serves 4-6**

HEALTHIER HASH BROWNS

1 lb/450 g potatoes
3 tablespoons/45 ml oil
1 egg, beaten

Scrub the potatoes thoroughly and grate them coarsely into a large bowl of cold water. Pour the oil into a 9-inch 22.5-cm round non-stick sandwich tin. Place in the oven at Mark 7 — 220°C — 425°F for 5 minutes. Drain the potatoes in a sieve and press gently to remove the excess water.

Place the potatoes in a bowl and mix in the beaten egg with salt and plenty of freshly ground black pepper. Press the potato mixture evenly into the preheated tin and bake for 45 minutes until a brown crust forms on the under side. To serve, turn out the potatoes so that the browned side is uppermost. Serve with eggs. **Serves 4**

FENNEL ROAST POTATOES

3 tablespoons/45 ml oil
1 oz/25 g butter
2 lb/900 g potatoes, cut into quarters
2 fennel bulbs
3 oz/75 g stoned black olives
3 sprigs rosemary

Place the oil and butter in a roasting tin and heat at Mark 6 — 200°C — 400°F for 5 minutes. Add the potatoes, turning them in the oil. Return to the oven for 15 minutes. Trim the fennel and remove the outer coarse leaves. Cut each into quarters, lengthways. Add the fennel, olives and rosemary to the potatoes, turning them to coat. Season with freshly ground black pepper. Return to the oven for ½ hour, basting occasionally, until the vegetables are crispy on the outside but soft inside. **Serves 6**

BAKED POTATOES

Preparation. Choose even-sized floury types of potatoes for baking, such as King Edward or Maris Piper. Look for specially packed large potatoes for baking in supermarkets. Scrub well, dry and prick skins with a fork. Rub with oil and sprinkle with salt for a crispy finish.

Oven Baking. Place on a baking tray and bake at Mark 6 — 200°C — 400°F for about 1 hour or until soft when squeezed. Metal potato prongs produce fluffy baked potatoes which need less cooking.

Microwaving. Saves time for small numbers, but does not produce a crispy skin. Prick well and cook 4 (6-8 oz/175-225 g) potatoes on full power for 12 to 16 minutes. Allow to stand for 5 minutes before filling.

POTATO FILLINGS

Each filling is enough for 4 freshly baked medium potatoes. Cut a thin slice lengthways from the top of each potato. Scoop out the flesh taking care not to pierce the shell. Mash flesh with a fork, season and stir in any of the following fillings before putting back in the shells. Reheat for 5 minutes before serving.

Nutty Bacon. Mix in 6 rashers crumbled, cooked streaky bacon, 6 tablespoons/ 90 ml chopped watercress and 4 tablespoons/60 ml browned slivered almonds. Top with fresh sliced pineapple and watercress.

Prawn and Asparagus. Mix in 4 oz/125 g cooked shelled prawns, 1 (8-oz/225 g) can drained and chopped asparagus spears, 1 oz/25 g melted butter and a pinch of curry powder. Top with a fresh prawn.

Chicken, Grape and Mushroom. Mix in 1 chopped cooked chicken breast, 3 oz/75 g halved seedless white grapes, 2 oz/50 g sliced fried mushrooms, 4 tablespoons/60 ml Greek yogurt and a few drops of Tabasco sauce. Top with fresh chives.

Danish Royal. Mix in 1 tablespoon/15 ml whole-grain lumpfish roe, 1 chopped hard-boiled egg and 2 tablespoons/30 ml Greek yogurt. Top with lemon and parsley.

MEAL IN A POTATO

Eggs Baked in Potato Shells. Slice a lid from a baked potato. Scoop most of the flesh from the shell. Season and add a knob of butter to the shell. Break in an egg. Return to oven for 10 to 15 minutes until lightly set. Sprinkle with chives.

Crunchy Skins. Very thickly peel scrubbed potatoes. Deep fry skin pieces in hot fat 190°C (375°F) until deep golden brown. Drain thoroughly on kitchen paper. Serve hot with **Creamy Herb Dip.** To make dip, blend 2 oz/50 g cream cheese and 4 oz/ 125 g natural yogurt. Season. Add 3-4 drops Tabasco sauce and 1 tablespoon/15 ml chopped parsley.

Soufflé Potatoes. Slice a lid from 6 baked potatoes. Scoop out most of the flesh and mash it with 4 egg yolks, 4 oz/125 g finely grated cheese, 4 oz/125 g melted butter and 2 tablespoons/30 ml cream. Season. Stiffly whisk the egg whites and fold into the mixture. Pile back into shells and bake at Mark 6 — 200°C — 400°F for 20 to 25 minutes until golden brown and risen. Sprinkle with a little Parmesan cheese to serve.

POTATO TOPPINGS

Cut a deep cross in the top of each baked potato, cutting into the flesh. Gently squeeze round the base of the potato until the cross opens and the fluffy inside is exposed. Then top with any of the following. Each topping is enough for four freshly baked medium potatoes.

Frankfurter. Slice 2 large hot frankfurters and mix with 1-2 tablespoons/15-30 ml mild mustard, if liked. Garnish with parsley.

Cheese and Onion. Mix 6 oz/175 g grated Cheddar with raw onion rings or 3 tablespoons/45 ml sweet pickle.

Bacon 'n' Beans. Mix 6 rashers grilled, chopped, streaky bacon with 8 tablespoons/120 ml hot baked beans in tomato sauce.

Blue Cheese. Mix 4 oz/125 g crumbled Danish Blue or Stilton cheese with 2 tablespoons/30 ml thick mayonnaise and 2 finely chopped celery stalks.

Ham and Sweetcorn. Mix 6 oz/175 g minced or finely chopped lean cooked ham with 4 tablespoons/60 ml drained canned sweetcorn kernels, 2 teaspoons/ 10 ml chopped spring onion and 2 tablespoons/30 ml mayonnaise.

POTATO AND CELERIAC PUREE

1½ lb/700 g potatoes
1 celeriac, about 1½ lb/700 g
lemon juice
3 oz/75 g butter, melted
To garnish: paprika, celery leaves

Peel the potatoes and celeriac and coarsely chop. Put in a large saucepan. Cook in boiling salted water with a little lemon juice for 15 to 20 minutes or until tender. Drain and pass through a sieve. Return to the pan. Add butter, season and stir until combined. Serve sprinkled with paprika and garnished with celery leaves. ***Serves 6***

MIXED BEANS WITH GARLIC

1 (14-oz/397-g) can haricot beans
1 (14-oz/397-g) can flageolet beans
1 oz/25 g butter
1 garlic clove, peeled and crushed
2 tablespoons/30 ml chopped parsley

Heat beans in their can liquid until hot. Drain well. Return to the pan and add the butter and garlic. Stir gently until evenly combined. Add parsley and serve. ***Serves 6***

CARROT AND ORANGE PUREE

1½ lb/700 g carrots
juice of 1 large orange
½ oz/15 g butter
dash of Pernod or other aniseed spirit

Peel and slice carrots. Cook in boiling water for 15 minutes. When tender, purée in a food processor or liquidiser with orange juice. Return to the pan, add butter, Pernod and black pepper and heat through. ***Serves 4***

JERUSALEM ARTICHOKES PAYSANNE

Baby turnips could be substituted for the Jerusalem artichokes.

1½ lb/700 g Jerusalem artichokes
2 teaspoons/10 ml lemon juice
1 tablespoon/15 ml vegetable oil
1 onion, chopped
4 streaky bacon rashers, derinded and chopped
4 tablespoons/60 ml wholemeal breadcrumbs
1 tablespoon/15 ml finely chopped parsley

Scrub and peel the artichokes. Cook them in boiling water with the lemon juice to prevent discolouring until just tender, about 10 minutes. Drain and thickly slice.

Meanwhile, heat the oil in a frying pan, add the onion and fry until transparent. Add the bacon and fry until crisp, then add the artichoke slices and fry, turning, for a further 2-3 minutes. Transfer to a serving dish and keep warm.

Add the breadcrumbs to the pan and stir over moderate heat until crisp. Mix with the parsley and sprinkle evenly over artichokes. **Serves 4**

MIXED RADISH WITH CARROT AND ORANGE

8 oz/225 g mooli radish
8 oz/225 g carrots
juice of ½ large orange
juice of ½ lemon
thinly pared rind of 1 orange, cut into julienne strips
2 tablespoons/30 ml clear honey
6 or 7 red radishes, thinly sliced

Peel the mooli radish and carrots and slant-cut them by slicing at a 45-degree angle, then turn the vegetable 180 degrees towards you and slice again.

Steam the mooli radish and carrots until just tender, about 20 minutes. Heat the orange and lemon juice, rind and honey in a small saucepan. Bring to boil and reduce by half. Transfer the mooli radish and carrot to a heated serving dish,

mix with the red radishes and pour over the hot honey and orange mixture.
Serves 4

MEXICAN-STYLE CHOW CHOW

Chow chow (also called chayote, vegetable pear or christophine) could be replaced with courgettes or cucumber.

1 chow chow, peeled, stoned, and sliced lengthways
juice of ½ lemon
1 (14 oz/397 g) can tomatoes, drained and sieved
2 tablespoons/30 ml Greek yogurt
1 teaspoon/5 ml paprika
1 small fresh green chilli, deseeded and very finely sliced

Sprinkle the chow chow with lemon juice and steam for about 10 minutes or until tender. Cook the tomatoes in a large frying pan until thick and pulpy. Stir in the yogurt and paprika. Transfer the steamed chow chow to a heated serving dish, pour over the creamy tomato sauce and garnish with chilli. **Serves 4**

CRUNCHY TRICOLOUR CABBAGE

8 oz/225 g each red, green and white cabbage, shredded
1 tablespoon/15 ml oil
1 oz/25 g butter
6 oz/175 g streaky bacon, derinded and chopped
2 oz/50 g button mushrooms, chopped
4 oz/125 g fresh white or brown breadcrumbs
2 tomatoes, peeled, seeds and core removed, chopped
pinch of dried oregano

Steam cabbage until just tender. Meanwhile, heat oil and butter in a large frying pan and fry the bacon for 2 minutes. Add mushrooms, breadcrumbs and plenty of freshly ground black pepper and fry, turning for 5 minutes or until the crumbs are crisp and golden. Stir in tomatoes and oregano and scatter the mixture over the hot cabbage. **Serves 6**

LEFT FROM THE TOP: JERUSALEM ARTICHOKES
PAYSANNE, MIXED RADISH WITH CARROT AND
ORANGE, MEXICAN-STYLE CHOW CHOW
RIGHT: CRUNCHY TRICOLOUR CABBAGE

SPINACH SALAD

6 oz/175 g baby spinach
8 oz/225 g potatoes
4 tablespoons/60 ml vegetable oil
2 tablespoons/30 ml mayonnaise
3 oz/75 g blue cheese, crumbled
5 oz/150 g Greek yogurt
1 egg, hard-boiled, peeled and sliced
4 cooked langoustines or 8 prawns

Spine the spinach, wash gently and dry. Place in a salad bowl. Cut the potatoes into ½-inch/1-cm cubes and slice. Heat the oil in a frying pan and fry the potatoes for 10 minutes. Keep hot. Blend the mayonnaise, cheese and yogurt until smooth. Spoon into a serving dish. Add potatoes, egg and langoustines. Serve with the blue cheese dressing. **Serves 4**

CHINESE LEAVES WITH PEANUT DRESSING

1 head Chinese leaves
2 tablespoons/30 ml crunchy peanut butter
2 tablespoons/30 ml white wine vinegar
4 tablespoons/60 ml olive oil
To garnish: lemon wedges

Separate the leaves, wash gently and dry. Tear diagonally across the leaves into thickish strips. Place in a salad bowl. Place the peanut butter, wine vinegar and olive oil in a small pan and heat gently, stirring. Pour over the salad and toss. Garnish with lemon wedges. **Serves 4-6**

SALAD WITH HOT DRESSING

½ large crisp lettuce
½ head of radicchio
1 lime
1 garlic clove, peeled
6 slices streaky bacon, rinds removed

Twist the core out of the lettuce and ease out the centre leaves. Save the outer leaves for another salad. Wash gently, dry. Place lettuce and radicchio leaves in a salad bowl.

Very thinly pare the rind from the lime and cut into tiny julienne strips. Squeeze

the juice. Reserve.

Crush the garlic into the base of a grill pan. Arrange the bacon on the rack and grill until crisp and golden. Finely chop the bacon. Stir the lime juice into the bacon fat in grill pan, add the chopped bacon and place under the grill to heat through. Pour the hot bacon mixture over the leaves and toss to coat. Sprinkle with lime and serve at once. **Serves 4**

SHREDDED LEEK SALAD

Raw leeks are crispy and crunchy and look very delicate served thinly sliced.

2 leeks, cut into thin slices
2 tablespoons/30 ml oil
4 oz/125 g button mushrooms, sliced
2 hard-boiled eggs, shelled
5 tablespoons/75 ml olive oil
2 tablespoons/30 ml wine vinegar
pinch of dry mustard
pinch of dried mixed herbs

Place the leeks in a large serving bowl and separate the slices into rings. Heat the oil, fry the mushrooms for 2 minutes and add to the leeks. Press the egg yolks through a sieve and chop the whites finely. Whisk the olive oil, vinegar and mustard together. Add freshly ground black pepper and herbs and toss through the leeks. Top with the egg yolk and white. **Serves 6-8**

OMELETTE SALAD

2 oz/50 g butter
6 eggs
4 tablespoons/60 ml water
4 large tomatoes, sliced
1 (15-oz/425-g) can artichoke hearts, drained, sliced
2 tablespoons/30 ml olive oil
2 oz/50 g black olives, stoned
1 tablespoon/15 ml chopped fresh basil

Melt half the butter in an 8- or 9-inch/20- or 22.5-cm non-stick frying pan. Beat 3 eggs with 2 tablespoons/30 ml water, season. Pour into pan when butter sizzles. Cook over high heat, stirring with a fork. When set, slip the omelette on to a large plate. Cook the remaining eggs in the same way. Roll omelettes up tightly.

Allow to cool, then cut into thin slices. Arrange the omelette slices, tomatoes, and artichoke hearts on a bed of lettuce in a dish. Season, then pour over the oil and sprinkle with olives and basil. **Serves 3-4**

MINT AND LETTUCE SALAD

1 cos lettuce
1 oz/25 g fresh mint leaves
4 tomatoes
½ cucumber, peeled
4 tablespoons/60 ml olive oil
juice of 3 lemons

Remove the outer leaves from the lettuce, wash gently and dry. Roughly chop and place in a bowl. Trim the centre leaves and reserve. Chop the mint leaves, tomatoes and cucumber. Add to the chopped lettuce. Mix the oil and lemon juice together and pour some into a small bowl. Place the bowl in the middle of a large plate and stand the centre leaves in the bowl. Pour the remaining dressing over the lettuce and mint mixture, toss, then spoon around the bowl on the plate. **Serves 4**

RED CABBAGE SLAW

Red cabbage makes an unusual change from white in this coleslaw and you'll be surprised at how tender it is.

½ red cabbage, very finely shredded
1 tablespoon/15 ml salt
8 oz/225 g seedless white grapes, halved
3 oz/75 g dried apricots, sliced
2 oz/50 g hazelnuts, halved
Dressing:
4 tablespoons/60 ml oil
2 tablespoons/30 ml wine vinegar
pinch of dry mustard
pinch of sugar
1 teaspoon/5 ml lemon juice

Layer the cabbage and salt alternately into a large bowl. Cover and leave to stand for 4 hours. Rinse the cabbage to remove excess salt. Drain. Stir in the fruit and nuts. Whisk all the dressing ingredients together until evenly blended. Season with freshly ground black pepper. Toss the dressing through the salad and check the seasoning before serving as a side dish. **Serves 6-8**

SALADS

Many of our green-leafed wild plants make excellent salad ingredients — don't forget even the common lettuce was wild itself once. Sorrel, lamb's lettuce, curly endive and watercress are well-known and popular wild foods found all over the British Isles, but chickweed, wintercress and young dandelions and daisy leaves are equally tasty in a salad. Wash, shred and serve them with chopped apple or crispy bacon and croûtons. Chopped marjoram or borage can be added to a salad with a French dressing spiced with wild garlic, apple mint and chives.

Clockwise from centre top: winter purslane, ground elder, sorrel, curly endive, nettles, salad burnet, garden cress, lovage, pansy, lemon balm, oyster mushroom, marjoram, fennel, daisy, chives, chickweed, borage flowers, red-veined dock, green celery, spinach, salad rape.

CAESAR SALAD

1 large crisp lettuce
1 oz/25 g butter
1 tablespoon/15 ml vegetable oil
2 garlic cloves, peeled and crushed
4 thick slices white bread, crusts removed and cubed
1 tablespoon/15 ml white wine vinegar
2 teaspoons/10 ml anchovy essence
3 tablespoons/45 ml olive oil
1 large egg
1 tablespoon/15 ml grated Parmesan cheese

Wash the lettuce gently, dry and cut into shreds. Place in a salad bowl. Melt the butter with the vegetable oil and add the garlic and cubes of bread. Fry over moderate heat until browned and crisp. Drain on kitchen paper and keep hot.

Beat the wine vinegar, anchovy essence and seasoning together. Gradually beat in the olive oil. Cook the egg in its shell in boiling water for 1 minute only, to coddle.

Add the croûtons to the lettuce with the dressing and Parmesan. Break the egg over the salad and toss well. Serve at once. **Serves 4**

CHICORY WITH ORANGE AND WATERCRESS

3 heads of chicory
3 large oranges
2 bunches of watercress
3 tablespoons/45 ml groundnut oil

Trim the chicory, separate into leaves, wash gently and dry. Place in a salad bowl.

Pare the rind from 1 orange. Cut into julienne strips and place in a small bowl. Squeeze the juice from this orange and add to the rind.

Peel the remaining 2 oranges, making sure all the white pith is removed. Cut down between each segment, leaving the membranes behind. Add the orange

LEFT TOP: CAESAR SALAD; BELOW: CHICORY WITH ORANGE AND WATERCRESS

segments to the chicory. Trim the watercress and add the leaves to the bowl.

Season the orange juice and rind and beat in the oil. Pour the dressing over the salad in the bowl and toss well. Serve at once. **Serves 4**

GARDEN SALAD

This is a marvellous mixture of the leaves and flowers you can grow in your garden – or buy.

2 small bunches lamb's lettuce, leaves separated
few sorrel leaves
1 oak leaf lettuce
1 rougette
2 teaspoons/10 ml wine vinegar
2 tablespoons/30 ml sunflower oil
***To garnish:* 1 mimosa spray, few rose petals, few primroses, few violas**

Wash all the leaves and dry gently. Place in a salad bowl. Beat the vinegar with seasoning, then beat in the oil. Pour over the leaves and toss gently. Arrange on individual plates. Pick off the mimosa from the stalks and garnish the salad with these, the rose petals, primroses and violas. **Serves 6**

ENDIVE, GOAT'S CHEESE AND WALNUT SALAD

1 curly endive
5 oz/150 g walnut halves
6 oz/175 g goat's cheese, cubed
1 tablespoon/15 ml cider vinegar
3 tablespoons/45 ml walnut oil

Trim the curly endive, wash gently and dry. Break off into sprigs. Place in a salad bowl with the walnuts and goat's cheese. Beat the vinegar with seasoning, then beat in the oil. Pour the dressing over the salad and toss well. Serve at once. **Serves 6**

RIGHT TOP: GARDEN SALAD; BELOW: ENDIVE, GOAT'S CHEESE AND WALNUT SALAD

TOMATO AND ONION SALAD

3 ripe beef steak tomatoes, thinly sliced

1 medium onion, thinly sliced

juice of 1 lemon

2 tablespoons/30 ml olive oil

2 tablespoons/30 ml fresh chopped parsley

Arrange tomatoes and onion on a plate. Pour over the lemon juice, olive oil and parsley and season with freshly ground black pepper.

Serves 2

ROCKET WITH SESAME SEED DRESSING

If you can't get rocket or dandelion use any salad leaves.

1 bunch rocket or dandelion leaves

1 tablespoon/15 ml tahini (sesame seed) paste

1 tablespoon/15 ml water

2 tablespoons/30 ml oil

1 teaspoon/5 ml lemon juice

½-inch/1-cm piece root ginger, peeled and grated

4 spring onions

Separate the rocket or dandelion leaves, wash gently and dry. Place in a bowl. Beat the tahini paste with the water. Beat in the remaining ingredients, except the spring onions. Arrange the leaves in a circle on individual plates. Finely chop the spring onions and arrange in the centre of each plate. Dribble over the dressing, serve at once.

Serves 2-3

SPICED RICE CHICKEN SALAD

If you haven't time, you don't have to blanch the peppers — but it does make them more digestible.

8 oz/225 g (dry weight) long grain rice, cooked

½ red pepper, cored, deseeded and sliced

½ green pepper, cored, deseeded and sliced

3 tablespoons/45 ml olive oil

¼ teaspoon/1.25 ml ground cinnamon

¼ teaspoon/1.25 ml ground nutmeg

2 teaspoons/10 ml crushed coriander seeds

8 cardamom pods

1 tablespoon/15 ml wine vinegar

2 teaspoons/10 ml soy sauce

2 cooked chicken quarters, skinned and boned

To garnish: fresh coriander, cinnamon sticks

Drain the cooked rice well. Pour boiling water over the peppers to blanch and leave for 5 minutes. Heat the oil in a pan and cook spices for 2 minutes. Add freshly ground black pepper, the vinegar and soy sauce and cook a little longer. Pour the sauce over the rice and add the drained peppers. Cut the chicken into pieces and stir through the rice. Serve garnished with coriander and cinnamon.

Serves 4-6

MIXED PEPPER SALAD

1 red pepper

1 green pepper

1 yellow pepper

8 oz/225 g back bacon, derinded

3 oz/75 g button mushrooms, finely sliced

1 (14-oz/397-g) can chickpeas, drained

6 oz/175 g feta cheese, crumbled

Dressing:

4 tablespoons/60 ml olive oil

1 tablespoon/15 ml wine vinegar

1 teaspoon/5 ml lemon juice

1 garlic clove, peeled and crushed

1 teaspoon/5 ml chopped fresh parsley

1 teaspoon/5 ml chopped fresh tarragon

1 teaspoon/5 ml chopped fresh chervil

pinch of caster sugar

pinch of dry mustard powder

Roast peppers under preheated grill until they collapse and skins blister and char. Remove and cover with a damp tea-towel to cool. Carefully peel off skins, remove cores and seeds, slice. Retain juices. Grill bacon until crisp. Finely chop. Mix the peppers, mushrooms, bacon, chickpeas and cheese.

Whisk together all dressing ingredients. Add pepper juices. Season. Toss through the salad.

Serves 4

POTATO SAUSAGE SALAD

2 lb/900 g new potatoes, cooked in their skins, halved

8 oz/225 g pepperoni or salami sausage, rinds removed, and sliced

1 tablespoon/15 ml snipped chives

4 hard-boiled eggs

4 tablespoons/60 ml mayonnaise

In a salad bowl mix the potatoes, sausage and chives. Remove the yolks from the eggs and press through a sieve. Chop the whites finely, and sprinkle over the salad. Spoon the mayonnaise in the centre. Sprinkle over the egg yolk.

Serves 4

SPICED RICE CHICKEN SALAD

Herbs and Spices

Fresh aromatic herbs are one of the true joys of cooking and, though parsley, thyme and sage are available all year round from supermarkets and good greengrocers, the season for most herbs is short unless you grow your own, so make the most of them, for dried herbs don't have the aroma of fresh ones. Some herbs have become traditional partners to particular foods — mint or rosemary with lamb, tarragon with chicken, fennel or dill with fish, and basil or oregano with tomatoes. Experiment is the key to discovering new combinations, but remember that herbs should enhance rather than dominate, and never mix a pungent herb with a delicate one. Rosemary, thyme and sage are all strong and should be used judiciously, while parsley, dill, chervil and marjoram are more delicately fragrant and you can afford to be more generous.

● Store fresh herbs with a sprinkling of water in a polythene bag; inflate the bag with air, tie it and keep it in the bottom of the fridge, where the herbs will stay fresh for up to a week.

● Historically, spices have been prized and the images they conjure up are exotic — of wealthy traders and Arabian nights — yet they are nothing more than the dried buds, bark, berries, seeds or roots of aromatic plants or, in the case of saffron, the stigmas of purple crocus.

● Spices are often used singly, or in a 'sorcerer's' mix: Indian garam masala; Chinese five-spice powder, an aromatic mix of star anise, cloves, fennel, cinnamon and peppercorns; the French *quatre épices*, which consists of nutmeg, peppercorns, cloves and cinnamon, similar to our own mixed spice. These are not the same as commercial seasoning mixes, which often contain salt, monosodium glutamate and artificial flavourings, and are to be avoided.

● It's best to buy whole spices and grind your own with a pestle in a mortar or in a spice mill. Always buy small quantities, store in a dark, cool, dry place for up to three months.

HOT AND SPICY PORK

1 3 lb/1.4 kg loin of pork — on the bone
1 to 2 teaspoons/5 to 10 ml chilli powder
1 teaspoon/5 ml ground cinnamon
1 teaspoon/5 ml ground black pepper
2 teaspoons/10 ml salt
1 teaspoon/5 ml dried rosemary
about 20 cloves
2 fl oz/60 ml clear honey
1 tablespoon/15 ml brown sugar

Trim the fat from the top inch of the pork bones. Scrape bones clean. Separate rib bones from the flesh but leave attached at the base. Score the skin and fat. Mix together chilli powder, cinnamon, black pepper, salt and rosemary. Rub the mixture over the joint. Insert cloves into the cuts in the scored skin. Place joint in a roasting tin. Pour over the honey and sprinkle with sugar. Cover with foil. Cook at Mark 6 — 200°C — 400°F for 25 minutes per pound. Uncover for the last 30 minutes. **Serves 4**

A SELECTION OF SPICES

CLOCKWISE FROM THE LEFT: SPICED MARBLE CAKE, MIXED FRUIT COMPÔTE, MARINATED MUSHROOMS, BEETROOT AND TOMATO SOUP, PLAICE AND FENNEL SAUTÉ, CHICKEN TIKKA, QUICK-FRIED RIBBONS OF BEEF, PISTACHIO AND CARDAMOM ICE CREAM, YORKSHIRE CURD TART

CHICKEN TIKKA

4 boneless chicken breasts, skinned
Marinade:
¼ teaspoon/1.25 ml ground chilli
1½ teaspoons/7.5 ml ground ginger
3 garlic cloves, peeled and crushed
2 teaspoons/10 ml paprika
1 tablespoon/15 ml lemon juice
1 teaspoon/5 ml ground cumin
1 teaspoon/5 ml ground coriander
1 teaspoon/5 ml salt
1 (5 oz/150 g) carton natural yogurt
½ teaspoon/2.5 ml cochineal
2 oz/50 g butter, melted
Garnish: lime wedges, onion rings and
   shredded lettuce

Cut chicken into 1-inch/2.5-cm cubes. Combine all marinade ingredients. Add chicken and marinate for at least 12 hours, covered, in a cool place. Remove chicken from marinade, thread on to skewers. Brush with melted butter. Grill, turning once, for 15 to 20 minutes. Garnish. **Serves 4**

SPICED MARBLE CAKE

7 oz/200 g butter or polyunsaturated
   margarine
3 oz/75 g soft dark brown sugar
1 tablespoon/15 ml black treacle
2 eggs, separated
11 oz/325 g self-raising flour
½ teaspoon/2.5 ml ground cinnamon
½ teaspoon/2.5 ml ground cloves
½ teaspoon/2.5 ml allspice
½ teaspoon/2.5 ml nutmeg
6 fl oz/180 ml milk
4 oz/125 g caster sugar
1 oz/25 g ground almonds
3 oz/75 g crystallised ginger, chopped
Icing:
5 oz/150 g icing sugar, sieved
1 tablespoon/15 ml hot water
1 tablespoon/15 ml lemon juice

Grease and flour a 3-pint/1.75-litre Kugelhupf (fluted ring) cake tin. Cream 4 oz/125 g butter with the sugar and treacle until light and fluffy. Beat in the egg yolks. Sift 6 oz/175 g flour with the spices and fold into the mixture with 4 fl oz/120 ml milk. Keep to one side. Cream remaining butter with caster sugar. Fold in remaining flour and ground almonds with rest of milk. Whisk egg whites until stiff and fold into the mixture with 2 oz/50 g of the chopped ginger. Spoon alternate amounts of mixtures into the prepared tin and bake in a moderate oven (Mark 4 — 180°C — 350°F) for about an hour until risen and firm to touch. Cool in the tin. Beat icing sugar with water and lemon juice until smooth. Remove cake from tin and spoon over icing. Decorate with reserved ginger.

MIXED FRUIT COMPOTE

6 whole cloves
2 (2-inch/5-cm) cinnamon sticks
¼ teaspoon/1.25 ml ground ginger
3 oz/75 g sugar
½ lemon, pared rind and juice
10 fl oz/300 ml medium dry white wine
8 oz/225 g apricots, halved and stoned
8 oz/225 g plums, halved and stoned
2 large bananas, peeled and sliced
2 kiwi fruit, peeled and sliced.

Place cloves, cinnamon, ginger, sugar, lemon rind and juice and white wine in a wide, shallow pan. Heat gently to dissolve sugar then bring to the boil. Remove rind. Reduce heat, add apricots and plums and poach until just tender. Leave to cool, transfer to serving dish to go cold. Add banana and kiwi fruit. **Serves 6**

PLAICE AND FENNEL SAUTE

2 oz/50 g unsalted butter
1 tablespoon/15 ml oil
1 oz/25 g almond nibs
2 oz/50 g fennel, finely chopped
2 teaspoons/10 ml fennel seeds
4 plaice fillets, skinned and halved
   lengthways
1 teaspoon/5 ml paprika
2 tablespoons/30 ml lemon juice
Garnish: sprigs of fennel

Melt half the butter and the oil. Fry almonds and fennel until golden. Remove with slotted spoon and keep warm. Add remaining butter to pan with fennel seeds. Fold plaice fillets in half and fry gently, four at a time, for about 5 minutes, until cooked. Transfer to a serving dish and keep warm. Add paprika and lemon juice to pan and bring to the boil. Spoon juices over fish, spoon fennel and almonds in centre of dish, garnish and serve. **Serves 4**

PISTACHIO AND CARDAMOM ICE CREAM

1 (14 oz/400 g) can evaporated milk
20 cardamom pods, seeds removed
   and crushed, or ½ teaspoon/2.5 ml
   ground cardamom
2 oz/50 g caster sugar
2 teaspoons/10 ml powdered gelatine
5 fl oz/150 ml single cream
1 oz/25 g pistachio nuts, chopped
½ teaspoon/2.5 ml rosewater
To decorate: edible flower petals

Warm the evaporated milk with the cardamom and sugar, until sugar dissolves. Bring just to the boil and leave to cool. Dissolve gelatine in 2 tablespoons/30 ml water and stir into the milk with remaining ingredients. Transfer to rigid container and freeze until thick. Beat well, then freeze until solid. Or, transfer to dariole moulds before final freezing. Turn out and decorate with petals. **Serves 6**

BEETROOT AND TOMATO SOUP

1 oz/25 g butter
8 oz/225 g raw beetroot, peeled and
   grated
1 small onion, peeled and chopped
1 teaspoon/5 ml ground cumin
½ teaspoon/2.5 ml ground cinnamon
¼ teaspoon/1.25 ml ground cloves
1½ pints/900 ml chicken stock
8 oz/225 g tomatoes, peeled, deseeded
   and chopped
Garnish: lemon slices, parsley

Melt butter and gently fry the beetroot and onion until the onion is transparent. Add spices and cook, stirring for 1 to 2 minutes. Add stock and tomatoes, season with freshly ground black pepper. Cover and simmer for about 30 minutes, stirring occasionally, until beetroot is tender. Cool, liquidise until smooth. Reheat and garnish. **Serves 4**

MARINATED MUSHROOMS

2 tablespoons/30 ml oil
1 small onion, peeled and chopped
8 oz/225 g button mushrooms, wiped
1 tablespoon/15 ml ground coriander
1 tablespoon/15 ml wine vinegar
3 tablespoons/45 ml dry vermouth
***To garnish*: natural yogurt and fresh**
    coriander

Gently fry the onion until transparent. Add mushrooms and coriander and fry quickly for 3 minutes. Add remaining ingredients, season with freshly ground black pepper, bring to the boil and cook until only a little liquid remains. Chill and garnish. ***Serves 4***

YORKSHIRE CURD TART

4 oz/125 g plain flour
1 oz/25 g butter
1 oz/25 g lard
2 tablespoons/30 ml cold water
1½ oz/40 g caster sugar
1½ oz/40 g butter, melted
12 oz/350 g curd or sieved cottage cheese
2 small eggs, beaten
1 oz/25 g currants
grated rind of ½ lemon
½ teaspoon/2.5 ml ground nutmeg

Sift flour with a pinch of salt. Rub in the butter and lard, then mix to a firm dough with water. Roll out and use to line an 8-inch/20-cm fluted flan tin. Mix all remaining ingredients together, pour into pastry case and bake in a moderately hot oven (Mark 5 — 190°C — 375°F) for 35 to 40 minutes. Serve just warm or cold.
Serves 6

QUICK FRIED RIBBONS OF BEEF

8 oz/225 g rump steak, cut in thin strips
2 teaspoons/10 ml five spice powder
1½ teaspoons/7.5 ml cornflour
1 teaspoon/5 ml sugar
1 tablespoon/15 ml light soy sauce
2 tablespoons/30 ml oil
4 oz/125 g carrots, peeled and cut in strips
4 oz/125 g celery, trimmed, cut in strips
1 garlic clove, peeled and chopped
8 spring onions, trimmed and sliced
    diagonally
1 tablespoon/15 ml medium sherry
2 tablespoons/30 ml stock or water
***Garnish*: celery leaves**

Combine the beef with the five spice powder, cornflour, sugar and soy sauce and marinate for 45 minutes. Heat the oil in pan and fry carrots and celery, stirring for 2 minutes over high heat. Remove from pan with slotted spoon. Fry beef strips over high heat for 30 seconds, stirring. Add garlic. Return vegetables to pan with remaining ingredients and beef. Bring to the boil, stirring. Garnish and serve with boiled rice. ***Serves 2-3***

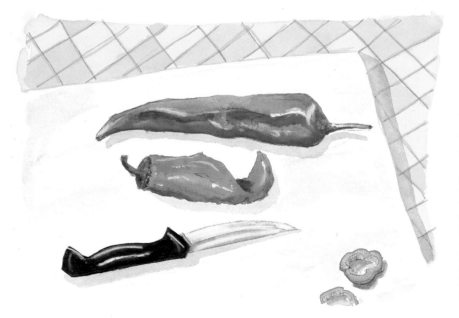

ORIENTAL DRESSING

5 oz/150 g natural yogurt
½ teaspoon/2.5 ml ground ginger
½ teaspoon/2.5 ml soy sauce
1 teaspoon/5 ml grated lemon rind
1 tablespoon/15 ml chopped fresh chives
pinch chilli powder

Blend all the ingredients together. Store in a screw top in the fridge for up to 1 week.

HOT CROSS BUNS

1½ lb/700 g strong plain flour
2 teaspoons/10 ml mixed spice
1 teaspoon/5 ml salt
1 sachet easy blend dried yeast
3 oz/75 g caster sugar
4 oz/125 g currants
2 oz/50 g chopped mixed peel
3 oz/75 g butter, melted and cooled
1 egg
12-14 fl oz/350-400 ml warm milk and
    water, half and half
For crosses:
4 oz/125 g shortcrust pastry
To glaze:
4 fl oz/120 ml milk
2 tablespoons/30 ml caster sugar

In a mixing bowl combine the flour, spice, salt, yeast, sugar, currants and peel. Stir in the butter, egg and half the milk mixture and mix until the dough forms a ball. Add enough of the remaining liquid to make a soft dough. Knead on a lightly floured surface for about 5 minutes until smooth and elastic. Place in an oiled plastic bag and leave in a warm place until doubled in size. Roll out the pastry to a 5 by 8-in/12.5 by 20-cm rectangle. Cut into 14 strips, then cut each strip in half. Turn out the dough and knead until original size. Divide into 14 pieces and knead into smooth rounds. Place well spaced on greased baking trays. Cover with oiled polythene and leave to prove for 30 minutes. Brush with milk and arrange pastry strips in crosses on top. Bake in a hot oven (Mark 7 — 220°C — 425°F) for 15-20 minutes. Meanwhile mix the sugar with the remaining milk and use to glaze the buns immediately they are removed from the oven. Cool on a wire rack. ***Makes 14***

HAM AND CITRUS MINT SALAD

There are many varieties of mint all of which are sweet and refreshing. Mint is a perfect partner for citrus fruit with savoury overtones provided by a little tarragon.

1 grapefruit
1 orange
2 sprigs fresh mint
1 sprig fresh tarragon
1 (2-inch/5-cm) piece cucumber, cut into matchsticks
1 tablespoon/15 ml olive oil
pinch of dried mustard
lettuce leaves
2 oz/50 g Parma ham
***To garnish:* few whole mint leaves**

With a sharp knife, cut skin and bitter white pith from grapefruit and orange. Cut segments free from membrane over a bowl to catch the juice. Reserve the fruit. Squeeze membrane to extract all juice. Add the mint and tarragon leaves and crush lightly. Put the orange, grapefruit and cucumber into a shallow bowl and pour over the juice and herbs. Cover and leave for 1 hour. Strain. Discard herbs and reserve juice. Blend juice with olive oil and mustard. Season with black pepper. Arrange the fruit and cucumber on lettuce leaves. Garnish with mint and serve with Parma ham and dressing. ***Serves 4***

EGGS WITH HERB BEURRE BLANC

Commonly used in sauces, especially Béarnaise, and to flavour vinegar, tarragon has a pungent flavour which marries well with egg in this classic fines herbes mix.

4 eggs
2 tablespoons/30 ml white wine vinegar
2 oz/50 g unsalted butter, chilled
1 tablespoon/15 ml mixed chopped herbs — tarragon, chervil and chives

Crack eggs into barely boiling water in a large shallow pan. Turn heat to low. Cover and leave for 5 minutes. Meanwhile, bring vinegar to boil and reduce by half. Whisk in the butter a little at a time. Remove from heat and stir in the herbs. Strain eggs with a slotted spoon. Pour over a little sauce and serve with hot toast. ***Serves 4***

CHICKEN WITH CORIANDER AND MINT

Coriander is one of the most highly perfumed herbs, characteristic of Asian cooking. A good partner, too, for lamb, fish and vegetables. Mint lends a touch of sweetness.

4 (6 oz/175 g) chicken breasts, skinned and boned
2 oz/50 g butter, cubed
1 carrot, cut into matchsticks
4 spring onions, trimmed and shredded
1 tablespoon/15 ml chopped coriander
1 tablespoon/15 ml chopped mint
2 fl oz/60 ml dry white wine or chicken stock

Place chicken breasts skinned side down between non-PVC film and beat with a rolling pin until ¼-inch/5-mm thick. Take care not to break the flesh. Divide the butter, vegetables and herbs between the four breasts. Season with freshly ground black pepper and roll up to form a sausage shape. Make sure the edges are firmly sealed. Wrap each breast in foil, pour over a little wine or stock. Seal well and bake at Mark 5 — 190°C — 375°F for 15 to 20 minutes. Serve in slices with juices. **Serves 4**

RED MULLET WITH THYME AND FENNEL

The combination of fennel's pronounced aniseed flavour and fish cannot be faulted. A touch of thyme adds robustness.

4 red mullet, scaled and cleaned
1 tablespoon/15 ml olive oil
juice of 1 lemon or lime
1 teaspoon/5 ml fresh thyme
2 sprigs fresh fennel, chopped

Wash the fish carefully inside and out and dry. Slash both sides 3 times. Mix the oil, lemon or lime juice and herbs together and coat the fish, rubbing into the slashes and cavity. Cover and chill for one hour. Grill for 10 minutes, turning once. Serve with new potatoes and salad. **Serves 4**

CLOCKWISE FROM TOP LEFT: HAM AND CITRUS MINT SALAD, PASTA WITH HERB YOGURT SAUCE, CHICKEN WITH CORIANDER AND MINT, EGGS WITH HERB BEURRE BLANC, RED MULLET WITH THYME AND FENNEL

PASTA WITH HERB YOGURT SAUCE

There are many varieties of origanum, of which marjoram is the sweetest and oregano the most pungent. Feathery dill adds a delicate touch of anise.

8 oz/225 g spaghetti or tagliatelle
2 tablespoons/30 ml olive oil
1 clove garlic, peeled and crushed
5 oz/150 g Greek yogurt
1 tablespoon/15 ml each fresh
    marjoram and parsley, chopped
1 teaspoon/5 ml chopped fresh dill
½ oz/12 g Parmesan cheese, grated

Boil the pasta in a large saucepan for 12 to 15 minutes, until *al dente*. Drain well. Heat oil in a frying pan and sauté garlic over low heat until softened. Do not brown. Add the yogurt and stir well to combine. Return pasta to the pan and pour over the yogurt sauce, herbs, Parmesan and plenty of freshly ground black pepper. Toss well.

Serves 4 as a starter

SAVOURY BUTTERS

These will flavour, moisten and garnish grilled or barbecued meat, fish and vegetables.

Beat 8 oz/225 g unsalted butter until soft and add one of the following:

- 2 oz/50 g fresh mixed herbs
- Grated peel and juice of 2 lemons
- 6 stoned black olives and 2 soaked anchovy fillets, pounded
- 2 tablespoons/30 ml Dijon mustard

When ingredients are thoroughly mixed, form into a roll and chill. Cut into ¼-inch/5-mm slices to serve. **Serves 16**

HERBAL TEAS

Herbal teas or tisanes are infusions of boiling water and herbs taken as refreshing drinks to aid digestion and provide beneficial properties. Keep a separate teapot, use 2 teaspoons chopped fresh leaves per cup, add to the warmed pot, cover with boiling water and infuse for 7-10 minutes. Drink hot without milk or serve with ice cubes, fresh herb sprigs and mineral water.

MARINADES

The role of a marinade is threefold: to protect food from drying out, especially in the fierce heat of a grill or barbecue; to tenderise; and to flavour. Oil-based marinades are the protective ones, good for grilling fish and meat with little natural fat, while acidic marinades based on wine, vinegar and fruit juices perform a tenderising function and also counteract fat in oily foods such as pork, herring or mackerel. Yogurt tenderises, too, and is the basis of many Indian dishes, especially Tandoori ones. The time you marinate foods depends on the effect you want to create. To flavour and protect, allow about four hours at room temperature or overnight in the fridge; for tenderising, you can double this time. Fish and shellfish deteriorate quickly and should be left only for an hour at room temperature or two hours in the fridge.

CITRUS MARINADE

Use for pork and other meats and fish high in natural fat. A good complement to poultry.

3 limes
2 lemons
3 oranges
4 tablespoons/60 ml olive oil
2 bay leaves
1 garlic clove, peeled and crushed

Thinly pare the rind from 2 of the limes, lemons and oranges. Squeeze juice. Mix with the oil, bay leaves and garlic. Thinly slice remaining lime and orange. Stir well and pour over meat or fish.

RED WINE MARINADE

Use for loin of pork or leg of lamb, for roasting, cubed beef for a casserole, steak or venison.

8 fl oz/250 ml red wine
2 fl oz/60 ml olive oil
1 small onion, finely sliced
1 small carrot, finely sliced
1 celery stick, finely sliced
½ teaspoon/2.5 ml dried thyme
6 black peppercorns, crushed

Mix all the ingredients together and pour over the meat.

TANDOORI MARINADE

1 teaspoon/5 ml coriander seeds
1 teaspoon/5 ml cumin seeds
2 cloves garlic, peeled
1 teaspoon/5 ml fresh root ginger, peeled
    and grated
10 fl oz/300 ml natural yogurt
juice of 2 lemons
2 tablespoons/30 ml wine vinegar
1 teaspoon/5 ml red chillies
1 small onion, finely sliced
½ teaspoon/2.5 ml cayenne pepper

In a pestle and mortar grind the coriander and cumin seeds. Add the garlic and ginger and pound to a paste. Transfer to a bowl and add remaining ingredients.

DRY SPICE MARINADE

Use to rub into scored fat of pork.

1 tablespoon/15 ml juniper berries
½ teaspoon/2.5 ml black peppercorns
½ teaspoon/2.5 ml allspice berries
1 teaspoon/5 ml dried thyme
3 to 4 blades of mace
pinch ground bay leaves
5 oz/150 g coarse sea salt

In a pestle and mortar grind the herbs and spices. Add the salt and grind briefly. Rub into the scored fat of pork.

WHITE WINE MARINADE

Use for fresh salmon steaks, rainbow trout, plaice or whiting, prawns or chicken.

8 fl oz/250 ml dry white wine
2 fl oz/60 ml olive oil
2 shallots or 1 small onion, finely sliced
1 garlic clove, peeled and crushed
juice of 1 small lemon
1 teaspoon/5 ml chopped fresh tarragon
    or dill
6 black or green peppercorns, crushed

Mix all ingredients together and pour over fish or meat.

**CLOCKWISE FROM THE LEFT: DRY SPICE MARINADE,
RED WINE MARINADE, TANDOORI MARINADE,
WHITE WINE MARINADE, CITRUS MARINADE**

SWEET AND SOUR MARINADE

Use for spare ribs, chicken joints.

5 fl oz/150 ml dry sherry
5 fl oz/150 ml unsweetened pineapple juice
3 tablespoons/45 ml soy sauce
2 tablespoons/30 ml wine vinegar
2 tablespoons/30 ml olive oil
2 tablespoons/30 ml brown sugar
pinch of mustard powder
dash of Worcestershire sauce
2 garlic cloves, peeled and crushed

Mix all the ingredients together and pour over meat.

OILS AND VINEGARS

For general cooking choose oils high in polyunsaturates: sunflower, safflower and soya bean; for flavour, and especially for salad dressings, virgin olive oil is favourite. More expensive nut oils such as walnut and hazelnut are very rich in flavour and best used in conjunction with another, lighter oil.

The combination of oil and vinegar in a vinaigrette is the perfect dressing for a salad and, while red and white wine vinegars and cider vinegars are the most common, herb, fruit and, more recently, pungent balsamic vinegar can all be substituted. Dressings should enhance not mask, just coat food not drown it. Dress cooked ingredients such as potatoes, rice and pasta while still warm, but leave leafy salads to the last moment to avoid wilting. Also, make sure they are dry so that the dressing is not diluted.

SELECTION OF HERB AND FRUIT VINEGARS AND OILS

Cooking with Fruit

As gardeners with fruiting trees already know, and those of us getting hooked on the booming Pick-Your-Own market are fast discovering, cooking with fruit does not begin with packing them into pies and end with jam-making. Nor has it ever for, as familiar favourites like redcurrant sauce with lamb, cranberry with turkey and apple sauce with pork indicate, fruit and meat have long been successful partners. Apart from strawberries, most berries and currants as well as 'top fruits' such as apples, cherries and plums, have a high acid content, so their tart flavours help to balance rich meats such as pork and lamb (hence their success as spicy relishes); and they work well in salads too (see page 104).

● You can add fruit whole to a stir-fry or risotto (see recipes, pages 98 and 101). Grapes, sweet and juicy, are classic with seafood and fish (see recipe, page 105), and stone fruits such as peaches, apricots and nectarines complement not only ham but also nuts and salad leaves, making all sorts of luscious late-summer combinations cheap and accessible. You can purée fruits to make dazzlingly coloured sauces (see Redcurrant Stuffed Chicken Breasts on page 100), or add puréed kiwi fruit to dressings for chicken, apple and horseradish for fish, citrus and lemon juices in dressings for ham. Purées of fruit and fruit juices can also provide the acid element in dressings.

● While imports are extending the fresh fruit season right round the year, our own soft fruit season starts with the first cherries in May and goes on until September's blackberrying expeditions, followed by the season of plums and orchard fruits. For generations we have stored fruit for winter by bottling and drying as well as preserving them in jams and chutneys, and to these we can now add freezing. All soft fruit bar strawberries freeze well, and even strawberries, which lose their shape and texture on defrosting, freeze well in a purée. Others should be open-frozen and then packed in bags. Apples and pears keep fresh through winter, choose perfect specimens and keep in a cold place, wrapped in paper and packed in boxes.

PANCAKES FILLED WITH SWEET SOUR REDCURRANTS

4 oz/125 g plain flour
pinch of salt
1 egg, beaten
10 fl oz/300 ml milk
1 oz/25 g melted butter
1 tablespoon/15 ml oil
1 clove garlic, peeled and crushed
6 oz/175 g streaky bacon, derinded and chopped
8 oz/225 g broccoli, cut into florets
4 oz/125 g button mushrooms, wiped and sliced
2 tablespoons/30 ml fresh chopped parsley
8 oz/225 g redcurrants
1 tablespoon/15 ml caster sugar
To garnish: cucumber slices

Sieve the flour and salt into a bowl. Make a well in the centre and pour in the egg. Gradually beat in the milk with a wooden spoon until smooth.

Heat a 5-inch/12.5-cm frying pan and brush with a little melted butter. Pour in just enough batter to cover the bottom and swirl to coat evenly. Cook for 30 seconds, turn over and cook the other side for 30 seconds. Make the remaining pancakes in the same way and layer between sheets of greaseproof paper.

Melt the oil in a frying pan and fry the garlic and bacon for 2 minutes. Stir in the broccoli florets and cook for 5 minutes. Then add the mushrooms, parsley, redcurrants, sugar and freshly ground black pepper, and fry for a further 2 minutes. Divide the mixture between the pancakes and fold them in half and half again. Serve garnished with cucumber.
Makes 18

STRAWBERRY LIVER RISOTTO

SEAFOOD GOOSEBERRY PIE

12 oz/350 g gooseberries

1 oz/25 g caster sugar

12 oz/350 g monkfish, trimmed

3 oz/75 g peeled prawns

½ red pepper, cored, deseeded and diced

1 lb/450 g puff pastry, thawed if frozen

Place 8 oz/225 g gooseberries, the sugar and 1 tablespoon/15 ml water in a saucepan. Bring to the boil, cover and simmer gently for 10 minutes. Sieve. Cut the remaining gooseberries in half. Cut the monkfish into small cubes and mix with the gooseberries, half the purée, prawns, red pepper and season with freshly ground black pepper.

Roll out two-thirds of the pastry to ⅛-inch/2-mm thick. Cut out six 4½-inch/11-cm circles and use to line six 3½-inch/9-cm fluted tartlet tins. Chill for 30 minutes. Prick the bases well and line with greaseproof paper or foil and fill with baking beans. Bake blind at Mark 6 — 200°C — 400°F for 30 minutes.

Remove the beans and paper and allow to cool slightly. Divide the filling between the pastry cases. Brush the edges with beaten egg. Roll out the remaining pastry to ⅛-inch/2-mm thick and cut out six 3½-inch/9-cm circles. Cover the pies and seal the edges firmly.

Decorate with pastry fish cut from the trimmings and brush with a little beaten egg. Bake at Mark 6 — 200°C — 400°F for a further 20 to 25 minutes until golden. Heat the reserved gooseberry purée and serve with the pies. **Serves 6**

RASPBERRY STIR-FRY

3 × 6 oz/175 g pork steaks, trimmed

2 tablespoons/30 ml oil

1 inch/2.5-cm piece fresh root ginger, cut into julienne strips

2 carrots, cut into matchsticks

½ head Chinese leaves, thickly shredded

8 oz/225 g raspberries

1 tablespoon/15 ml dark soy sauce

Cut the pork into ½ × 3-inch/1-cm × 7.5-cm strips. Heat the oil in a wok or frying pan until almost smoking. Add the ginger and stir-fry for 30 seconds. Add the pork and cook for 2 minutes. Add the carrots, cook for 2 minutes then toss in the Chinese leaves and raspberries and stir-fry for a further minute. Pour over the soy sauce and serve. **Serves 4**

SEAFOOD GOOSEBERRY PIE RASPBERRY STIR-FRY

PASSION FRUIT AND CRAB SALAD

1 (10-oz/300-g) can peeled lychees, drained
3 passion fruit
3 Sharon fruit, cored
4 oz/125 g white crab meat, thawed if frozen
1 tablespoon/15 ml lemon juice
To garnish: **toasted flaked almonds**

Cut the lychees in half and place in a large bowl. Cut the tops off the passion fruit and scoop out the seeds into the bowl. Slice the Sharon fruit and add to the bowl with the crab meat and the lemon juice. Toss gently and divide between individual serving plates. Top with flaked almonds and serve with wholewheat bread. ***Serves 4-6***

REDCURRANT STUFFED CHICKEN BREASTS

REDCURRANT STUFFED CHICKEN BREASTS

6 oz/175 g redcurrants
4 oz/125 g skimmed milk cheese (quark)
4 × 5 oz/150 g chicken breasts, skinned and boned
2 tablespoons/30 ml oil
4 fl oz/120 ml chicken stock
2 fl oz/60 ml dry white wine
2 fl oz/60 ml double cream

Mix together 2 oz/50 g of the redcurrants, skimmed milk cheese and freshly ground black pepper.

Make a 1½-inch/3.5-cm deep horizontal cut in the side of each chicken breast to form a pocket. Fill each with 1 heaped tablespoon/15 ml of the cheese mixture.

Heat the oil in a frying pan over a high heat and quickly brown the chicken breasts on both sides. Pour over the stock and wine and bring to the boil. Cover, and simmer for 10-15 minutes until tender.

Remove the chicken breasts with a slotted spoon and keep warm. Rapidly boil the juices until reduced by two-thirds. Stir in the cream and remaining redcurrants and simmer gently for 1 minute. Spoon over the chicken breasts and serve immediately with minted new potatoes. ***Serves 4***

STRAWBERRY PLAICE PAUPIETTES

The sweetness of the strawberries is offset by the spicy coriander.

1 lb/450 g strawberries, hulled
4 tablespoons/60 ml fresh chopped coriander
10 × 3-oz/75-g plaice fillets, skinned
6 fl oz/180 g fish stock

Finely chop 12 oz/350 g of the strawberries and halve the rest. Blend together the coriander, two plaice fillets and freshly ground black pepper in either a food processor or liquidiser until

smooth. Stir in the chopped strawberries.

Divide the filling between the remaining plaice fillets and roll up from the wider end of the fillet. Place the fillets side by side in a small frying pan and pour over the stock. Bring to the boil, cover and poach for 10 minutes, until the fish begins to flake. Carefully remove the fish with a slotted spoon, taking care not to break them, and keep warm.

Rapidly boil the juices until reduced by two-thirds. Toss in the remaining halved strawberries and simmer gently for 10 seconds. Serve the fish with the sauce poured over. **Serves 4**

CHEESE AND APPLE PIE

A wonderful combination, hence the old saying "apple pie without cheese is like a kiss without a squeeze".

8 oz/225 g self-raising wholewheat flour
2 oz/50 g polyunsaturated margarine or butter
2 oz/50 g vegetable shortening
3-4 tablespoons/45-60 ml iced water
Filling:
4 cooking apples, peeled, cored and sliced
3 oz/75 g Cheshire cheese, thinly sliced
finely grated zest of 1 lemon
½ teaspoon/2.5 ml freshly grated nutmeg
2 tablespoons/30 ml sugar

Place the flour in a large bowl and rub in the margarine or butter and shortening. Mix in just enough water to make a firm dough. Use three-quarters of the pastry to line a deep, 8-inch/20-cm pie plate. Layer the apple and cheese into the pie case and sprinkle with the lemon zest, nutmeg

and sugar. Use the remaining pastry to make a lid for the pie. Crimp the crust and brush the top with water. Sprinkle with a little more sugar. Bake at Mark 6 — 200°C — 400°F for 35-40 minutes until the pastry is golden. **Serves 6**

PEAR AND WALNUT PIE

8 oz/225 g plain flour
3 oz/75 g walnuts, finely ground
1 oz/25 g icing sugar, sifted
2 oz/50 g butter
2 tablespoons/30 ml cold water
Filling:
3 conference pears, halved, cored and peeled
1 egg, beaten
2 oz/50 g soft brown sugar
grated rind of 1 lemon and 1 teaspoon/ 5 ml lemon juice
1 oz/25 g butter, melted

For the pastry: mix the flour, walnuts and icing sugar in a bowl. Rub in the butter and stir in just enough water to mix to a firm dough. Chill, wrapped in polythene, for at least 30 minutes. Use three-quarters of the pastry to line an 8-inch/20-cm pie dish.

For the filling: arrange the pears cut side down in the base of the pie. Beat the egg with the sugar until well blended. Stir in the lemon rind, juice and butter. Pour over the pears. Arrange the remaining pastry in a lattice pattern over the pie. Bake at Mark 7 — 220°C — 425°F for 10 minutes, then reduce the heat to Mark 4 — 180°C — 350°F for 1 hour. **Serves 6**

STRAWBERRY LIVER RISOTTO

STRAWBERRY LIVER RISOTTO

1 pint/600 ml chicken stock
6 oz/175 g risotto rice
1 lb/450 g pigs' liver, trimmed
2 tablespoons/30 ml oil
1 yellow pepper, cored, deseeded and sliced
1 bunch spring onions, trimmed and sliced
12 oz/350 g strawberries, halved

Bring the stock to the boil and add the rice. Cover and simmer for 15-20 minutes, until the rice is tender.

Slice the liver into thin strips about ¼-inch/5-mm by 3-inches/7.5-cm. Heat the oil in a pan and fry the peppers for 4 minutes until softened. Add the liver and spring onions and fry for 2 to 3 minutes. Add the strawberries and fry for a further 30 seconds. Gently stir into the rice and serve immediately. **Serves 4**

BLACKCURRANT KEBABS WITH RASPBERRY SAUCE

8 oz/225 g lean minced beef
1 tablespoon/15 ml fresh chopped coriander
3 oz/75 g blackcurrants, sieved
12 small onions, peeled
12 button mushrooms, wiped
12 small tomatoes
8 oz/225 g raspberries, sieved
1 tablespoon/15 ml soy sauce
2 teaspoons/10 ml caster sugar

Mix together the minced beef, coriander, blackcurrant purée and seasoning. Divide the mixture into twelve and roll into balls. Chill for 30 minutes.

Blanch the onions in boiling water for 2 minutes and drain. Thread on to four skewers, alternating with the mushrooms, beef and tomatoes. Brush with a little oil. Grill for 8-10 minutes, turning occasionally. Meanwhile, bring the raspberry purée, soy sauce and sugar to the boil, stirring until the sugar dissolves, and season to taste with freshly ground black pepper.

Serve the kebabs with boiled rice sprinkled with chopped herbs and the raspberry sauce. **Serves 4**

TROPICAL HAM SALAD

1 pawpaw, peeled, deseeded
½ small pineapple, peeled, cored
4 oz/125 g mange-tout, trimmed
3 oz/75 g sliced cooked ham, cut into
    strips
Dressing:
3 tablespoons/45 ml mayonnaise
3 tablespoons/45 ml soured cream
1 bunch watercress, trimmed and finely
    chopped
To serve: chicory leaves

Cut the fruit into pieces and place in a bowl. Blanch the mange-tout in boiling water for 1 minute. Plunge into iced water, drain and add with ham to fruit.

Combine ingredients for the dressing and season with freshly ground black pepper. Pile the fruit mixture into a rosette of chicory leaves and spoon dressing on top. **Serves 4**

GINGERED PEARS

3 firm pears, peeled, cored
2 ripe fresh figs
3 large oranges
1-inch/2.5-cm piece fresh root ginger
1 tablespoon/15 ml green peppercorns,
    drained
3 tablespoons/45 ml white wine vinegar
2 tablespoons/30 ml caster sugar
Dressing:
4 tablespoons/60 ml olive oil
2 tablespoons/30 ml lemon juice
pinch dry mustard
large pinch ground cinnamon
large pinch ground coriander

Slice pears and figs into a bowl. Thinly pare the rind from oranges and set aside. Remove pith and divide oranges into segments. Add to the fruit. Peel and finely grate the ginger and add with the peppercorns. Cut the orange rind into thin strips. Place in a pan with the vinegar and sugar. Heat gently until sugar is dissolved. Bring to the boil and simmer for 5 minutes. Remove the rind and drain.

Whisk the dressing ingredients together with plenty of freshly ground black pepper until well blended. Toss through the salad and garnish with the orange rind. **Serves 4-6**

MANGO, MUSHROOM AND MOZZARELLA SALAD

6 oz/175 g black grapes, peeled
2 red apples, cored
1 ripe mango, peeled and stoned
1 tablespoon/15 ml lemon juice
2 oz/50 g button mushrooms, sliced
6 oz/175 g Mozzarella cheese, cut into
    small cubes
6 fresh basil leaves
6 black peppercorns, crushed
2 tablespoons/30 ml olive oil
1 tablespoon/15 ml white wine vinegar

Halve the grapes and remove seeds. Slice the apples and mango and toss in the lemon juice. Add to grapes with the mushrooms. Transfer to serving plates and sprinkle with Mozzarella cubes. Shred the basil leaves and mix with the peppercorns, oil and vinegar. Sprinkle the dressing over each salad. Serve chilled. **Serves 4-6**

SALMON AND STRAWBERRY

4 oz/125 g strawberries, hulled
3-inch/7.5-cm piece cucumber, thinly
    sliced
2-3 oz/50-75 g smoked salmon, thinly
    sliced
6 small mint sprigs
Dressing:
4 oz/125 g strawberries, puréed
2 tablespoons/30 ml oil
1 teaspoon/5 ml lemon juice
To garnish: mint leaves

Slice the strawberries lengthways, and place in a bowl with the cucumber. Cut the salmon into diamond shapes and mix with the fruit. Add the mint. Whisk dressing ingredients together with plenty of freshly ground black pepper. Pour over the salad and turn to coat thoroughly. Garnish with mint. **Serves 2-4**

APPLE AND PEAR CHEESE

A fruit cheese is similar to both a jam and a jelly but is firm in texture and can be sliced. Originally called "cheeses" because they were eaten instead of a cheese course.

Store for 2 to 3 months before eating. Will keep for up to 12 months.

1½ lb/700 g cooking apples, washed and
    roughly chopped
1½ lb/700 g pears, washed and roughly
    chopped
juice of 1 lemon
pinch ground nutmeg
1 lb/450 g sugar to each 1 lb/450 g fruit
    purée

Place the prepared fruit in a heavy pan and half cover with water. Cover and simmer until very soft and pulpy. Press the fruit through a sieve to make a smooth purée. Weigh the purée and return it to the cleaned pan with lemon juice and nutmeg. Simmer until thick. Stir in the required quantity of sugar until it dissolves. Cook gently for about 1 hour, stirring to prevent burning. The cheese must be stiff enough for a spoon to leave a clean line when drawn across the bottom of the pan. Skim if necessary.

Pour the fruit cheese into a tin or jar from which it can be turned out and served on a plate or dish. Press waxed paper discs on the cheese and cover with non-PVC film. Store in a cool, dry place. Serve the fruit cheese cut into wedges or slices and eat with bread and cheese or with cold meats. **Makes 2-3 lb/900 g-1.4 kg**

GRAPE AND SEAFOOD SALAD

Fruit blends perfectly with juicy prawns.

4 oz/125 g white grapes, peeled
½ ogen melon, deseeded and cubed
4 sticks celery, sliced
6 oz/175 g cooked prawns, shelled
Dressing:
4 tablespoons/60 ml olive oil
2 tablespoons/30 ml lemon juice
½ teaspoon/2.5 ml wholegrain mustard
1 tablespoon/15 ml fresh chopped mint
To serve: curly endive, few unshelled
prawns, fresh mint

Halve grapes and remove seeds. Place in a bowl with the melon cubes, celery and prawns. Toss together. In another small bowl place the oil, lemon juice, mustard, and chopped mint. Whisk together until evenly blended. Arrange salad on a bed of curly endive with a few unshelled prawns, pour over dressing and garnish with mint. **Serves 4**

KIWI AND MELON SALAD

1 ogen melon, seeds removed
1 head chicory
6 oz/175 g cherry tomatoes
3 kiwi fruit, peeled, cut into segments
Dressing:
finely grated rind of 1 lime
1 tablespoon/15 ml lime juice
½ teaspoon/2.5 ml whole coriander
   seeds, crushed
5 fl oz/150 ml soured cream
few drops Tabasco sauce
To garnish: fresh chopped parsley

Cut the melon into balls using a vegetable baller or teaspoon (or cut into cubes), reserve juice. Using a stainless steel knife, remove the central core and thinly slice the chicory. Halve the cherry tomatoes. Arrange on individual serving plates with the kiwi fruit.

Mix all the dressing ingredients together with the melon juices and chill for 10 minutes, spoon a little on each salad and sprinkle with chopped parsley. Serve as a starter. **Serves 4-6**

HANDY JELLY HINTS

- Fruit must not be over-ripe.
- Frozen fruit can be used.
- Fruit must be thoroughly washed but not stalked, cored or peeled: much of the setting quality is in the pips and skin.
- The fruit requires long, slow initial cooking in water until soft and pulpy.
- Straining is all-important. Special jelly bags are available. Scald the bag with boiling water before use.
- Suspend the jelly bag from the legs of an upturned stool and place a large bowl under it to catch the juice.
- Make sure the bag does not touch the juice as it collects.
- Allow plenty of time for straining; at least 1 hour, or overnight.
- Never squeeze the bag while straining, as it will cloud the jelly.
- Use granulated sugar for jelly making, or preserving sugar which creates less scum.
- Test for setting point as for jam: with a thermometer — 220°F/105°C — or do the saucer test: put a teaspoon of the jelly on a cold saucer and see if the surface wrinkles when pushed with a finger.
- The jelly must be quickly skimmed to remove any scum, poured at once into warmed, sterilised jars and covered immediately.
- Make sure the jars are filled to the brim, as the jelly will shrink as it cools.
- Use small jars for jelly (maximum size 1 lb/450 g) as this aids setting.
- Do not move the jars until the jelly has set firmly.
- Jelly should be stored in a cool, dry place away from direct sunlight.

QUINCE JELLY

4 lb/1.8 kg quinces, chopped
6 pints/3.5 litres water
1 lb/450 g granulated or preserving
   sugar per pint of juice

Put the quinces into a preserving pan or large heavy saucepan and add the water. Bring to a simmer, then simmer for about 1 hour until very soft and pulpy. Mash well, then strain.

Measure the strained juice into the rinsed-out pan and add 1 lb/450 g sugar per pint/600 ml of juice. Heat until the sugar is dissolved, then boil rapidly until setting point is reached. Skim quickly,

then pour immediately into warmed jars, top with waxed discs and cover the jars.
Makes 3 lb/1.4 kg

REDCURRANT AND APPLE JELLY

2 lb/900 g redcurrants, washed
3 lb/1.4 kg cooking apples, washed and
   roughly chopped
about 2 pints/1.1 litre water
1 lb/450 g granulated or preserving
   sugar per pint/600 ml of juice

Follow same method as Quince Jelly.
Makes 3-4 lb/1.4-1.8 kg

BLACKBERRY AND APPLE JELLY

2 lb/900 g blackberries, washed
4 lb/1.8 kg cooking apples, washed and
   cut up roughly
2 pints/1.1 litre water
1 lb/450 g granulated or preserving
   sugar per pint/600 ml of juice.

Follow same method as Quince Jelly.
Makes 5 lb/2.3 kg

MINT JELLY

6 lb/2.7 kg cooking apples, washed and
   roughly chopped
1 pint/600 ml white wine vinegar
juice of 4 lemons
about 2 pints/1.1 litre water
1 bunch fresh young mint, bruised
1 lb/450 g granulated or preserving
   sugar per pint/600 ml of juice
3 tablespoons/45 ml very finely chopped
   fresh mint

Put the apples into a preserving pan or large heavy saucepan and add the lemon juice, vinegar and enough water to barely cover. Add the mint, divided in sprigs. Bring to the boil, then simmer for about 1 hour until very soft and pulpy. Mash well then strain. Measure the juice into the rinsed out pan and add 1 lb/450 g sugar per pint/600 ml of juice. Heat until sugar is dissolved then boil rapidly until setting point is reached. Skim quickly then stir in the chopped mint. Pour immediately into warmed jars, top with waxed discs and cover the jars.

Desserts

We may feel guilty if we satisfy the all-too-familiar desire for something sweet at the end of a meal with rich and lusciously creamy concoctions, but the arrival of quark and its French cousin *fromage frais*, both skimmed milk cheeses, thick and creamy Greek yogurt and reduced-fat creams have made it possible to enjoy desserts and not feel too indulgent. Desserts arouse strong passions and some hostesses feel the urge to show off with three or even four choices. After a substantial main course, though, one simple creation is enough to tantalise palates, and often a light and refreshing fruit-based sweet is the best choice: a simple fruit salad, perhaps, with the addition of something exotic like a couple of passion fruit or a mango. Don't drown your fruit with a heavy syrup: fruit juice and a splash of brandy or a liqueur such as Cointreau are all you need.

● Gone are heavy, calorie-laden cheesecakes and full-cream mousses. For a simple lightweight dessert, stir Greek yogurt or any of the skimmed-milk cheeses into a fruit purée and top it with toasted nuts, or mix the purée into a chilled custard lightened with egg whites and fold in just a spoonful or two of whipped cream. Make fruit tarts in the French style: spoon over a layer of custard or crème pâtissière (page 124) and fill with the fruit of the season, fresh or poached. Ice cream and sorbets remain firm favourites for all — see our list on pages 112-13.

● If you are an ice cream or sorbet fan, it's worth investing in an ice cream maker or sorbetière, so you don't have to bother about beating and re-freezing, the machine will do it for you. To save time when serving ice cream, especially if you are entertaining, allow the ice cream to soften sufficiently for scooping and return scoops and remaining ice cream to the freezer. Thirty minutes before serving, arrange scoops on the plates and leave in the fridge. When serving sorbets, always chill dishes thoroughly so that the sorbet doesn't melt too quickly.

LOW FAT CREME BRULEE

8 fl oz/250 ml fresh skimmed milk
10 fl oz/300 ml low-fat single cream
grated rind of 1 lemon
5 egg yolks
2 oz/50 g caster sugar
2 tablespoons/30 ml hazelnuts, finely chopped
2 tablespoons/30 ml demerara sugar

Bring the milk, cream and lemon rind to the boil. Remove from heat. Whisk the egg yolks and caster sugar together until pale and stir into the milk until well blended. Strain and pour into four 5 fl oz/150 ml lightly buttered ramekins. Place the ramekins in a roasting tin, and half fill the tin with boiling water. Bake at Mark 4 — 180°C — 350°F for 40 minutes until set. Allow to cool, cover the ramekins and chill overnight.

Sprinkle the hazelnuts evenly over the top of the creams and then do the same with the demerara sugar. Place under a very hot grill for about 2 minutes, rotating occasionally until evenly browned. Watch to prevent burning. Cool, then chill for a further 30 minutes before serving.
Serves 4

ORANGE-FLOWER WATER JUNKET

Rennet essence is available in bottles from supermarkets and delicatessens.

2 pints/1.1 litre fresh skimmed milk
2 tablespoons/30 ml caster sugar
1 teaspoon/5 ml rennet essence
few drops of orange-flower water

Place the milk and sugar in a saucepan and stir over a gentle heat until the sugar has dissolved. Remove from the heat and allow to cool slightly until lukewarm. Stir in the rennet and the orange-flower water and pour into a serving bowl. Leave the junket to stand at room temperature for about 2 hours until set. *Serves 6*

RASPBERRY SORBET WITH SUMMER BERRY SAUCE

1 lb/450 g raspberries, sieved
2 oz/50 g sugar
juice ½ orange
2 egg whites
8 oz/225 g mixed strawberries/
 redcurrants, sieved

Mix the raspberry purée with the sugar and the orange juice. Pour into a freezer container and freeze for 45 minutes.

 Beat the egg whites until stiff and fold into the raspberry mix. Freeze for a further 1 hour. Beat until smooth. Refreeze until firm. To serve: remove from the freezer ½ hour before serving. Place in a piping bag with ½-inch/1-cm star nozzle and pipe into individual dishes, or serve in scoops. Serve with the sieved fruit. **Serves 4**

TARTE TATIN

1¼ lb/575 g Cox's apples
2 oz/50 g unsalted butter, melted
3 oz/75 g sugar
12 oz/350 g puff pastry

Peel and core the apples and slice thickly. Pour half the melted butter into an 8-inch/20-cm cake tin. Sprinkle over half the sugar. Arrange the apples in concentric rings. Top with remaining butter and sugar. Bake at Mark 5 — 190°C — 375°F for 30 minutes. Allow to cool slightly. Roll out the pastry to form a circle about 8½ inches/21 cm in diameter. Place on top of the apples. Bake for a further 50 minutes until golden and caramelized. Invert on to a plate and serve hot or cool. **Serves 4-6**

SPICED GINGER PEARS

The vine leaves we used were preserved in brine, but if fresh ones are available these can be used instead.

4 pears, peeled, halved and cored
lemon juice
1 oz/25 g preserved ginger, sliced
few cloves
8 vine leaves
1 pint/600 ml sweet cider
2 oz/50 g caster sugar

Sprinkle the pear halves with lemon juice. Divide the ginger and cloves equally between them. Put the halves back together and wrap in vine leaves. Pack tightly into a dish and pour over the cider. Cover and bake at Mark 3 — 170°C — 325°F for 30 minutes or until the pears are softened. Leave to go cold then strain off the cooking liquid and boil with the sugar for 15 minutes, or until reduced to a quarter. Serve cold with pears. **Serves 4**

RASPBERRY SORBET WITH SUMMER BERRY SAUCE   **SPICED GINGER PEARS**

CLOCKWISE FROM TOP LEFT: LYCHEE AND CHAMPAGNE ICE CREAM, STRAWBERRY AND BLACK PEPPER ICE CREAM, BLACKCURRANT ICE CREAM, TANGARINE ICE CREAM; CENTRE: STRAWBERRY AND ALMOND ICE CREAM WITH RASPBERRY PURÉE

CUSTARD-BASED VANILLA ICE CREAM

This is a rich ice cream and should be served in small portions.

1 pint/600 ml milk
1 vanilla pod or few drops of vanilla essence
6 egg yolks
4 oz/100 g caster sugar
5 fl oz/150 ml double cream, whipped

Scald the milk with the vanilla pod, if using, and leave to infuse for 15 minutes. Strain. Whisk the egg yolks with the sugar until pale and thick. Gradually stir in the strained milk and vanilla essence, if using. Cook over very low heat, stirring constantly, for about 3 to 4 minutes until the custard thickens and coats the back of a wooden spoon. Do not allow to boil, otherwise the eggs will curdle.

Press a circle of greaseproof paper or cling film on to the surface and leave until cold.

Fold in the whipped cream (and chosen flavouring if not using vanilla).

Spoon into a shallow container and freeze for 40 minutes or until the ice cream begins to harden round the edges. Turn into a chilled bowl and whisk to break up the ice crystals. Return to the container and repeat the freezing and beating process once or twice more, depending on the required smoothness.

Makes 1½ pints/900 ml

ICE CREAM FLAVOURS

Apricot and Brandy
Soak 8 oz/225 g dried apricots in 2 tablespoons/30 ml brandy and 5 fl oz/150 ml water overnight. Purée all but 1 oz/25 g in a food processor. Chop remainder. Fold into ice cream.

Blackcurrant
(pictured on page 111)
Poach 10 oz/300 g trimmed blackcurrants with 2 oz/50 g sugar and 2 fl oz/60 ml water until soft. Fold into ice cream

Blackberry and Apple Ripple
Poach 12 oz/350 g blackberries in 5 fl oz/150 ml water with 2 oz/50 g sugar until soft. Drain and rub through a sieve. Peel, core and slice 1 lb/450 g cooking apples and poach in 3 fl oz/90 ml water and juice of ½ lemon with 2 tablespoons/30 ml sugar until soft. Drain and purée in a food processor. Fold the apple purée into the ice cream. Spoon into the shallow container. Lightly swirl in the blackberry purée.

Coffee and Brazil Nut
Dissolve 3 teaspoons/15 ml instant coffee in 2 tablespoons/30 ml boiling water. Pour into ice cream with 3 oz/75 g (shelled weight) chopped Brazil nuts.

Crème de Menthe
Stir 3 tablespoons/45 ml crème de menthe into the ice cream.

Brown Bread
Trim the crusts from 4 oz/125 g wholemeal bread and process to breadcrumbs in a food processor. Mix with 4 oz/125 g demerara sugar. Toast at Mark 7 — 220°C — 425°F, stirring frequently, for 12 minutes. Cool, crush with a rolling pin. Fold into ice cream with 3 tablespoons/45 ml sherry. Freeze.

Chestnut
Fold 8 oz/225 g canned sweetened chestnut purée into ice cream with 3 tablespoons/45 ml rum.

Chocolate and Cointreau
Melt 6 oz/175 g plain chocolate, cool and stir in 4 tablespoons/60 ml Cointreau. Stir into ice cream.

Chocolate and Marshmallow
Melt 4 oz/125 g plain chocolate with 4 oz/125 g white marshmallows. Cool slightly, beat into ice cream.

Chocolate Fudge
Melt 2 oz/50 g plain chocolate, 1 tablespoon/15 ml cocoa powder, 2 tablespoons/30 ml golden syrup, 2 oz/50 g sugar and 4 tablespoons/60 ml water together over a low heat. Boil until the temperature reaches 116°C (240°F) on a sugar thermometer. Cool slightly then stir into warm ice cream, made with 2 oz/50 g sugar.

Coffee and Hazelnut
Finely chop 4 oz/125 g blanched hazelnuts and toast under a hot grill. Fold into ice cream with 1 tablespoon/15 ml coffee essence.

English Toffee
Dissolve 8 oz/225 g sugar in 3 fl oz/90 ml water over low heat. Boil until the temperature reaches 154°C (310°F) on a sugar thermometer. Remove from the heat and pour on to an oiled baking tray. Leave until hard then crush with a rolling pin. Stir into ice cream made with 1 oz/25 g sugar.

Fig
Drain 1 (14 oz/397 g) can figs in syrup and remove stalks. Purée. Fold into ice cream.

Irish Coffee
Dissolve 3 teaspoons/15 ml instant coffee in 2 tablespoons/30 ml boiling water. Stir in 1 tablespoon/15 ml demerara sugar and 4 tablespoons/60 ml whisky. Stir into ice cream.

Kiwi and Guava
Peel 3 kiwi fruit. Purée with 1 (14 oz/397 g) can guavas in syrup. Stir into ice cream with 1 tablespoon/15 ml finely chopped mint.

Macaroon and Amaretto
Stir 4 oz/125 g crushed macaroons and 3 tablespoons/45 ml Amaretto liqueur into ice cream.

Mint with Chocolate Flake
Fold a few drops peppermint essence, a few drops of green food colouring and 3 oz/75 g crumbled chocolate flakes into ice cream.

Muesli
Fold 4 oz/125 g of your favourite unsweetened muesli mix into ice cream.

Pistachio
Fold 4 oz/125 g (shelled weight) pistachio nuts, a few drops green food colouring and a few drops almond essence into ice cream.

Praline
Dissolve 8 oz/225 g sugar with 3 fl oz/90 ml water over low heat. Boil until the temperature reaches 154°C (310°F) on a sugar thermometer. Stir in 2 oz/50 g toasted chopped almonds. Pour on to an oiled baking tray and leave until hard. Crush with a rolling pin and stir into ice cream made with 1 oz/25 g sugar.

Port and Raisin
Soak 8 oz/225 g raisins in 4 fl oz/120 ml port overnight or until plumped up and all the liquid has been absorbed. Stir into ice cream.

Strawberry and Almond
Purée 1 lb/450 g hulled strawberries with 1 oz/25 g ground almonds. Fold into ice cream.

Tangerine
(pictured on page 110)
Thinly pare the rind of 6 tangerines, cut into tiny julienne strips and blanch in boiling water for 2 minutes. Drain and cool. Squeeze the juice from the tangerines and fold into ice cream with the rind.

Tutti-frutti

Soak 6 oz/175 g mixed dried fruit, 3 oz/75 g chopped mixed peel and 2 oz/50 g glacé cherries in 5 fl oz/150 ml sweet white wine for 6 hours or until plumped up and all the liquid has been absorbed. Fold into ice cream.

Lychee and Champagne

Drain 1 (1 lb 4 oz/575 g) can lychees and rinse well. Purée with 10 fl oz/300 ml champagne or sparkling white wine. Fold into ice cream.

Maple Syrup

Stir 2 tablespoons/30 ml maple syrup into ice cream.

Melon and Ginger

Peel and deseed 1 charantais melon and purée the flesh with ¼ teaspoon/1.25 ml ground ginger. Fold into ice cream.

Mint and Redcurrant

Poach 8 oz/225 g trimmed redcurrants in 3 fl oz/90 ml water until soft. Rub through a sieve and stir in 2 oz/50 g sugar. Stir in 2 tablespoons/30 ml finely chopped fresh mint. Fold into ice cream.

Orange and Grand Marnier

Mix the finely grated rind and juice of 1 large orange with 3 tablespoons/45 ml Grand Marnier. Stir into ice cream.

Pawpaw and Lime

Peel 2 pawpaws, halve and remove the seeds. Purée with the grated rind and juice of 1 lime. Stir into ice cream.

Peach and Mango

Peel and stone 1 mango and 4 fresh peaches. Or use 1 (14 oz/397 g) can peaches in natural juice, drained. Purée in a food processor. Fold into ice cream.

Pear and Sauternes

Peel, core and slice 4 pears and soak in 10 fl oz/300 ml Sauternes for 4 hours. Purée in a food processor, fold into ice cream.

Pineapple and Kirsch

Purée 1 drained (1 lb 13 oz/825 g) can pineapple in natural juice with 4 tablespoons/60 ml Kirsch. Leave to soak for 4 hours if wished. Fold into ice cream.

Rhubarb and Orange

Poach 12 oz/350 g trimmed rhubarb in the juice of 1 large orange for 4 minutes until soft. Drain and rub through a sieve. Cool and stir in the grated rind of 1 large orange. Fold into ice cream.

Rose Petal

Stir 1 teaspoon/5 ml rosewater concentrate, ½ oz/15 g each crystallised rose and violet petals, crushed, and a few drops of pink food colouring into ice cream.

Strawberry and Black Pepper

(pictured on page 111)
Purée 1 lb/450 g hulled strawberries with ¼ teaspoon/1.25 ml ground black pepper. Fold into ice cream.

BAY LEAF BAKED CUSTARD

15 fl oz/450 ml low-fat single cream
5 fl oz/150 ml fresh skimmed milk
1 vanilla pod, split
8 fresh bay leaves
3 eggs
2 oz/50 g caster sugar
pinch ground nutmeg

Place the cream, milk, vanilla pod and 2 bay leaves in a pan and gently bring to the boil. Remove from the heat. Whisk the eggs and sugar together and gradually blend into the strained cream. Strain again into six 5 fl oz/150 ml lightly buttered ramekins. Sprinkle ground

nutmeg on to each and top with a bay leaf. Place the ramekins in a roasting tin, half fill the tin with boiling water and bake at Mark 4 — 180°C — 350°F for 20-25 minutes, until set. Allow to cool and serve with biscuits. *Serves 6*

LEMON HONEYCOMB MOULD

18 fl oz/500 ml fresh skimmed milk
4 fl oz/120 ml low-fat single cream
pared rind and juice of 2 lemons
3 eggs, separated
2 oz/50 g caster sugar
1 (½-oz/11-g) sachet gelatine, dissolved in 2 tablespoons/30 ml of boiling water
To decorate: lemon slices

Bring the milk, cream and lemon rind to the boil and remove from heat. Whisk the egg yolks and sugar together until pale and pour into the milk, whisking until well blended. Continue stirring over a low heat until thickened enough to coat the back of a wooden spoon. Do not allow to boil. Remove custard from the heat and strain. Allow to cool.

Add the lemon juice to the cooled, dissolved gelatine and blend into the custard. Whisk the egg whites until stiff. Fold into the custard, pour into a 1½-pint/ 1-litre mould and chill until set.

To turn out, dip the base of the mould into very hot water for 30 seconds and turn out on to a serving plate. Decorate.
Serves 6

TAPIOCA FRUIT PUDDING

1½ pints/900 ml fresh skimmed milk
grated rind of 1 lemon
1 tablespoon/15 ml demerara sugar
2 oz/50 g tapioca
¼ teaspoon/1.25 ml cinnamon
1 oz/25 g sultanas
2 eating apples, peeled, cored and sliced
1 oz/25 g hazelnuts, chopped

Bring the milk, lemon rind and sugar to the boil, stirring until the sugar has dissolved. Add the tapioca and simmer for 10 minutes. Remove from the heat and stir in the remaining ingredients. Pour into a lightly greased ovenproof dish. Bake at Mark 3 — 160°C — 325°F for 1 hour until golden. *Serves 4*

LEMON-SCENTED GERANIUM CREAM WITH FRUIT COMPOTE

5 fl oz/150 ml low-fat single cream

1 tablespoon/15 ml caster sugar

2 lemon-scented geranium leaves

5 oz/150 g Greek yogurt

12 oz/350 g skimmed milk cheese, softened

juice of 1 orange

8 oz/225 g strawberries

8 oz/225 g raspberries

4 oz/125 g frozen blackberries, defrosted

Bring the cream, sugar and geranium leaves to the boil, remove from heat and allow to cool. Whisk in the yogurt and skimmed milk cheese until smooth. Cover and leave in a cool place overnight.

Bring the orange juice to the boil, add the fruit and simmer gently for 2 minutes until just soft. Cool. Strain the cream mixture, then whip until soft peaks form. Serve with the fruit. **Serves 6**

BLACKCURRANT FOOL

1 lb/450 g blackcurrants

2 oz/50 g caster sugar

2 fl oz/60 ml water

10 fl oz/300 ml double cream

2 egg whites

Drain the blackcurrants and poach in the sugar and water for 10 minutes. Strain from the liquid and rub through a sieve. Stir in the cream. Whisk the egg whites until stiff and carefully fold into the mixture. Pour into glasses and chill for 1 to 2 hours. **Serves 4**

PLUM AND BRAMBLE FOOL

2 lb/900 g plums, stoned

15 fl oz/450 ml thick custard

2 egg whites

4 oz/125 g blackberries, sieved

Poach the plums with 3 tablespoons/45 ml water for 10 minutes until tender. Drain and sieve. Cool.

LEFT: ROSE PETAL ICE CREAM; RIGHT: PLUM AND BRAMBLE FOOL

Blend plum purée and custard in a food processor or liquidiser until smooth. Whisk egg whites until stiff and fold into the plum mixture. Pour into individual dishes. Spoon a little blackberry purée on each, swirl through with a skewer.

Serves 4

LEMON SYLLABUB

grated rind and juice of 1 lemon

1 tablespoon/15 ml brandy

1 tablespoon/15 ml sweet sherry

8 fl oz/240 ml fresh skimmed milk

10 fl oz/300 ml low-fat double cream

1½ tablespoons/22.5 ml clear honey

To decorate: julienne strips of lemon rind

Mix the lemon rind and juice, brandy and sherry together in a bowl. Cover and leave to stand for 1 hour. Add the remaining ingredients and whisk until thickened. Spoon into individual glasses and chill. Decorate with julienne strips of lemon rind. **Serves 8**

CARAMEL CUSTARD

4 oz/125 g caster sugar

4 tablespoons/60 ml water

15 fl oz/450 ml fresh skimmed milk

1 vanilla pod, split

4 eggs

Bring 3 oz/75 g sugar and the water to the boil, stirring until the sugar has dissolved. Continue to boil rapidly, without stirring, until golden. Quickly pour into four 5 fl oz/150 ml ramekins and swirl around to cover base and sides.

Bring milk and vanilla pod gently to the boil. Meanwhile, whisk the eggs and remaining sugar together until pale. Strain the milk and gradually whisk it into the eggs. Strain again, then divide mixture between the ramekins.

Place the ramekins in a roasting tin, and half fill the tin with boiling water. Bake at Mark 4 — 180°C — 350°F for 40 minutes until set. Allow to cool, then turn out on to plates. **Serves 4**

115

STRAWBERRY KIWI SWIRL

3 eggs

3 oz/75 g caster sugar

3 oz/75 g plain flour, sifted twice

Filling:

4 oz/125 g quark (skimmed milk cheese)

4 oz/125 g Greek yogurt

1½ oz/40 g caster sugar

4 oz/125 g strawberries, puréed (to make 2½fl oz/75 ml)

2½ teaspoons/12.5 ml gelatine

1½ tablespoons/22.5 ml lemon juice

1 tablespoon/15 ml water

1 tablespoon/15 ml strawberry liqueur, (optional)

2 kiwi fruit, peeled and thinly sliced

To decorate: **sliced strawberries, mint leaves, icing sugar**

Whisk eggs and sugar together until very light and thick. Fold in flour. Pour into greased, lined, 9-inch/23-cm by 13-inch/33-cm Swiss roll tin. Bake at Mark 7 — 220°C — 425°F for 10 to 12 minutes until risen and golden. Turn out on to waxed paper sprinkled with caster sugar. Trim sponge edges and roll up with waxed paper inside.

For the filling: whisk quark, yogurt and sugar together until smooth. Stir in purée. Sprinkle the gelatine over the lemon juice and water in a small pan. Heat until dissolved. Cool. Stir into strawberry mixture with liqueur, if using. Chill until almost set. Unroll sponge, remove paper and arrange kiwi slices over sponge. Spread with mousse and roll up carefully. Chill. Decorate and dust with icing sugar.

Serves 6-8

RASPBERRY SOUFFLE WITH BLACKCURRANT GLAZE

4 oz/125 g blackcurrants

2 oz/50 g caster sugar

3 eggs, separated

10 oz/300 g Greek yogurt

1 lb/450 g raspberries, sieved

½ oz/15 g sachet gelatine dissolved in 3 tablespoons/45 ml boiling water

To decorate: **fresh rosemary**

To collar a 1½-pint/1-litre soufflé dish or 4 ramekins, wrap a band of double-thickness greaseproof paper around the dish to stand about 2-inches/5-cm above the top. Secure with an elastic band or string. Gently simmer blackcurrants and 1 tablespoon/15 ml of sugar in a small saucepan for 5 minutes. Sieve and reserve. Beat yolks and remaining sugar until pale and fluffy. Fold in the yogurt, raspberry purée and gelatine. Whisk whites until stiff and gently fold into the raspberry mixture. Pour into soufflé dish or ramekins. Chill for at least 2 hours until set. Carefully remove the greaseproof paper, spoon some blackcurrant purée on top and smooth with a knife. Decorate and serve with thin biscuits and remaining blackcurrant purée. **Serves 4**

RASPBERRY SOUFFLÉ WITH BLACKCURRANT GLAZE   **STRAWBERRY KIWI SWIRL**

Baking

Home baking is making a comeback, and that's a revival of one of our best traditions, for you can create far healthier and more wholesome breads, cakes and biscuits than you can buy and it's much cheaper too, especially if you batch-bake. Healthy baking means using wholemeal flour where possible, or half white and half brown. Wholemeal self-raising flour is now fine enough for most baking, although I haven't tried wholemeal for choux pastry. Refined sugar is loaded with 'empty' calories and nothing else apart from the ability to rot your teeth: replace it with dried fruits such as apricots, bananas, sultanas and raisins, which are high in natural sugar but also in fibre, vitamins and minerals, and in flavour. To reduce saturated fat, substitute polyunsaturated margarine or oils for butter or, if you miss the flavour, use half and half.

● In this chapter you'll find a delicious selection of savoury breads, all based on two quick recipes, as well as Danish pastries, healthier biscuits, and a few special-occasion pastries — some *not* so healthy, like the luscious mille-feuilles on page 124.

● If you have difficulties with yeast baking, follow the simple guidelines on page 128, and if croissants have always defeated you look at page 120. Choux pastry is, for some, another area of baking mystery best left to the talents of the pastry chef, yet in fact it is one of the easiest of all doughs to make as there's no rubbing in or rolling out and no worry about hot hands.

● Choux pastry bakes to a golden crisp shell, perfect for sweet or savoury fillings, from the familiar and favourite éclairs and profiteroles to creamy mushroom filling (see pages 122-3). Choux pastry can also be flavoured with grated cheese and baked, sprinkled with extra cheese and perhaps a few poppy or caraway seeds, a perfect accompaniment to chicken, fish or vegetables cooked in a creamy white sauce.

DANISH PASTRIES

For the best results the dough must be kept cool while you work. Always rest it in the fridge and quickly return it if the butter starts to become sticky during the rolling and folding process.

1 lb/450 g strong plain flour
½ teaspoon/2.5 ml salt
1 oz/25 g fresh yeast
8 fl oz/250 ml lukewarm milk
1 egg
2 oz/50 g butter, melted
6 oz/175 g butter, chilled

Sift flour and salt into a large bowl. Blend yeast with milk. Beat in the egg with the melted butter. Add the yeast and egg to the flour. Mix to a smooth dough with a wooden spoon. Knead for about 10 minutes, until silky and elastic. Leave to rest in the fridge in an oiled polythene bag for 15 minutes. Knock back dough and knead until silky smooth again. Roll dough to a long 5-inch/13-cm by 16-inch/40-cm rectangle. Divide the chilled butter in half. Dot small flakes of half the butter over the top two-thirds of the dough. Fold up the bottom third over the centre and the top third down on top of these two. Press edges firmly to seal. Chill for 20 minutes. Give dough a quarter turn, clockwise. Roll out to the same size as before. Dot with remaining butter and repeat folding. Chill and repeat rolling and folding, without butter, twice more. Leave dough to rest in the fridge overnight or for at least 4 hours.

To use dough, roll out required amount to about ¼-inch/5-mm thick. Trim square. Shape and fill.

Before baking, allow pastries to rise for 20 minutes covered in oiled non-PVC film on greased baking trays. Remove film. Glaze with beaten egg. Bake at Mark 7 — 220°C — 425°F for 10 to 12 minutes until risen and golden. Cool the pastries on a wire rack before decorating.

Makes about 20

A SELECTION OF DANISH PASTRIES

USING DRIED YEAST

For this Danish Pastries recipe, sprinkle ½ oz/15 g dried yeast on to the lukewarm milk with 1 teaspoon/5 ml sugar. Whisk in with a fork. Leave in a warm place for 15 to 20 minutes until frothy. Continue the recipe as for fresh yeast. Allow a little extra proving time before baking.

SHAPING AND FILLING

Here we give the combinations of shapes and fillings shown in the picture below. The fillings are, of course, interchangeable between the shapes. You can devise your own favourites.

THE SHAPES

Windmills. Roll a quarter of the dough to a 4-inch/10-cm by 16-inch/40-cm strip. Cut into four (4-inch/10-cm) squares. Place 1 walnut-sized ball of **hazelnut marzipan** on each square. Make a cut in towards the centre from each corner. Brush the corners with beaten egg. Then bring four alternate tips, in turn, up on to the filling. Press into place (see picture below – top left). After baking, brush with warm apricot jam and sprinkle with chopped roasted hazelnuts.

Lemon twists. Roll a quarter of the dough to a 6-inch/15-cm by 12-inch/30-cm rectangle. Spread evenly with **lemon curd filling.** Fold the bottom third of the rectangle up over the centre third, then fold the top third down over these. Cut into six strips across the folds. Twist each strip once (see picture below – bottom left) before placing on a baking tray. After baking, brush with warmed lemon curd, sprinkle with lemon rind.

Cockscombs. Roll a quarter of the dough to a 4-inch/10-cm by 16-inch/40-cm strip. Cut into four (4-inch/10-cm) squares. Place 1 teaspoon/5 ml **apple and ginger filling** on each square. Brush the edges of the squares with egg. Fold dough squares over to make oblong pockets. Seal edges. On each shape, make four cuts in folded edge and spread slightly (see picture below – top right). After baking, brush with a little egg white, then sprinkle with caster sugar and toasted flaked almonds.

Pinwheels. Roll half the dough to a 10-inch/30-cm square. Spread evenly with **apricot and walnut filling.** Roll up from one edge like a Swiss roll. Cut the roll into six pieces. Make two slashes in each piece and spread out to expose the filling (see picture below – bottom right). After baking, brush with warm apricot jam and sprinkle with preserving sugar.

Croissants. Roll half the dough to a large rectangle. Cut into four long triangles (see diagram 1). Place 1 teaspoon/5 ml **cherry mincemeat filling** on the base of each. Brush the tips with beaten egg. Roll up each triangle from its base, enclosing the filling. Bake, brush with warm apricot jam.

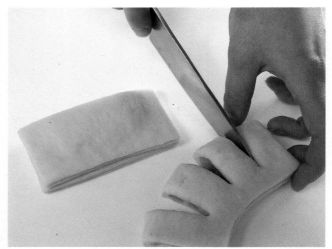

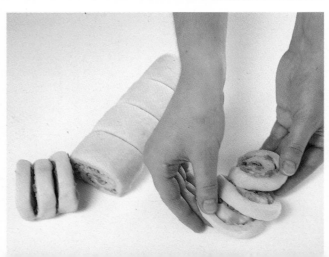

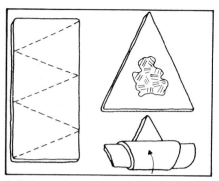

1. Croissants. Cut the dough into four triangles. Add 1 teaspoon/5 ml filling to each and roll up from the base.

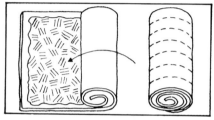

2. Whirls. Roll up the dough which is spread with the filling, Swiss roll style. Slice across into pieces.

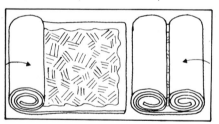

3. Scrolls. Roll up both short ends of the dough towards the centre. Cut across to give six pieces.

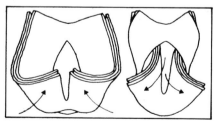

4. Slips. Push one end of the strip through the central slit, pull through and flatten out slightly.

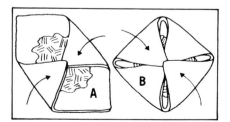

5. Envelopes and Tivolis. A — bring opposite corners of the square into the centre. B — repeat with other corners.

Whirls. Roll half the dough to an 8-inch/20-cm by 10-inch/30-cm rectangle. Spread with **sultana spice filling**. Roll up from the shorter side like a Swiss roll. Slice the roll into seven pieces (see diagram 2). Lay pieces on their sides on a baking tray. After baking, brush with warmed golden syrup and sprinkle with chopped blanched almonds.

Scrolls. Roll out half the dough to an 8-inch/20-cm by 14-inch/35-cm rectangle. Spread with **apple, almond and date filling**. Roll up both short sides to meet in the centre (see diagram 3). Slice the double roll into six pieces. Lay pieces on their sides on a baking tray. After baking, brush with warm apricot jam and sprinkle with chopped roast hazelnuts.

Orange slips. Roll half the dough to a 6-inch/15-cm by 12-inch/30-cm rectangle. Cut into two (3-inch/7.5-cm) strips. Spread one strip with **orange filling**. Place the other strip on top to make a sandwich. Cut the sandwich across at 2-inch/5-cm intervals to make six strips. Cut a slit down the centre of each (see diagram 4). Tuck one end of each strip into the slit (shown from below), then pull this up and out through the slit (shown from above). Flatten slightly on a baking tray. After baking, brush with melted marmalade.

Envelopes. Roll out the dough and cut into four squares as for windmills. Brush the corners with beaten egg. Place 1 teaspoon/5 ml **chocolate filling** on the centre of each square. Bring all corners together in the centre and press down (see diagram 5 A and B). After baking, drizzle with glacé icing and sprinkle with chopped dark chocolate.

Tivolis. Roll dough and cut into four squares as for cockscombs. Place 1 teaspoon/5 ml **macaroon filling** on the centre of each square. Bring two opposite corners of each square up over the filling. Seal with beaten egg (see diagram 5A). After baking, drizzle a little glacé icing over each and sprinkle with chopped glacé cherries.

THE FILLINGS

These fillings are enough for the shapes described.

Hazelnut marzipan. Mix together 3 oz/75 g ground blanched hazelnuts, 2 oz/50 g icing sugar, 1 oz/25 g caster sugar and 1 egg yolk. Knead until smooth.

Lemon curd. Beat together 1 oz/25 g each of caster sugar and butter and 1 tablespoon/15 ml lemon curd.

Apple and ginger. Very gently cook 1 small, peeled, cored and sliced cooking apple in ½ tablespoon/8 ml lemon juice until soft. Add 2 pieces chopped stem ginger and 1 teaspoon/5 ml sugar. Cool before using.

Apricot and walnut. Beat together 1 oz/25 g caster sugar and 2 oz/50 g butter until soft. Stir in 3 oz/75 g chopped dried apricots and 3 oz/75 g chopped walnuts.

Cherry mincemeat. Blend 2 tablespoons/30 ml mincemeat with 2 oz/50 g chopped maraschino cherries and 1 teaspoon/5 ml brandy.

Sultana spice. Beat 2 oz/50 g caster sugar, 2 oz/50 g butter and 1 teaspoon/5 ml mixed spice. Mix in 5 oz/150 g sultanas.

Apple, almond and date. Beat together 2 oz/50 g caster sugar, 1 oz/25 g butter and 1 oz/25 g ground almonds. Stir in 4 tablespoons/60 ml apple purée and 2 oz/50 g chopped dates.

Orange. Beat together 1 oz/25 g caster sugar, 2 oz/50 g butter, 3 tablespoons/45 ml marmalade and the finely grated rind of 1 orange.

Chocolate. Beat together 1 oz/25 g caster sugar and 1 oz/25 g butter. Stir in 2 oz/50 g plain cake crumbs and 2 oz/50 g chopped plain chocolate.

Macaroon. Beat together 1 oz/25 g each caster sugar, butter and crushed macaroons or almond biscuits.

FREEZING

As the preparation time for Danish pastries is lengthy, it can be helpful to make up a batch or two for the freezer. When required you can serve fresh, warm pastries in a matter of moments. They may be frozen for up to six weeks. Open-freeze unbaked, shaped pastries. To serve, thaw for 1½ hours at room temperature. Allow to prove for 20 minutes. Bake as before. Alternatively, open-freeze baked pastries before finishing. Thaw for 30 minutes, then warm through in microwave or moderate oven before finishing.

CHOUX PASTRY

This quantity of choux pastry will make 14 large or 26 small buns or éclair shapes.

2½ oz/65 g strong plain flour, sifted
5 fl oz/150 ml water
2 oz/50 g butter
2 eggs, beaten

Sift flour on to a sheet of greaseproof paper. Place the water and butter in a small pan and heat gently until the butter melts. Bring to the boil and immediately add the flour. Beat rapidly over the heat for about 1 minute until smooth. Remove from the heat and beat for about 5 minutes until cooled. Gradually beat in just enough egg to form a smooth, glossy, stiff paste. Shape as required.

Bake on a lightly oiled baking tray at Mark 7 — 220°C — 425°F for about 30 to 40 minutes depending on size. Cool on a wire rack.

CHOUX PASTRY

Pointers to success
● Do not allow the water to boil until the butter has melted (it will evaporate too much water).
● Add the flour all at once. Make sure the water is boiling when the flour is added. Continue to beat the mixture over the heat for 1 minute to cook the flour.

● Allow the paste to cool slightly before adding the eggs.
● Add the eggs little by little, beating very thoroughly between each addition until the mixture is smooth. The paste should be very smooth, glossy and stiff enough to stand in soft peaks. If large eggs are used, this stage may be reached before all the egg is added.
● Use greased baking trays and cook in a hot oven until crispy. The pastry should, ideally, be eaten within one to two days, but do not store in an airtight container as the pastry softens.

PARIS BREST

This is said to be the creation of a chef who wished to honour the famous bicycle race of the same name. He made the cake circular and inflated like a bicycle wheel!

1 quantity choux pastry
egg white, to glaze
½ oz/15 g flaked almonds
Praline cream:
1 oz/25 g whole blanched almonds
3 oz/75 g caster sugar
**½ quantity Crème Pâtissière made with
   2 oz/50 g sugar (see page 124)**
To decorate: icing sugar

Shape or pipe choux pastry into one 8-inch/20-cm ring or several small rings on a greased baking tray. Bake for 30 minutes. Pierce the sides to release steam,

then cool for 10 minutes. Brush with egg white and sprinkle with flaked almonds. Return to oven for about 5 minutes until brown and crisp. Cool on a wire rack.

Make praline cream filling. Place blanched almonds and sugar in a heavy-based pan. Heat gently until the sugar melts. Stir briefly. Pour on to an oiled baking tray. Cool. Grind or finely crush into a powder. Stir into crème pâtissière.

Slice through the choux rings, fill with praline cream and replace tops. Dust with icing sugar. **Serves 4-6**

PROFITEROLES

PARIS BREST

CREAMY MUSHROOM CHOUX

1 quantity of choux pastry (see recipe)
Filling:
1 tablespoon/15 ml oil
1 clove garlic, peeled and crushed
1 small onion, finely chopped
**4 oz/125 g button mushrooms, finely
   chopped**
2 teaspoons/10 ml lemon juice
2 oz/50 g fromage frais
**1 tablespoon/15 ml fresh chopped
   parsley**
pinch cayenne pepper
To garnish: paprika

Make the choux pastry as directed in the main recipe. Fill a piping bag fitted with a

CREAM ECLAIRS

Using a large piping bag and ½-inch/1-cm plain or star nozzle, pipe the choux pastry into 3-inch/7.5-cm fingers on to a greased baking tray. Bake for 20 to 30 minutes until brown and very crisp. Cool on a wire rack. Split. Dip the tops of the buns in melted chocolate or glacé icing and fill bases with whipped cream or crème pâtissière. Sandwich together.

PROFITEROLES

For a contrasting texture and temperature; fill the profiteroles with ice cream.

1 quantity choux pastry
5 fl oz/150 ml double cream
5 fl oz/150 ml single cream
½ teaspoon/2.5 ml vanilla essence
Chocolate sauce:
6 oz/175 g soft brown sugar
5 fl oz/150 ml boiling water
1 teaspoon/5 ml instant coffee powder
1 tablespoon/15 ml cocoa powder
1 tablespoon/15 ml brandy
3 oz/75 g butter
1 tablespoon/15 ml golden syrup

Using a large piping bag and ½-inch/1-cm plain nozzle, make 26 1-inch/2.5-cm balls of choux pastry on a baking tray. Bake for 25 to 30 minutes until crisp. Cool. Meanwhile, make the sauce. Place all the ingredients for the sauce in a pan and heat gently until smooth. Boil for about 10 minutes until thickened. Stand for 30 minutes.

Whip the creams and vanilla together. Split the balls and fill with cream. Pile up the filled balls into a pyramid. Serve the sauce over the profiteroles. **Serves 4-6**

POTATO BEIGNETS

2 oz/50 g butter
4 fl oz/120 ml water
3 oz/75 g plain flour
2 eggs
4 oz/125 g smoked ham, finely chopped
4 oz/125 g cooked potato, mashed and sieved
2 oz/50 g mature Cheddar, finely grated
To serve: freshly grated Parmesan

Melt the butter in the water over a low heat. Bring to the boil. Off the heat, immediately add the flour. Return to a medium heat and beat until the mixture forms a ball and leaves the sides of the pan. Cool slightly. Gradually add the eggs and beat thoroughly. Stir in the remaining ingredients and season with freshly ground black pepper. Deep fry heaped teaspoonfuls of the mixture at 190°C — 375°F for about 5 minutes until golden brown. Drain on absorbent paper and serve hot sprinkled with the cheese.
Makes about 35

½-inch/1-cm plain nozzle and pipe about 15 small balls on to a baking sheet. Bake at Mark 6 — 200°C — 400°F for 20 to 30 minutes.

For the filling, heat the oil in a small saucepan and fry the garlic and onion over a medium heat until softened and transparent. Add the mushrooms and lemon juice and cook for about 10 minutes. Stir in the remaining ingredients. Cut the tops off the choux balls and fill with the mushroom mixture. Replace tops and serve sprinkled with paprika. **Makes about 15**

CHEESE GOUGERE

1 quantity of choux pastry (see recipe)
3 oz/75 g Gruyère cheese, finely grated

Draw a 10-inch/25-cm circle on to a sheet of non-stick paper. Make the choux pastry as in the main recipe. Stir in 2 oz/50 g of the cheese. Spoon the mixture around the edge of the circle, to make a ring about 2 inches/5 cm in diameter. Scatter with the remaining cheese and bake at Mark 6 — 200°C — 400°F for 35 minutes. Serve with chicken, ham, or vegetables in a creamy white sauce. **Serves 4**

CREAM ÉCLAIRS

MILLE-FEUILLES

When soft summer fruits are in season, use as an alternative to the jam.

8 oz/225 g puff pastry
6 tablespoons/90 ml raspberry
jam
10 fl oz/300 ml whipped cream
Icing:
4 oz/125 g icing sugar
2 oz/50 g plain chocolate, melted

Roll out the pastry on a lightly floured surface into a 10-inch/30-cm by 15-inch/37.5-cm rectangle, about ¼ inch/5 mm thick. To ensure that the dough rises evenly and does not buckle during cooking, prick all over with a fork. Trim the edges, cut into three strips each 5-inches/7.5-cm wide and place on dampened baking trays. Cover the trays with cling film and refrigerate for 30 minutes. Bake in a hot oven (Mark 7 — 220°C — 425°F) for 15 to 20 minutes until well risen and golden. Remove from trays and allow to cool completely on a wire rack — warm pastry would melt the filling. Stack pastry on a chopping board and trim with a large sharp knife.

For the icing, sieve the icing sugar into a bowl to remove any lumps. Make a well in the centre and add 1 tablespoon/15 ml warm water. Stir the mixture carefully, gradually incorporating all the sugar until the icing is smooth and glossy.

Take one of the pastry layers, turn over so the flat side is uppermost. Pour the icing into the centre and spread evenly towards the edges with a palette knife dipped in hot water. Put the melted chocolate into a small piping bag fitted with a writing nozzle. Pipe straight lines across the width of the wet icing about 1-inch/2.5-cm apart. With the tip of a sharp knife, drag through the piped chocolate at right angles first in one direction, then in the other in alternate lines to give the classic feathered effect. Allow the icing to set slightly, then cut into six equal slices using a long sharp knife dipped into hot water before each cut.

To assemble, place first pastry layer on a flat platter and spread with half the raspberry jam and half the whipped cream. Place a second pastry layer on top and spread with the remaining jam and cream. Place the six iced slices in a layer on top. Chill for 15 to 20 minutes, then cut into six using a long sharp knife and serve immediately.

MILLE-FEUILLES WITH VARIOUS FILLINGS AND DECORATION

PASTRY CREAM FILLINGS (CREME PATISSIERE)

Pastry cream is often used as a filling for mille-feuille. It is a light egg custard mixture thickened with a little flour, it can be flavoured with vanilla, lemon, chocolate, liqueurs or chopped nuts. Whipped cream is folded into the finished cream to add lightness and create a soft, velvety texture.

4 oz/125 g caster sugar
4 eggs
1 oz/25 g plain flour
pinch of salt
1 pint/450 ml milk
1 vanilla pod
2 strips of lemon peel
pinch of ground mace
5 fl oz/150 ml double cream, whipped

Beat together the sugar and eggs until thick, light and creamy. Sift the flour with a pinch of salt and gradually work into the mixture until smooth. Put the milk in a pan with the vanilla pod, lemon peel and mace and bring slowly to the boil. Remove from heat and leave to stand for 5 minutes for the flavours to infuse. Strain. Gradually pour the milk on to the egg mixture, stirring constantly. Return pastry cream to the pan, bring almost to the boil, stirring all the time to prevent the mixture burning. Simmer, but do not boil, for about 2 minutes until thickened. Strain. Leave to cool. To prevent a skin from forming, rub the surface with a knob of butter or press non-PVC film directly on to the surface. Refrigerate until needed. Pastry cream will keep for 2 days. Before serving beat the mixture until smooth, stir in whipped cream.

DECORATION

For a different decorative topping, thickly dredge the top layer of the mille-feuille with icing sugar from a small sieve. Hold a fine metal skewer in a flame until red hot, then place it diagonally across the sugar at regular intervals. Rest the skewer on the sugar for a couple of seconds — just enough time for the sugar to caramelize. Reheat the skewer if necessary.

For an even simpler finish, ice the top with glacé icing. Cut into slices, then reassemble on base. Spread sides of the mille-feuille with a little whipped cream. Gently press on the reserved pastry trimmings with a palette knife. Cut into slices.

GINGER AND PARSNIP CAKE

In Elizabethan times root vegetables were used to sweeten cakes when the last of the autumn fruits had been eaten.

1½ lb/700 g self-raising flour
¼ teaspoon/1.25 ml salt
1 teaspoon/5 ml bicarbonate of soda
1 teaspoon/5 ml freshly grated nutmeg
1 tablespoon/15 ml ground ginger
1 lb/450 g parsnips, peeled and grated
8 oz/225 g sultanas
12 oz/350 g unsalted butter
10 oz/300 g clear honey
2 eggs
2 tablespoons/30 ml milk
To decorate: apricot jam, sieved, parsnip cut into shapes

Sift the flour, salt, bicarbonate of soda, nutmeg and ginger into a bowl. Stir in the parsnips and sultanas and mix well. Melt the butter with the honey. Make a well in the centre of the flour and pour in the melted butter and honey mixture. Add the eggs and milk and mix well. Spoon into a greased and base-lined 9-inch/23-cm round tin. Bake at Mark 3 — 170°C — 325°F for 2 hours or until firm to the touch and a skewer inserted comes out clean.

Leave to cool in the tin for 10 minutes, then turn out on to a wire rack. Heat the apricot jam and brush over the top of the cake. Brush the parsnip shapes with jam and brown under hot grill. Arrange on top of the cake. Serve cold.

Makes one 9-inch/23-cm cake

GINGER AND PARSNIP CAKE

BASIC BREADMAKING

If you have difficulties with yeast cookery here are a few simple guidelines.

Buy fresh yeast from chill cabinets in health food stores (some supermarkets sell it, too) and let it stand in the warmth of your kitchen for 30 minutes. Yeast is most active in warm temperatures, so keep all bowls and utensils warm. The flour can also be warmed in the oven on very cold days — stir to distribute the heat. While the dough is rising, keep it covered loosely with oiled polythene draped with a tea towel to stop any draughts.

Put it in a warm airing cupboard, the top oven of a double-oven cooker or an enclosed grill compartment. Once bread has proved, treat it gently, don't knock or jolt it and bake as quickly as possible after glazing. Cover loaves with foil to prevent burning. After baking, remove from the tins and allow them to cool on a wire rack so that the moisture can evaporate from the crust and prevent sogginess.

USING DRIED YEAST

Dried yeast is a convenient substitute for fresh and a good store cupboard standby. It will keep for up to a year in an unopened packet or tin and up to four months after opening if stored in a small airtight container.

With dried yeast use half the quantity given for fresh yeast; for instance, if the recipe calls for 1 oz/25 g fresh yeast use ½ oz/15 g dried yeast. Sprinkle the dried yeast over the hand-hot liquid, add 1 teaspoon/5 ml of sugar and whisk together with a fork. Leave in a warm place until frothy then use as the recipe requires.

With Easy Blend Yeast simply stir in one sachet of yeast to the basic quantity of dry flour mixture before adding the hand-hot liquid as specified in the recipe.

QUICK BROWN BREAD

½ oz/15 g fresh yeast
10 fl oz/300 ml hand-hot water
1 lb/450 g wholemeal flour
1½ teaspoons/7.5 ml salt
½ oz/15 g margarine

Blend the yeast and water together. Mix the flour and salt together in a bowl. Rub in the margarine. Pour in the yeast liquid and any flavourings, and mix all the ingredients until the sides of the bowl are left clean.

Turn out the dough on to a lightly floured surface and knead until silky smooth for about 10 minutes. Shape the dough as required. Cover and leave in a warm, draught-free place for about one hour or until doubled in size. Glaze and decorate as needed. Bake at Mark 8 — 230°C — 450°F for 45-50 minutes for a loaf or 10-15 minutes for rolls.

Makes 1 large loaf

QUICK WHITE BREAD

1 oz/25 g yeast
15 fl oz/450 ml hand-hot water
1 25-mg tablet vitamin C (or ascorbic acid), crushed
1½ lb/700 g strong white plain flour
2 teaspoons/10 ml salt
1 tablespoon/15 ml sugar
1 oz/25 g margarine

Blend the yeast and water. Stir in the crushed vitamin C tablet. Sift the flour, salt and sugar into a bowl. Rub in the margarine. Stir in the yeast liquid, and any flavourings, and mix to a soft dough. Turn out to a floured surface and knead until silky smooth and elastic — about 10 minutes.

Shape the dough as required. Cover with oiled cling film and leave in a warm draught-free place until doubled in size (about 50 minutes). Glaze and decorate. Bake at Mark 8 — 230°C — 450°F for 45-50 minutes for a loaf, 10-15 minutes for rolls.

Makes 1 large loaf

OATMEAL SODA BREAD

1 lb/450 g wholemeal flour
1 teaspoon/5 ml salt
2 oz/50 g lard
4 tablespoons/60 ml coarse oatmeal
1 teaspoon/5 ml bicarbonate of soda
10 fl oz/300 ml milk
½ teaspoon/2.5 ml lemon juice

Mix the flour, soda and salt. Rub in the lard then mix in the oatmeal. Gradually stir in enough milk to make a firm dough. Divide into two equal pieces. Turn on to a floured board and shape into a flattened ball (5 inches/12.5 cm in diameter).

Place on two floured baking trays, score each bread lightly into quarters, and bake at Mark 7 — 220°C — 425°F for 30 minutes, or until the bread is browned. Cool on a wire rack. **Makes two loaves**

OLIVE AND ANCHOVY BREAD

1 oz/25 g fresh yeast
15 fl oz/450 ml hand hot water
1 (75-mg) vitamin C tablet, crushed
1½ lb/700 g strong white flour
4 oz/125 g black olives, stoned and roughly chopped
½ oz/15 g anchovy fillets, finely chopped
1 teaspoon/5 ml semolina
1 tablespoon/15 ml olive oil
3 sprigs fresh rosemary

Blend the yeast, water and vitamin C tablet. Sift the flour into a warmed bowl. Add the olives and chopped anchovies and stir thoroughly. Make a well in the centre. Add the oil and yeast mixture and mix to a dough. Turn out on to a floured surface and knead until smooth and elastic — about 10 minutes. Shape into a round.

Cover with oiled non-PVC film and leave in a warm, draught-free place until doubled in size — about 50 minutes. Remove polythene, brush with milk and sprinkle with semolina. Slash 3 times and lay a sprig of fresh rosemary in each cut. Bake at Mark 8 — 230°C — 450°F for 40 minutes until well browned. Cover with foil if browning too quickly.

Makes 1 large loaf

WHEATEN BREAD

5 oz/150 g wheatmeal flour
5 oz/150 g wholemeal flour
2 oz/50 g plain flour
1 teaspoon/5 ml salt
1½ teaspoons/7.5 ml baking powder
1½ oz/40 g butter or margarine
12 fl oz/360 ml buttermilk, soured fresh milk, or blend 8 fl oz/240 ml fresh milk with 5 oz/150 g natural yogurt

Blend the flours, salt and baking powder. Rub in the fat. Stir in the liquid and mix to a soft dough. Knead very lightly. Press into an oiled 9-inch/23-cm round cake tin. Mark into four quarters and sprinkle with a little flour. Bake at Mark 8 — 230°C — 450°F for 35 minutes.

Turn out and wrap in a clean tea towel to keep in the steam and prevent the bread hardening. This bread freezes well.

Makes one loaf

SAVOURY BREAD

Each quantity of flavouring ingredients is sufficient for one quantity of basic quick dough.

Beetroot and Lemon Bread

Grate 1 lb/450 g raw beetroot. Sprinkle with 2 tablespoons/30 ml of salt. Stir and allow to stand for 1 hour. Rinse thoroughly and squeeze out all the excess juice. Add to white dough with the finely grated rind of 1 lemon. Shape into two loaves. After proving, brush with beaten egg.

Carrot and Celeriac Bread

Grate 8 oz/225 g carrot and 8 oz/225 g celeriac. Sprinkle with 2 tablespoons/30 ml of salt. Stir and allow to stand for one hour. Rinse and squeeze the vegetables to remove all excess juice and add to white dough. Shape into a round loaf. After proving, brush with beaten egg, sprinkle with poppy seeds and slash the top in a cross with a sharp knife.

Caraway and Brown Rice Bread

Add 1 tablespoon/15 ml caraway seeds and 2 oz/50 g (raw weight) of cooked brown rice to brown dough. Shape into two loaves. After proving, brush with milk and sprinkle with caraway seeds if liked.

Cottage Loaf

Divide risen dough into two, one piece twice the size of the other. Knead both into rounds, indent the centre of each. Place smaller on top of larger and indent with fingers to secure.

Bacon and Pinenut Bread

Grill 8 oz/225 g smoked bacon until crisp and chop it finely. Add to white dough with 1 oz/25 g pinenuts. Shape into five equal long rolls and pack side by side into a large loaf tin. After proving, brush with milk and sprinkle with some alfalfa or fenugreek seeds.

Onion and Walnut Bread

Add one large grated onion, juice drained, and 2 oz/50 g chopped walnuts to brown dough. Shape into a large cottage loaf. Roll one third and two thirds of the dough into large rounds, place the smaller one on top of the other and press a floured wooden spoon handle down through the centre of both. After proving, brush with beaten egg and sprinkle with chopped walnuts.

Pepper Bread

Shred half a red, half a green and half a yellow pepper. Dry well on kitchen paper. Add to white dough. Shape into a flowerpot loaf. After proving, brush top with milk and sprinkle with rolled oats.

Olive and Anchovy Bread

Add 3 oz/75 g chopped stuffed green olives and ½ oz/15 g small chopped anchovy fillets to brown dough. Shape into small loaf tins. After proving, brush with milk and sprinkle with coarse oatmeal.

Cheddar Bagels

Add 4 oz/125 g grated Cheddar cheese to white or brown dough. Shape into 12 small rounds and make a hole in the centres to form rings. Poach the bagels, four at a time, in simmering water for about 20 seconds, until they start to puff up. Remove them with a slotted slice and place on a greased baking sheet. Brush with beaten egg and sprinkle with poppy seeds if liked.

Marbled Stilton Bread

For this bread use a half quantity of both brown and white doughs. Cut the dough into small pieces and flatten them with the palm of the hand. Sprinkle 4 oz/125 g crumbled Stilton over the brown pieces. Layer the pieces of dough into a loaf tin in a haphazard pattern. After proving, brush top with beaten egg and sprinkle with chopped pistachio nuts.

Peanut Butter Bread

Add 4 tablespoons/60 ml of crunchy peanut butter to brown dough. Shape the dough into seven round pieces. Arrange in a regular pattern in a 9-inch/23-cm deep round tin. After proving, brush with milk and sprinkle with coarse salt.

Sunflower Seed Bread

Add 2 oz/50 g sunflower seeds to brown dough. Shape into a large bloomer loaf. After proving, brush with beaten egg. Slash the loaf diagonally at intervals with a sharp knife.

Pumpkin Seed Bread

Add 2½ oz/65 g pumpkin seeds to white dough. Shape into two French sticks. After proving, dust with flour.

Saffron and Cumin Bread

Add ¼ teaspoon/1.25 ml powdered saffron and ½ teaspoon/2.5 ml ground cumin to white bread dough. Shape into two round loaves. After proving, brush with milk and sprinkle with semolina. Slash the tops of the loaves in a criss-cross pattern with a sharp knife.

SHORTBREAD

5 oz/150 g wholemeal flour
1 oz/25 g rice flour
1 oz/25 g molasses sugar
4 oz/125 g polyunsaturated margarine

Mix the flours and sugar together in a bowl. Rub the margarine into the mixture and knead to form a soft dough. Press into a lightly floured 7-inch/17.5-cm round shortbread mould. Carefully turn out on to a lightly oiled baking sheet and bake at Mark 3 — 160°C — 325°F for 30-40 minutes until golden. Cool. **Makes 8**

SHORTBREAD CRESCENTS: Divide the basic recipe into walnut size pieces. Roll into 3-inch/7.5-cm sausages. Brush with beaten egg and roll in 3 oz/75 g finely chopped blanched almonds. Turn edges in to form crescents and bake for 30 minutes. **Makes 22**

SHORTBREAD STARS: Roll out the basic mixture to ¼-inch/5-mm thick and cut out 3-inch/7.5-cm stars. Cut 1-inch/2.5-cm plain circles from the centre of half the stars. Brush the remaining stars with beaten egg and top with the holed stars. Bake for 30 minutes. Cool. Fill each centre with a teaspoon of low-sugar jam. **Makes 15**

ORANGE SHORTBREAD: Add the grated rind of 1 orange to basic mixture. Roll out to ¼-inch/5-mm thick and cut into 2-inch/5-cm squares. Mark with the back of a knife to form pattern. Bake for 30 minutes. **Makes 18**

CAROB SHORTBREAD: Substitute 1 oz/25 g carob powder for rice flour in basic

mixture. Roll to ¼-inch/5-mm thick and cut into 3 by 1-inch/7.5-cm by 2.5-cm rectangles. Brush with egg. Sprinkle over 2 oz/50 g finely chopped hazelnuts. Bake for 20 minutes. **Makes 20**

APRICOT AND ALMOND SHORTBREAD: Spread basic mixture into a 7½ by 11½-inch/19 by 29-cm Swiss roll tin. Spread with 3 oz/75 g low-sugar apricot jam, sieved, and sprinkle with 3 oz/75 g nibbed or flaked almonds. Bake for 45 minutes. Cut into bars. **Makes 16**

PEANUT SHORTBREAD: Roll out basic mixture to a 12 by 6-inch/30 by 15-cm rectangle. Mix together 3 tablespoons/45 ml honey and 4 oz/125 g finely chopped unsalted peanuts. Spread over the shortbread and roll up. Slice at ¼-inch/5-mm intervals. Bake for 30 minutes. **Makes 20**

BRANDY SNAPS

2 oz/50 g polyunsaturated margarine
2 oz/50 g caster sugar
1 tablespoon/15 ml honey
2 oz/50 g flour
¼ teaspoon/1.25 ml ground ginger
1 tablespoon/15 ml brandy, optional
To serve: 5 fl oz/150 g low-fat double cream, whipped

Heat the margarine, sugar and honey in a saucepan, stirring occasionally until the margarine has melted. Remove from the heat and stir in the remaining ingredients until well blended. Place teaspoonfuls of the mixture on to a lightly oiled baking sheet, spacing them 4 inches/10 cm apart. Bake at Mark 4 — 180°C — 350°F for 8-10 minutes until golden. Cool slightly, about 1 minute, then carefully but quickly remove the biscuits with a palette knife and wrap around a lightly oiled wooden spoon handle. Allow to cool completely. Serve filled with cream. **Makes 16**

ALMOND SNAPS: Add 1 oz/25 g flaked almonds to the basic mixture. Bake as above. Mould around a rolling pin. **Makes 16**

LEMON SNAPS: Add the grated zest of 1 lemon to basic mixture. Bake. Carefully fold the biscuits in half and half again. **Makes 16**

CANDIED SNAPS: Add 1 oz/25 g candied peel to basic mixture. Bake, then wrap around a horn-shaped mould. Allow to cool completely. Melt 1 (2½ oz/65 g) orange carob bar. Dip one end of the snap in the carob to coat. Allow to set. **Makes 16**

FRUITY SNAPS: Add 1 oz/25 g roughly chopped raisins, sultanas and currants to the basic mixture. Bake as above. Mould around rolling pin. **Makes 16**

SESAME SEED SNAPS: Add 2 tablespoons/30 ml sesame seeds to the basic mixture. Bake as above. Mould around a rolling pin. **Makes 16**

FLAPJACKS

4 oz/125 g polyunsaturated margarine
1 oz/25 g molasses sugar
3 tablespoons/45 ml clear honey
8 oz/225 g rolled oats

Melt margarine, sugar and honey in a pan over a medium heat. Stir in the oats until coated. Spoon into a lightly oiled 7½-inch/19-cm square tin. Bake at Mark 5 — 190°C — 375°F for 30-40 minutes until golden. Cool slightly then cut into 12 bars. Cool completely in the tin. **Makes 12**

BANANA FLAPJACKS: Stir 2 oz/50 g roughly chopped banana chips into the basic mixture and place tablespoonfuls on to a baking sheet 2 inches/5 cm apart. Bake for 20 minutes. **Makes 20**

DATE FLAPJACKS: Chop 2 oz/50 g dried dates and 2 oz/50 g dried apricots, and add to basic mixture. Spoon into a tin as above. Bake for 30 minutes. Melt 1 (2½ oz/65 g) orange carob bar and half dip each cooled flapjack into it. **Makes 12**

FRUIT FLAPJACKS: Add the grated zest of 1 lemon, 1 oz/25 g toasted flaked coconut, 1 peeled, cored and finely chopped apple to the basic mixture. Spoon a little into paper cases and bake for 20 minutes. **Makes 20**

MUESLI FLAPJACKS: Substitute 8 oz/225 g unsweetened muesli for the rolled oats in the basic mixture. Spread into a lightly oiled 7½ by 11½ inch/19 by 29 cm Swiss roll tin. Bake for 30 minutes. Cool slightly and cut into bars. **Makes 16**

VIENNESE BISCUITS

8 oz/225 g polyunsaturated margarine
2 oz/50 g icing sugar
6 oz/175 g plain flour
2 oz/50 g cornflour

Beat together margarine and sugar until pale. Fold in remaining ingredients until well blended. Using ½-inch/1-cm star nozzle, pipe 2-inch/5-cm fingers on to a baking sheet. Bake at Mark 4 — 180°C — 350°F for 20 minutes until golden.

Makes 36

VIENNESE ALMONDS: Substitute 1 oz/25 g ground almonds for 1 oz/25 g of plain flour in basic mixture. Using a ½-inch/1-cm star nozzle, pipe ring shapes. Bake for 20 minutes. *Makes 36*

HAZELNUT VIENNESE: Substitute 1 oz/25 g ground hazelnuts for 1 oz/25 g of flour in basic mixture. Lightly oil madeleine tins, and dust with flour. Spread the mixture into each shell and bake for 20 minutes. Allow to cool. *Makes 24*

CHERRY VIENNESE: Add 2 oz/50 g finely chopped glacé cherries to basic mixture. Using a ½-inch/1-cm plain nozzle, pipe 1-inch/2.5-cm rounds on to a baking sheet. Bake for 20 minutes. Melt 1 (2½ oz/65 g) Bran 'n' Raisin carob bar as before and half dip each biscuit into it.

Makes 36

LEMON VIENNESE: Add the grated zest of 1 lemon to basic mixture. Using a ½-inch/1-cm star nozzle, pipe the mixture into 2-inch/15-cm rounds. Bake for 20 minutes. *Makes 18*

PEANUT VIENNESE: Substitute 1 oz/25 g ground unsalted peanuts for 1 oz/25 g plain flour in basic mixture. Place tablespoonfuls on to a baking sheet. Sprinkle with 2 oz/50 g finely chopped peanuts and bake for 20 minutes.

Makes 24

COCONUT VIENNESE: Add 1 oz/25 g desiccated coconut to basic mixture. Using ½-inch/1-cm plain nozzle, pipe crescent shapes and sprinkle with 1 oz/25 g roasted flaked coconut. Bake for 20 minutes. *Makes 36*

MIXED NUT VIENNESE: Add 2 oz/50 g chopped mixed nuts to basic mixture. Place tablespoonfuls of the mixture on to a baking sheet. Bake for 20 minutes.

Makes 24

Fast and Budget Meals

Even when there seems absolutely no time for proper cooking for the family, let alone for yourself, there is no need to resort to expensive prepared and pre-packaged dishes. All the recipes in this chapter are based on ingredients that are simple to prepare and quick to cook, and they are designed to prove that in the time it takes to open a packet and heat something through you really can whip up, say, a speedy stir-fry and, in just a few extra minutes, a starter or a dessert to extend it into a proper meal. Lean meats like chicken and pork fillet are speedily cooked, eggs and cheese take virtually no time, and fish is the ultimate convenience food since all you have to do is light the grill and pop it under. The meals chosen for one or two people will take no longer than 20 minutes to get on the table, those for a family perhaps 10 minutes longer. All the ingredients can be picked up from the supermarket on the way home from work — *and* they are all healthy.

● Satisfying a family and keeping them healthy when you're on a tight budget presents a different set of problems, but we've cracked them too, so read on. There are recipes to appeal both to kids and their mums. Even kids with junk-food tastes can be steered towards healthier habits since you can imitate their favourite take-away fast foods with healthy and cheaper alternatives. Encourage them to use only pepper to season foods at table. Buy them tomato sauce without added sugar and salt, and serve plenty of crisp salads and crusty wholemeal bread with meals. Use fresh fruit instead of sugar to sweeten desserts, serve low-fat spreads and low-sugar jams and, instead of sugary fizzy drinks, give them fruit juice. Packed lunches need present no problem either — plan the week in advance so that you can vary each day's lunch. Include fresh or dried fruit or make up your own mixture of nuts, sunflower seeds, sultanas and toasted coconut flakes for a healthy snack, much cheaper than buying commercially prepared mixes. Pack salads and desserts in rigid containers with tight fitting lids.

HAM AND PEACH ROLLS

8 oz/225 g curd cheese
1 tablespoon/15 ml fresh chopped parsley
1 teaspoon/5 ml fresh chopped tarragon
2 teaspoons/10 ml fresh chopped chives
1 large peach, peeled, stoned and chopped
8 large slices of ham

Blend the cheese and herbs together, season with freshly ground black pepper and stir in the peach. Divide the mixture equally among the ham slices and roll each one up to make a cornet shape. Arrange on a serving dish and garnish with parsley. **Serves 4**

CHICKEN AND BEAN SALAD

4 chicken thighs, skinned and boned
1 tablespoon/15 ml soy sauce
grated rind and juice of 1 lemon
1 tablespoon/15 ml oil
4 oz/125 g French beans, blanched
4 spring onions, trimmed and shredded
2 tablespoons/30 ml natural yogurt
1 tablespoon/15 ml milk

Cube chicken and toss with soy sauce and lemon rind. Marinate for 1 hour. Heat the oil in a frying pan and cook the drained chicken for 5 minutes or until golden. Add the soy sauce and toss well. Arrange beans and spring onions on plates. Blend the yogurt and milk and spoon over the vegetables. Top with the hot chicken. **Serves 4**

COD WITH SESAME SEEDS AND CARROTS, CHICKEN AND BEAN SALAD

AVOCADO SOUP

2 avocados, peeled, stoned and chopped
1½ pints/900 ml chicken stock
1 tablespoon/15 ml chives, chopped
2 tablespoons/30 ml lemon juice
dash of Tabasco sauce

Blend avocados in a food processor or liquidiser until smooth. Add remaining ingredients, season with black pepper. Blend again. Serve chilled. *Serves 4*

PLAICE PROVENCAL

4 plaice fillets, skinned
4 tablespoons/60 ml creamed tomatoes
2 oz/50 g wholemeal breadcrumbs
3 oz/75 g Edam cheese, grated
1 clove garlic, peeled and crushed

Spread the fillets with creamed tomatoes. Mix together the remaining ingredients with a little black pepper and sprinkle evenly over the fish. Grill for 5 to 7 minutes. *Serves 4*

HOT GINGER GRAPEFRUIT

2 large grapefruit
3 tablespoons/45 ml ginger wine
1 tablespoon/15 ml demerara sugar
½ teaspoon/2.5 ml ground ginger

Halve the grapefruit. Mix together the remaining ingredients and spread over the grapefruit halves. Grill for about 5 minutes, until bubbling. *Serves 4*

ANTI PASTI

4 oz/125 g Parma ham
4 oz/125 g assortment of peppered, herbed and coarse salamis
1 (14-oz/397-g) can artichoke hearts, drained and sliced
1 beefsteak tomato, thinly sliced
1 Mozzarella cheese, sliced
To garnish: black olives, basil leaves

Arrange the ham, salamis and artichoke hearts on a large serving platter. Place the tomato and Mozzarella slices overlapping on one side of the platter. Garnish with olives and basil. *Serves 4*

PEARS WITH CHOCOLATE RUM SAUCE

4 oz/125 g plain chocolate
4 tablespoons/60 ml dark rum
½ oz/15 g butter
4 pears, peeled and cored
To garnish: chopped nuts

Melt the chocolate, rum and butter in a bowl over a saucepan of boiling water. Stir until smooth. Pour over the pears and sprinkle with chopped nuts. *Serves 4*

CHICKEN AND BROCCOLI CHOW MEIN

2 tablespoons/30 ml vegetable oil
2 chicken breasts, skinned and boned
4 oz/125 g broccoli florets
1 carrot, thinly sliced
4 oz/125 g mange-tout
2 spring onions, thinly sliced
1 tablespoon/15 ml soy sauce

Heat the oil in a wok or heavy frying pan until smoking. Cut the chicken into strips and stir-fry for 2 minutes. Remove with a slotted spoon and keep warm, add the broccoli and carrot and cook for a further minute. Add the mange-tout and soy sauce. Return the chicken. Toss well. Serve immediately with egg noodles. *Serves 4*

RASPBERRY MACAROON WHIP

4 fl oz/120 ml single cream
8 oz/225 g Greek yogurt
4 oz/125 g raspberries
8 ratafias, crushed
To garnish: fresh mint

Fold the cream into the yogurt and fold in remaining ingredients. Spoon into glasses or individual serving dishes. Garnish with fresh mint. *Serves 4*

CHICKEN AND BROCCOLI CHOW MEIN, RASPBERRY MACAROON WHIP

SPAGHETTI WITH CLAM SAUCE

8 oz/225 g wholewheat spaghetti
1 (14-oz/397-g) can chopped tomatoes
1 (7-oz/200-g) jar clams, drained
1 teaspoon/5 ml oregano
2 tablespoons/30 ml chopped parsley

Cook the spaghetti in boiling water for 10 to 15 minutes. Meanwhile, bring the tomatoes to the boil. Stir in the remaining ingredients and season with black pepper. Simmer for 5 minutes.

Drain spaghetti and toss in sauce. Serve with grated Parmesan cheese.

Serves 3-4

ZABAGLIONE

4 egg yolks
3 tablespoons/45 ml caster sugar
6 tablespoons/90 ml Marsala

Whisk the egg yolks, sugar and 2 tablespoons/30 ml of the Marsala in a large bowl over a saucepan of simmering

water until pale and frothy. Gradually pour in the remaining Marsala, whisking all the time, and continue to whisk until thickened and increased in volume. Pour into 4 tall glasses and serve at once.

Serves 4

SALMON AND LEMON PATE

1 (7-oz/200-g) can red salmon
juice 1 lemon
1 teaspoon/5 ml grated lemon rind
4 oz/125 g curd cheese

Remove skin and bones from salmon and mash with the lemon juice and rind. Beat in the cheese. Serve chilled with toast and fresh lemon. *Serves 4 as a starter*

RHUBARB ORANGE COMPOTE

1 lb/450 g rhubarb
2 oranges, segmented
juice and rind of 1 orange

Cut the rhubarb into 1-inch/2.5-cm lengths. Place in a saucepan with the

AVOCADO SOUP, PLAICE PROVENÇAL

remaining ingredients. Simmer for 10 to 12 minutes until tender. *Serves 4*

DEVILLED CHICKEN LIVERS

1 oz/25 g butter
1 lb/450 g chicken livers, halved and trimmed
½ teaspoon/2.5 ml mild curry powder
1 tablespoon/15 ml Dijon mustard
2 teaspoons/10 ml Worcestershire sauce
5 fl oz/150 ml chicken stock
To garnish: 2 oz/50 g long-grain rice, cooked and kept hot; 4 spring onions, finely chopped.

Melt the butter in a pan, add the chicken livers and fry, stirring gently, for 2 minutes. Stir in the curry powder, mustard, Worcestershire sauce and seasoning. Add the stock and cook over gentle heat, stirring, for 5 minutes. Mix the rice with the onion. Serve livers on individual plates, garnished with the rice.

Serves 6

CHICKEN AND TOMATO SOUP

1 pint/600 ml tomato juice
1 pint/600 ml chicken stock
1 teaspoon/5 ml mixed herbs
2 oz/50 g cooked rice
8 oz/225 g cooked chicken, shredded

Bring tomato juice, stock and herbs to the boil. Reduce heat. Stir in remaining ingredients, simmer for 2 minutes. Season with black pepper. Serve hot, garnished with chopped parsley. **Serves 4**

FLORENTINE EGGS

1 lb/450 g fresh spinach, stalks removed, washed and drained
8 oz/225 g frozen spinach, thawed
4 spring onions, trimmed and chopped
2 slices cooked ham, chopped
4 small eggs
pinch grated nutmeg
2 tablespoons/30 ml single cream

Place spinach in a pan and toss for 1 minute over heat. Put into 4 ovenproof dishes, top with spring onion and ham. Make a well in the centre and crack in an egg. Season with nutmeg and black pepper and spoon over the cream. Place dishes in a roasting tin, pour in boiling water to come halfway up the sides of the dish. Bake at Mark 5 — 190°C — 375°F for 15 to 20 minutes. Serve with crusty brown bread. **Serves 4**

ITALIAN RAREBIT

4 oz/125 g Lancashire cheese, grated
2 tablespoons/30 ml milk
1 teaspoon/5 ml Dijon mustard
1 teaspoon/5 ml dried oregano
1 teaspoon/5 ml tomato purée
2 thick slices wholewheat toast

Put the cheese, milk, mustard, herbs and tomato purée in a small pan and stir over a very low heat until combined. Place the toast on a flat ovenproof dish, spread with the cheese mixture and grill until bubbling. **Serves 2**

CHICKEN AND TOMATO SOUP, FLORENTINE EGGS

SCRAMBLED EGGS WITH ONION AND BACON

½ oz/15 g butter
8 spring onions, trimmed and chopped
4 back bacon rashers, derinded and
  chopped
8 eggs, beaten
1 tablespoon/15 ml fresh chopped
  parsley

Melt the butter in a small saucepan and fry the onions and bacon until soft, about 5 minutes. Pour in the eggs and parsley and cook gently, stirring continuously until the eggs begin to scramble. Season with freshly ground black pepper and cook until the desired consistency is reached. Serve with wholewheat toast.

Serves 4

AVOCADO DESSERT

2 ripe avocados, stones removed
juice and grated rind of ½ lemon
4 tablespoons/60 ml caster sugar
½ teaspoon/2.5 ml vanilla essence
10 fl oz/300 ml double cream, whipped
To garnish: flaked almonds, lemon and
  orange slices or strawberries

Mash or blend the avocado, lemon, sugar and vanilla essence. Stir in the cream. Spoon the mixture into glasses and decorate with flaked almonds, lemon and orange slices or strawberries. Prepare shortly before you eat it or the avocados might discolour.

Serves 4-6

LIVER AND MUSHROOM STROGANOFF

1 lb/450 g lamb's liver
1 tablespoon/15 ml vegetable oil
6 oz/175 g button mushrooms, sliced
3 tablespoons/45 ml quark or yogurt
1 teaspoon/5 ml paprika

Cut the liver into thin strips. Heat the oil, add the mushrooms and fry for 2 minutes until softened. Add liver and cook for a further 2 to 3 minutes until browned. Stir in the quark or yogurt, paprika and ground black pepper and heat gently. Serve with noodles.

Serves 3-4

VEGETABLE RISOTTO

1 tablespoon/15 ml oil
1 onion, chopped
2 sticks celery, finely chopped
1 red or green pepper, cored, deseeded
  and sliced
8 oz/225 g risotto rice
1 (12-oz/350-g) can sweetcorn, drained
4 oz/125 g frozen petit pois
1½ pints/900 ml vegetable stock
2 tablespoons/30 ml chopped parsley
3 oz/75 g Cheddar cheese, grated
1 tablespoon/15 ml grated Parmesan
  cheese
1 oz/25 g stuffed olives, sliced
pinch ground nutmeg
To garnish: 1 oz/25 g cashew nuts

Heat the oil in a saucepan and fry the onion, celery, pepper and rice until the rice turns chalky white. Add the sweetcorn, peas and stock. Simmer, uncovered, for 20 minutes. Stir in the remaining ingredients. Cook until the cheese has melted. Season with freshly ground black pepper. Serve sprinkled with a few cashew nuts. *Serves 4*

APRICOT ICE CREAM SUNDAES

4 crushed meringues
8 scoops vanilla ice cream
1 (14-oz/397-g) can apricots in natural
  juice, drained and sieved
1 tablespoon/15 ml apricot brandy
¼ teaspoon/1.25 ml ground cinnamon

In each of 4 sundae glasses place one meringue and 2 scoops of ice cream. Mix apricot purée with remaining ingredients and spoon over ice cream. *Serves 4*

SMOKED SAUSAGE STIR-FRY

2 tablespoons/30 ml oil
1 onion
½ red and green pepper, cored, deseeded
  and sliced
1 small cauliflower, broken into florets
1½ smoked pork rings, sliced
1 lb/450 g potatoes, cooked and diced
2 apples, peeled, cored and diced
6 fl oz/180 ml boiling water
1 tablespoon/15 ml soy sauce
2 tablespoons/30 ml tomato purée
dash Tabasco sauce
pinch of mixed spice
1 tablespoon/15 ml sesame seeds

Heat the oil in a wok or large shallow pan. Add the onion, peppers and cauliflower. Stir-fry for 5 minutes. Add the pork sausage, potatoes, apple, mixed spice and sesame seeds and cook for 5 minutes. Blend together the remaining ingredients. Stir into the pan and cook for a further 3 minutes. Serve with crusty bread. *Serves 4*

LEMON CRUNCH

6 digestive biscuits, crushed
1 egg yolk
1 oz/25 g caster sugar
grated rind and juice of 1 lemon
4 oz/125 g cream cheese
4 oz/125 g quark
To decorate: grated chocolate

Divide the biscuits between 4 glasses. Blend the remaining ingredients together

until smooth. Spoon over the biscuits and chill. Decorate with chocolate just before serving. *Serves 4*

FISH AND BACON KEBABS

1 lb/450 g cod fillet, skinned
4 bacon rashers, derinded
4 bay leaves
16 button mushrooms
8 cherry tomatoes
1 tablespoon/15 ml vegetable oil
2 teaspoons/10 ml lemon juice

Cut the cod fillet into 1-inch/2.5-cm pieces. Thread on four kebab skewers alternately with bacon, bay leaves, mushrooms and tomatoes. Mix oil and lemon juice and brush over kebabs. Season with black pepper and grill for 12 minutes, turning occasionally. Serve with a green salad. *Serves 4*

GINGER ADVOCAAT SYLLABUB

2 tablespoons/30 ml ginger marmalade
2 tablespoons/30 ml advocaat liqueur
4 tablespoons/60 ml single cream
4 oz/125 g Greek yogurt
To garnish: preserved ginger

Mix together marmalade and advocaat. Fold in cream and yogurt. Pour into glasses or sundae dishes and decorate with slivers of preserved ginger. Serve with crisp sweet biscuits. *Serves 4*

BELOW: FISH AND BACON KEBABS, GINGER ADVOCAAT SYLLABUB

TOP LEFT: VEGETABLE RISOTTO, APRICOT ICE CREAM SUNDAES

LEFT: SMOKED SAUSAGE STIR-FRY, LEMON CRUNCH

GRILLED SARDINES

Sprats are cheaper and smaller than sardines and if cooked in the same way, can be eaten whole, heads, tails and all. If using sardines, only eat the flesh.

12 small sardines or 1 lb/450 g sprats
flour
¼ teaspoon/1.25 ml cayenne pepper
***To garnish:* lemon slices**

Wash and dry the fish. Place the flour in a bag and season with cayenne, salt and pepper. Place each fish in the bag and shake to coat in flour. Shake off excess flour. Grill 4-5 minutes until golden brown, turning once. Serve with lemon.

Serves 4

SPANISH OMELETTE

3 tablespoons/45 ml oil
2 medium-sized potatoes, peeled and
   cubed
1 onion, sliced into rings
1 garlic clove, peeled and crushed
1 red pepper, cored, deseeded and cubed
4 streaky bacon slices, derinded and
   chopped
2 oz/50 g frozen peas
2 oz/50 g frozen green beans
2 tomatoes, peeled and chopped
1 tablespoon/15 ml tomato purée
6 (size 4) eggs, beaten
1 tablespoon/15 ml chopped fresh
   parsley

Heat the oil in a large frying pan and fry the potatoes for 5-7 minutes or until golden. Remove from the pan and reserve. Add the onion, garlic, red pepper and bacon and fry for 5 minutes, stirring. Add the peas, beans, tomatoes and tomato purée, with the potatoes, 2 fl oz/ 60 ml water and seasoning. Cook for a further 5 minutes.

Transfer the mixture to a shallow ovenproof dish. Pour over the eggs and sprinkle with the parsley. Bake at Mark 4 — 180°C — 350°F for 25 minutes. Serve cut into wedges.

Serves 4

GRILLED SARDINES, SPANISH OMELETTE

COD WITH SESAME SEEDS AND CARROTS

8 oz/225 g carrots, peeled, sliced
grated rind and juice of 1 orange
5 fl oz/150 ml fresh orange juice
1 lb/450 g cod, cubed
10 fl oz/300 ml fish stock
1 small onion, sliced
8 oz/225 g green noodles
1 tablespoon/15 ml cornflour
2 tablespoons/30 ml cold water
1 oz/25 g butter, softened

Marinate carrots in the orange rind and juice for 1 hour.

Poach the fish in stock and onion, for 5 minutes. Drain stock, strain and reserve. Meanwhile, cook the carrots in the orange marinade for 10 minutes. Drain carrots, reserving juice, and keep hot. Combine juice with stock and boil rapidly to reduce by half. Cook the noodles. Dissolve the cornflour in the water and stir into sauce. Whisk in butter and cook for 2 minutes, stirring.

Arrange noodles on plates. Top with fish, carrots and sesame seeds. Serve with the sauce. **Serves 4**

LIVER COURGETTE STIR-FRY

8 oz/225 g lamb's liver, thinly sliced
juice of 2 limes
2 tablespoons/30 ml light soy sauce
1 teaspoon/5 ml sesame oil
8 oz/225 g small courgettes
4 spring onions, trimmed
1½ tablespoons/22.5 ml vegetable oil
1 large clove garlic, peeled and cut into slivers

Cut the liver into narrow strips. Mix the lime juice, soy sauce and sesame oil in a shallow bowl. Add the liver and coat with the marinade. Set aside for 15 minutes.

Slice the courgettes and spring onions diagonally. Heat the vegetable oil in a preheated wok or frying pan, add the garlic and stir-fry for 1 minute. Remove the liver from the marinade and stir-fry for 1 minute. Remove with a slotted spoon and reserve. Add the spring onions and courgettes to the pan and stir-fry for 1 minute. Remove. Add marinade and boil briskly to reduce. Return the liver and vegetables and toss for 30 seconds. Serve immediately with egg noodles. **Serves 4**

SURPRISE HAMBURGERS

1 lb/450 g lean minced beef
1 clove garlic, peeled and crushed
2 teaspoons/10 ml tomato purée
½ teaspoon/2.5 ml mixed herbs
4 oz/125 g Danish blue cheese

Put the minced beef into a mixing bowl and add the garlic, tomato purée and herbs. Mash well together with a fork and season with freshly ground black pepper. Divide the meat mixture into 4 equal portions. Cut the cheese into 4 equal pieces and mould a portion of meat around each, shaping them into hamburgers. Grill for 10-15 minutes turning once, until browned and cooked through. **Serves 4**

PEANUT BUTTER COOKIES

2 tablespoons/30 ml golden syrup
5 oz/150 g polyunsaturated margarine
4 oz/125 g soft brown sugar
4 oz/125 g crunchy peanut butter
10 oz/300 g self-raising wholewheat flour

Heat the syrup, margarine, and sugar until melted. Stir in the peanut butter and flour. Roll into balls and place on greased baking sheets. Bake at Mark 4 — 180°C — 350°F for 15 to 20 minutes. Cool for a few minutes then transfer to a rack. **Makes 30**

CHICKEN AND BEAN BREAD BAKES

4 wholemeal rolls
4 oz/125 g cooked chicken, skinned, boned and diced
1 (7-oz/200-g) can low sugar and salt baked beans
2 oz/50 g low fat Cheddar cheese, grated

Cut the top off each roll. Scoop out the centres and mix with the remaining ingredients. Refill the bread rolls and place on a baking sheet. Bake at Mark 6 — 200°C — 400°F for 10-15 minutes until heated through. **Makes 4**

COD WITH SESAME SEEDS AND CARROTS, CHICKEN AND BEAN SALAD

SPINACH AND CHEESE PANCAKES, FRUIT SIMMERED
IN ORANGE JUICE

SPINACH AND CHEESE PANCAKES

Pancakes:
3 oz/75 g wholemeal flour
1 oz/25 g plain flour
1 egg
10 fl oz/300 ml milk
oil for frying
Filling:
2 lb/900 g spinach, stalks removed
**8 oz/225 g ricotta cheese or sieved
    cottage cheese**
1 teaspoon/5 ml freshly grated nutmeg
2 hard-boiled eggs, chopped
10 fl oz/300 ml béchamel sauce

First make the pancakes. Blend the flours,
egg and milk until smooth in a liquidiser.
Oil a 7-inch/18-cm frying pan and heat.
Add batter to the pan and swirl to coat the
base. Cook for 1½ minutes, flip over and
cook for 30 seconds. Make 8 pancakes.

Wash the spinach and cook in the water
clinging to the leaves for 4 minutes.
Drain. Mix with the cheese, nutmeg, eggs
and seasoning. Blend to a purée. Divide
between the pancakes and roll up.
Arrange in a dish and pour over the
sauce. Cook at Mark 4 — 180°C — 350°F
for 35 minutes. Serve with leeks.

Serves 4

FRUIT SIMMERED IN ORANGE JUICE

1 large orange, peeled, segmented
1 grapefruit, peeled, segmented
1 pear, peeled, cored, sliced
2 oz/50 g white grapes
2 oz/50 g black grapes
10 fl oz/300 ml fresh orange juice

Place fruit in a pan with the orange juice
and simmer for 2-3 minutes. Serve with a
little of the orange juice spooned over.

Serves 4

MUSTARD AND HONEY GLAZED GAMMON

4 gammon steaks
1 tablespoon/15 ml wholegrain mustard
3 tablespoons/45 ml clear honey

Snip the gammon rind at 1-inch/2.5-cm
intervals. Blend the mustard and honey
together and brush over the steaks. Place
under a preheated grill and cook for
about 5 minutes on each side. *Serves 4*

STRAWBERRY DIP

4 oz/125 g low-fat soft cheese
2 tablespoons/30 ml Greek yogurt
4 oz/125 g strawberries, sieved
2 teaspoons/10 ml caster sugar

Blend all the ingredients together until
smooth. Spoon into a bowl and serve with
crisp biscuits for dunking. *Serves 4*

BAKED PASTA

2 tablespoons/30 ml vegetable oil
1 onion, finely chopped
1 garlic clove, peeled and crushed
2 oz/50 g mushrooms, chopped
2 celery stalks, chopped
8 oz/225 g lean minced beef
1 (14-oz/397-g) can tomatoes
2 tablespoons/30 ml tomato purée
1 teaspoon/5 ml dried oregano
1 teaspoon/5 ml dried basil
8 oz/225 g pasta shapes, cooked
10 oz/275 g béchamel sauce
2-3 tablespoons/30-40 ml freshly grated
  Parmesan cheese

Heat the oil in a pan and fry the onion, garlic, mushrooms and celery until soft. Add the beef and fry until browned. Stir in the tomatoes, tomato purée, oregano, basil and seasoning. Cover and simmer for 1 hour. Toss the pasta with the meat sauce and place in a heatproof dish. Pour over the sauce and sprinkle with the cheese. Bake at Mark 4 — 180°C — 350°F for 40-45 minutes. **Serves 4**

FRUIT FOOL

8 oz/225 g dried apricots, soaked
  overnight
10 oz/300 g natural yogurt
2-3 tablespoons/30-45 ml apricot brandy
  (optional)

Purée the apricots in a food processor with the yogurt until smooth. Stir in the apricot brandy, if using. Spoon into individual glasses and swirl a little more yogurt on the top. Decorate with edible leaves (we used rose petals) and pieces of apricot. **Serves 4**

BAKED PASTA, FRUIT FOOL

HERBY MEAT PITTAS

8 oz/225 g lean minced beef
8 oz/225 g lean minced pork
1 egg
2 tablespoons/30 ml tomato relish
½ tablespoon/7.5 ml Worcestershire
   sauce
1 tablespoon/15 ml fresh chopped mint
1 tablespoon/15 ml fresh chopped
   parsley
2 oz/50 g fresh brown breadcrumbs
2 oz/50 g roasted peanuts, chopped
Barbecue Sauce:
4 tablespoons/60 ml unsweetened
   orange juice
1 tablespoon/15 ml liquid honey
1 tablespoon/15 ml soy sauce
1 teaspoon/5 ml vinegar
3 tablespoons/45 ml sugarfree tomato
   ketchup

Place the meats in a large bowl and knead with the hands until evenly blended. Work in the remaining ingredients with plenty of ground black pepper. Press into an oiled and lined 2-lb/ 1-kg loaf tin. Bake at Mark 4 — 180°C — 350°F for 1 hour. Allow to rest in the tin for 10 minutes.

Meanwhile make the sauce: combine all the ingredients in a small pan and simmer for 3 minutes, stirring often. Serve the meat loaf sliced in warm pitta breads, stuffed with shredded salad leaves and a little sauce. **Serves 4-6**

CREAMY RICE

1 pint/600 ml milk
3 oz/75 g pudding rice
1 tablespoon/15 ml custard powder
2-3 tablespoons/30-45 ml honey
5 oz/150 g Greek yogurt or low-fat cream
few drops vanilla essence
To serve: fresh or frozen blackberries,
   mint leaves

Place the milk and rice in a heavy-based pan and bring to the boil. Stir, simmer and cover for 1 hour or until the rice is tender. Blend the custard powder with the honey and yogurt and stir into the rice.

TOP: HERBY MEAT PITTAS; LEFT: CREAMY RICE

Cook until thickened. Remove from the heat and stir in the essence. Pour into lightly oiled moulds or dishes and chill until set. Unmould and serve with whole or puréed blackberries and decorate with mint leaves. **Serves 4**

SMOKED HADDOCK RISOTTO

1½ lb/700 g smoked haddock fillet, skinned and boned
1 lemon, finely grated rind and juice
1 onion, finely sliced
2 sticks celery, sliced
2 tablespoons/30 ml oil
6 oz/175 g long grain rice
10 fl oz/300 ml chicken stock
4 oz/125 g frozen peas
4 oz/125 g sweetcorn
2 hard-boiled eggs, chopped
To garnish: fresh chopped parsley

Place the fish, lemon rind and juice in a pan with just enough water to half cover the fish. Cover and simmer gently for 10 minutes. Drain the fish and reserve the liquor. Flake the fish flesh and remove bones. Fry the onion and celery in the oil for 3 minutes. Add the rice and cook until it turns chalky white. Add the stock and reserved fish liquor and cover. Simmer gently for 15 minutes until the rice is tender. Stir in the peas, corn, fish and eggs. Serve hot. **Serves 4**

JELLY WHIP

1 (½ oz/11 g) sachet gelatine dissolved in 4 tablespoons/60 ml boiling water
1 pint/600 ml orange juice
1 small can evaporated milk, chilled overnight
To decorate: grated chocolate or toasted flaked almonds

Mix the cooled gelatine with the orange juice and allow to stand until just beginning to thicken. Pour the evaporated milk into a chilled bowl and whip until very thick. Continue to whisk while slowly pouring in the jelly. Spoon into glasses and chill until set. Decorate with a little grated chocolate or flaked almonds. **Serves 4-6**

TOP: SMOKED HADDOCK RISOTTO; BELOW: JELLY WHIP

FRENCH FILLERS

Split a French loaf lengthways and spread each half with low-fat spread and sweet pickle. Cover one half with 2 oz/50 g thinly sliced cooked ham, 4 oz/125 g thinly sliced Edam cheese and 2 oz/50 g thinly sliced salami. Top with 2 sliced tomatoes, 2 oz/50 g sliced cucumber and a few shredded Chinese leaves and season with black pepper.

Cover firmly with the other half of loaf and cut diagonally into 4. Wrap individually in plastic film. ***Serves 4***

BANANA DATE LOAF

Mash 2 ripe bananas in a mixing bowl. Dissolve 1 teaspoon/5 ml bicarbonate of soda in 2 tablespoons/30 ml hot milk and mix with bananas. Add 4 oz/125 g polyunsaturated margarine, 6 oz/175 g caster sugar, 2 eggs, 8 oz/225 g sifted plain flour and 1 teaspoon/5 ml baking powder and beat well for 2 minutes until thoroughly combined. Stir in 4 oz/125 g chopped stoned dates.

Turn mixture into a greased and lined 2-lb/1-kg loaf tin and bake in a preheated oven Mark 4 — 180°C — 350°F for 1-1¼ hours, until the loaf is risen and golden-brown and a skewer inserted into the centre comes out clean. Turn out on to a wire rack and leave to cool completely. Slice and wrap individually in plastic film and freeze for up to 3 months. ***Serves 6***

SANDWICH FILLERS

1. Ham, sliced tomatoes and chopped olives.

2. Chicken, diced red peppers, curly endive or lettuce.

3. Equal amounts peeled prawns, diced hard-boiled eggs, plus a little yogurt, chopped fresh dill and lettuce.

4. Smoked sausage and chicken, topped with sliced cucumber.

5. Soused herring, sliced spring onions and chopped chives, stirred into a little Greek yogurt.

6. Flaked smoked mackerel, stirred into horseradish relish, topped with shredded Chinese leaves and sliced tomatoes.

7. Pâté, topped with sliced tomatoes and watercress.

TURKEY AND BACON ROLL

Split a wholewheat or granary roll and spread with low-fat mayonnaise. On one half of the roll place 2 oz/50 g thinly sliced turkey and 1 crisply grilled streaky bacon rasher, cut in half. Top with tomato slices and shredded lettuce. Cover with other half of roll and press down firmly. Wrap closely in non-PVC film. ***Makes 1***

JELLIED FRUIT SALAD

Dissolve 1 sachet powdered gelatine in 3 tablespoons/45 ml hot water and stir into 1 pint/600 ml apple juice. Peel and segment 1 large orange and 1 small pear. Halve 2 oz/50 g grapes and remove the pips. Stir the fruit into the apple juice and pour into 4 by 5 fl oz/150 ml containers. Chill until set firm. ***Serves 4***

PITTA NICOISE

Split a wholewheat pitta bread in half, leaving one long edge intact. Open out and spread both halves with low-fat mayonnaise, then spread with 1 small can of tuna, drained and mashed. Top with 1 sliced hard-boiled egg, 1 small sliced tomato, 4 sliced stuffed olives, ½ small green pepper, cored, deseeded and sliced, and ½ small onion, cut into rings. Season with black pepper and lemon juice. Press the pitta bread edges together firmly and wrap closely in plastic film. ***Serves 1***

APRICOT NUT YOGURT

Stir 4 chopped Brazil nuts and 4 chopped, no-soak dried apricots into a 5 oz/150 g carton of natural yogurt. Transfer to a rigid container with a lid. ***Serves 1***

TOP LEFT: FRENCH FILLERS, BANANA DATE LOAF
LEFT: TURKEY AND BACON ROLL, JELLIED FRUIT SALAD
RIGHT: PITTA NIÇOISE, APRICOT NUT YOGURT

Cooking Around the World

aking pride in a great national cuisine is not, regrettably, a British trait, and indeed it's often considered more fashionable to serve guests food that is anything but British. Even in our pubs, stronghold of British traditionalism, spaghetti Bolognese, sweet and sour pork and chicken curry feature on the menu at least as often as our own roast beef.

● This chapter contains a very personal selection of recipes, and memories of parched olive groves, hot, sunny days, terracotta roofs and noisy cicadas make Mediterranean food the first choice. The countries bordering the Mediterranean are blessed with a wealth of perfect, sun-ripened ingredients of pungent flavour — sweet, scarlet tomatoes, tender fragrant basil, rich virgin olive oil and fresh fish for the barbecue. This makes for a powerful but essentially simple cuisine since what could be more delicious than a tomato salad scattered with torn leaves of fresh basil and dressed with thick green olive oil, to be mopped up with rough peasant bread?

● Japanese food is food as art, and high on my list of favourites for its delicacy as well as the exquisite presentation. Having a passion for raw fish helps too! India has a very special place in my affections, and so has her food, although sometimes you may feel you have to be more of an alchemist than a cook to master all the spices used. It is precisely this subtle blending of spices that fascinates me, especially in the mildly spiced food of Kashmir, where sweet spices such as saffron, cinnamon and cardamom predominate over those dishes more commonly thought of as Indian, so packed with chilli as to blow off the top of your head.

● The inclusion of some regional French cooking is a must: we all have fond memories of the first time we tackled Coq au Vin (mine was the very first time I had to entertain friends for dinner). It wasn't quite what I had eaten in Burgundy, where the dish originates — perhaps it was the lack of French atmosphere. I have deliberately picked such familiar favourite recipes to include in this chapter, as these classics are so often bastardised, appearing as pale imitations of the real thing.

RATATOUILLE

The most typical Mediterranean vegetable dish — serve on its own with bread or with a main course.

1 aubergine, roughly chopped
2 cloves garlic, peeled and crushed
1 large onion, sliced
1 red pepper, cored, deseeded and cubed
1 green pepper, cored, deseeded and cubed
2 tablespoons/30 ml olive oil
1 lb/450 g courgettes, thickly sliced
1 (14-oz/397-g) can tomatoes, sieved
1 teaspoon/5 ml fresh chopped oregano

Put the aubergine in a colander, sprinkle with salt, weight with a plate and leave to drain for 30 minutes. Rinse. Fry the garlic, onion and peppers in the oil over a medium heat for 5 minutes. Add the remaining ingredients and seasoning, cook for a further 30 minutes, stirring occasionally. To thicken the juices, remove the vegetables with a slotted spoon and boil liquid until syrupy. Return vegetables and serve hot or cold.

Serves 8

CITRUS SPICED OLIVES

12 oz/350 g black or green olives
5 fl oz/150 ml olive oil
2 cloves garlic, peeled and bruised
1 tablespoon/15 ml coriander seeds
1 lemon, roughly chopped
1 orange, roughly chopped

Slash the olives. Mix the remaining ingredients together then stir in the olives. Pack into a glass jar, seal and marinate for 2 or 3 days in the fridge. Drain the olives and serve with drinks. Use the oil for salad dressings. The olives will keep for about two weeks in the fridge.

CLOCKWISE FROM TOP LEFT: ORANGE AND FENNEL SALAD, RATATOUILLE, CITRUS SPICED OLIVES, OLIVE, BACON AND MUSHROOM SAUCE, SALAD NIÇOISE, OLIVE AND ROSEMARY BREAD, CHICKEN WITH LEMON AND OLIVES

SALAD NIÇOISE

2 oz/50 g French beans
8 oz/225 g potatoes, cooked and chopped
4 hard-boiled eggs, shelled and cut into
    wedges
4 ripe tomatoes, roughly chopped
2 oz/50 g black olives
1 (14-oz/397-g) can artichoke hearts,
    drained and sliced
1 (14-oz/397-g) can tuna in brine,
    drained,
3-4 anchovies
vinaigrette dressing
To serve: lettuce leaves

Cook the beans in boiling water for 3 to 4 minutes until still crunchy, drain and cool. Place on a bed of lettuce leaves on a large platter or on individual plates. Arrange the remaining ingredients on top. Pour over a little vinaigrette dressing and serve. ***Serves 6***

OLIVE AND ROSEMARY BREAD

1 oz/25 g fresh yeast
15 fl oz/450 ml hand hot water
1 (75 mg) vitamin C tablet, crushed
1½ lb/700 g strong white flour
4 oz/125 g black olives, stoned and
    roughly chopped
2 tablespoons/30 ml fresh chopped
    rosemary
1 tablespoon/15 ml olive oil
1 teaspoon/5 ml semolina
3 sprigs fresh rosemary

Blend the yeast, water and vitamin C tablet. Sift the flour into a warmed bowl. Add the olives and chopped rosemary and stir thoroughly. Make a well in the centre. Add the oil and yeast mixture and mix to a dough. Turn out on to a floured surface and knead until smooth and elastic — about 10 minutes. Shape into a round.

Cover with oiled polythene and leave in a warm, draught-free place until doubled in size — about 50 minutes. Remove polythene, brush with milk and sprinkle with semolina. Slash 3 times and lay a sprig of fresh rosemary in each cut. Bake at Mark 8 — 230°C — 450°F for 40 minutes until well browned. Cover with foil if browning too quickly.

Makes 1 large loaf

CHICKEN WITH LEMON AND OLIVES

1 tablespoon/15 ml olive oil
1 clove garlic, peeled and crushed
4 chicken breasts, skinned and boned
5 fl oz/150 ml chicken stock
1 lemon, very thinly sliced
2 oz/50 g green olives, stoned
To garnish: fresh herbs

Heat the oil in a frying pan. Add the garlic and chicken and quickly seal both sides. Pour on stock and bring to the boil. Reduce the heat and add the remaining ingredients. Cover and simmer for 20 minutes. Remove the chicken and keep hot, increase heat to reduce liquor slightly. Pour over the chicken. Garnish with fresh herbs and serve with boiled rice or pasta. ***Serves 4***

ORANGE AND FENNEL SALAD

2 fennel bulbs
4 oranges
12 spring onions
3 oz/75 g black olives
1 bunch watercress, trimmed
vinaigrette dressing

Cut away any damaged or bruised outer leaves of fennel. Remove feathery leaves and reserve. Slice across into ¼-inch/5-mm rings with a sharp knife. Remove peel and bitter white pith from oranges. Slice into rounds. Trim and roughly chop the spring onions. Arrange fennel, oranges, spring onions, olives and watercress in a salad bowl. Pour over the vinaigrette, toss well and serve.

Serves 4-6

SALAMI AND STUFFED OLIVES

8 oz/225 g large green olives
2 anchovies, finely chopped
2 tablespoons/30 ml fresh white
    breadcrumbs
½ garlic clove, peeled and crushed
1 teaspoon/5 ml chopped fresh parsley
4 oz/125 g salami very thinly sliced
3 oz/75 g stoned black olives

Split the green olives and remove the stones. Mix together the anchovies, breadcrumbs, garlic and parsley and use to stuff the green olives. Arrange the salami, green and black olives on a serving plate. ***Serves 4***

OLIVE, BACON AND MUSHROOM SAUCE

1 tablespoon/15 ml olive oil
1 large onion, finely chopped
1-2 garlic cloves, peeled and crushed
4 thick rashers streaky bacon, derinded
    and chopped
4 oz/125 g small button mushrooms,
    wiped
1 oz/25 g pimiento stuffed olives, halved
1 oz/25 g green olives, stoned and
    chopped
4 tablespoons/60 ml skimmed milk
    cheese (quark)
To serve: 12 oz/350 g pasta, cooked, 2
    tablespoons/30 ml chopped fresh
    parsley, Parmesan cheese

Heat the oil and fry onion and garlic until softened slightly. Add the bacon and cook

for a further 5 minutes, stirring occasionally. Add the mushrooms, olives and freshly ground black pepper. Cook gently for 5 minutes, stir in the quark and heat through. Pour over the pasta of your choice, sprinkle with parsley and toss well. Serve immediately with freshly grated Parmesan cheese. **Serves 4**

TAPENADE

A Provençal spread served on toasted French bread or as a stuffing for hard-boiled eggs. Store in the fridge for one week.

- **1 (1¾-oz/50-g) can anchovy fillets, drained**
- **2 tablespoons/30 ml milk**
- **8 oz/225 g black olives, stoned**
- **2 oz/50 g capers, drained**
- **3 fl oz/90 ml olive oil**
- **1 tablespoon/15 ml brandy**

Soak the anchovy fillets in the milk for 10 minutes. Drain. Blend the olives, capers and anchovy fillets until smooth. With the processor running, gradually add the olive oil until evenly combined. Add the brandy, season with black pepper. Serve spread on toast or French bread or mash with the yolks of hard-boiled eggs and pile back into the whites. **Makes 12 fl oz**

CANNELONI

- **4 oz/125 g frozen chopped spinach, thawed**
- **2 oz/50 g ricotta cheese**
- **1 oz/25 g Parma ham, chopped**
- **¼ teaspoon/1.25 ml grated nutmeg**
- **4 canneloni tubes**
- **2 tablespoons/30 ml olive oil**
- **1 garlic clove, peeled and crushed**
- **1 onion, finely chopped**
- **1 (14-oz/397-g) can tomatoes, drained and sieved**
- **1 tablespoon/15 ml chopped fresh basil**
- **1 tablespoon/15 ml chopped fresh parsley**
- **2 tablespoons/30 ml grated Parmesan**

Mix the spinach, ricotta cheese, ham and nutmeg together and season. Use to stuff the canneloni tubes. Put the canneloni in a heatproof dish and set aside. Heat the oil in a pan and fry the garlic and onion

for 5 minutes. Stir in the tomatoes, basil and parsley and simmer for 15 minutes. Strain the sauce over the canneloni, season, and sprinkle with Parmesan. Bake at Mark 4 — 180°C — 350°F for 30 to 40 minutes until the pasta is cooked but *al dente*. **Serves 2**

SOUPE DE POISSON

- **4 tablespoons/60 ml olive oil**
- **2 garlic cloves, crushed**
- **1 large onion, sliced**
- **2 leeks, trimmed and finely sliced**
- **1 lb/450 g tomatoes, skinned, deseeded and chopped**
- **4 tablespoons/60 ml tomato purée**
- **1 bay leaf**
- **3¼ pints/2 litres fish stock**
- **2 lb/900 g mixed white fish, cleaned and cut into 1½-inch/3.7-cm cubes**
- **French bread**
- *Rouille:*
- **4 tablespoons/60 ml mayonnaise**
- **1 garlic clove**
- **½ red chilli, deseeded**
- *To garnish: paprika*

Heat 3 tablespoons/45 ml of the oil in a large saucepan and fry the garlic, onion and leeks until soft. Remove one quarter of the leeks and set aside. Add the tomatoes and tomato purée and cook for a further 3 minutes. Season, add the bay leaf and pour in the stock. Simmer for 15 minutes. Add the fish and cook covered, for 15 minutes or until the flesh flakes easily. Remove the fish with a slotted spoon and remove all skin and bones. Reserve half the fish cubes and put the remainder in a blender. Remove bay leaf from stock. Pour stock into blender with fish and blend until smooth.

Slice the French bread and brush with the remaining oil. Bake in an oven preheated to Mark 6 — 200°C — 400°F for 15 minutes. Blend all the rouille ingredients together in a blender or food processor until smooth. Spread a little on the French bread. Serve remainder separately, sprinkled with paprika. Return the stock mixture to pan, stir in reserved leeks and fish cubes. Reheat, float bread slices on top and serve.

Serves 6

GREEK SALAD

- **1 lettuce, washed and separated into leaves**
- **4 tomatoes, quartered**
- **1 small onion, sliced**
- **4 oz/125 g feta, Cheshire or Lancashire cheese, cut into 1-inch/2.5-cm cubes**
- **2 oz/50 g black olives**
- *To serve: olive oil, lemon juice*

Arrange the lettuce, tomatoes, onion and cheese on four serving plates. Scatter over the olives and dress with olive oil and lemon juice. **Serves 4**

SOUVLAKIA

A Greek classic. As a variation, the meat can be threaded on to rosemary twigs (remove most of the leaves) and cooked over a charcoal grill for about 15 minutes.

- **4 tablespoons/60 ml olive oil**
- **juice of 1 large lemon**
- **leaves from 1 sprig of fresh rosemary**
- **1 garlic clove, peeled and crushed**
- **2 lb/900 g shoulder or leg of lamb, cut into 1½-inch/3.5-cm cubes**
- *To garnish: shredded lettuce, lemon wedges*

Mix together the oil, lemon juice, rosemary and garlic in a shallow dish. Add the lamb and mix well. Cover the dish and leave to marinate for 3 hours at room temperature, stirring occasionally.

Thread the meat on to skewers and cook under a hot grill turning and basting frequently with the marinade. Cook for about 12 minutes, or until browned on the outside but pink and juicy inside.

Place on a bed of shredded lettuce with lemon wedges. Serve with Greek Salad. **Serves 4**

FIGS WITH LEMON FLAVOURED CREAM

- **8 fresh figs**
- **5 oz/150 g *fromage frais* or Greek yogurt**
- **grated rind of ½ lemon**
- *To decorate: mint leaves*

Cut the figs into quarters almost to the base, leaving the base intact. Open the quarters out slightly.

Fill figs with *fromage frais* or yogurt mixed with lemon rind, decorate with mint leaves. **Serves 4**

PAELLA

3 fl oz/90 ml olive oil

2 garlic cloves, crushed

1 large onion, chopped

1 lb/450 g tomatoes, skinned, deseeded
    and chopped

4 chicken thighs, skinned and chopped
    into 2 or 3 pieces

4 oz/125 g mild chorizo, thickly sliced

8 oz/225 g long-grain rice

½ teaspoon/2.5 ml saffron strands or
    turmeric

1 pint/600 ml chicken stock

3 oz/75 g frozen peas

1 small squid

1 oz/25 g butter

8 oz/225 g mussels

4 oz/125 g sliced green beans, blanched
    for 3 minutes

4 oz/125 g peeled prawns

To garnish: 8 unshelled prawns

Heat the oil in a paella pan or large heavy-based frying pan. Add the garlic and onion and fry for 5 minutes. Add the tomatoes and fry for 2 minutes. Add the chicken and chorizo and fry for 10 minutes. Stir in the rice and saffron and cook for 2 minutes. Pour in the stock, add the peas, cover and cook for 15 to 20 minutes until the rice has absorbed all the liquid.

Meanwhile, prepare the squid. Hold the head and pull away from the body, removing the innards. Discard head and innards. Cut off tentacles and pull out bony rib from body. Peel off dark skin. Cut the body into rings and chop the tentacles. Sauté in butter for 8 minutes until tender.

When rice is cooked stir in the squid, mussels, beans and peeled prawns. Cook for a further 5 minutes until heated through. Season to taste and serve garnished with the unshelled prawns.

Serves 4

CLOCKWISE FROM THE LEFT: FIGS WITH LEMON-FLAVOURED CREAM, SOUPE DE POISSON, GREEK SALAD, PAELLA, SOUVLAKIA, CANNELONI, SALAMI AND STUFFED OLIVES

CLOCKWISE FROM THE LEFT: MOGHLAI CHICKEN, KASHMIRI RICE, LASSI, FRAGRANT FISH FILLETS, CORIANDER SPICED POTATOES, LAMB MEATBALLS, CAULIFLOWER AND OKRA

KASHMIRI COOKING

Kashmir is a state in Northern India tucked serenely beneath the Himalayas, affectionately known as the jewel of the North. It was once a Mogul stronghold and the Persian influences are still apparent in both architecture and food. The cuisine, thanks to the Persians, is more lavish than anywhere else in India and at a Kashmiri wedding feast 20 or 30 individual dishes may be served.

The spices used are sweet rather than fiery, with particular emphasis on cinnamon, cardamom and saffron, which comes from the crocus flower and is widely grown in Kashmir — it is noted to be the finest in the world. While the beautiful golden colour of saffron can be achieved cheaply by substituting turmeric, this will not replace the fragrant perfumed flavour.

As with all Moslem countries, lamb predominates, although goat and chicken are also eaten. Yogurt is frequently used, both in cooking and as a refreshing drink, blended with water, salt or sugar and sometimes fruit to make Lassi. When planning an Indian menu, choose two meat dishes and one or two vegetables and serve with basmati rice or Indian bread. As a drink, serve chilled lager or Lassi. Finish with a selection of exotic fruits, mango, pawpaw or melon, and plenty of refreshing Kashmiri tea.

KASHMIRI RICE

If you like you can add turmeric to colour half the rice and keep half white. Then you can mix the two just before serving.

8 oz/225 g basmati or long grain rice
2 tablespoons/30 ml oil
3 1-inch/2.5-cm pieces of cinnamon stick
a few cloves
8 cardamom pods
1 pint/600 ml water
1 teaspoon/5 ml turmeric
½ teaspoon/2.5 ml salt

Wash the rice well under running water until the water runs clear, then soak in water for about 30 minutes. Heat the oil in a heavy-based saucepan and fry the spices, but not turmeric, for 2 minutes, over moderate heat. Drain the rice well. Rinse again and add to the pan, stirring. Add the water, turmeric and salt. Stir

again, cover and cook over a very low heat for 20 to 30 minutes until tender and all the liquid has been absorbed.
Serves 4

LASSI

Salty Lassi is often drunk with Indian food — here's a sweet alternative to have after a meal, or any time. Try adding a banana, a peach or a few strawberries.

10 oz/300 g natural yogurt
2 teaspoons/10 ml orange flower water or rosewater
2 teaspoons/10 ml caster sugar
1 tablespoon/15 ml chopped fresh mint
4 tablespoons/60 ml water
To garnish: fresh mint leaves

Place all the ingredients in a food processor or liquidiser and blend until smooth. Pour into glasses and serve garnished with mint leaves. *Serves 3*

MOGHLAI CHICKEN

A typical Kashmiri recipe for chicken.

a pinch of saffron threads
4 tablespoons/60 ml hot water
4 garlic cloves, peeled
1-inch/2.5-cm piece of fresh root ginger, peeled
5 oz/150 g natural yogurt
3½-lb/1.5-kg chicken
2 tablespoons/30 ml vegetable oil or clarified butter
1 large onion, sliced into rings
½ teaspoon/2.5 ml cumin seeds
2-inch/5-cm piece of cinnamon stick
5 whole cloves
2 bay leaves
10 cardamom pods, bruised
To garnish: fresh coriander

Soak the saffron in half the hot water for about 5 minutes. Blend the garlic and ginger with the remaining water in a liquidiser to form a paste. Stir in the strained saffron water and yogurt and rub this mixture all over the chicken, both inside and out. Leave for 1 hour.

Heat the oil or clarified butter in a large heavy-based saucepan and gently fry the onion until brown. Remove with a slotted spoon, drain on absorbent paper and reserve for garnish.

Remove chicken from the marinade and wipe off excess yogurt. Reserve marinade. Add chicken to the pan and fry on all sides until golden brown. Remove then fry the cumin, cinnamon, cloves, bay leaves and cardamom for 2 minutes until you can smell the aroma. Add the marinade, a tablespoon/15 ml at a time, stirring well after each addition. Return the chicken to the pan, cover and cook gently for 45 minutes, turning from time to time. Remove chicken and keep warm. Increase heat and reduce sauce until thickened. Pour over the chicken and serve garnished with the onion rings and fresh coriander, on a bed of Kashmiri rice.
Serves 6

CUCUMBER AND TOMATO RAITA

Serve this as a relish with any Indian meal.

1 cucumber
4 large tomatoes, peeled and deseeded
12 oz/350 g natural yogurt
½ teaspoon/2.5 ml ground cumin
a pinch of cayenne pepper
2 tablespoons/30 ml lemon juice

Peel and grate the cucumber. Place in a colander and sprinkle with salt. Stand for 30 minutes, then rinse well and squeeze firmly. Finely chop the tomatoes. Mix the yogurt with the ground cumin, cayenne pepper, lemon juice and seasoning. Stir in the vegetables. Cover and chill.
Serves 8

LAMB MEATBALLS

I was served these meatballs at a Kashmiri wedding banquet — the meat was ritually pounded for about 3 hours — but you can use a food processor.

8 oz/225 g finely minced lean lamb
¼ teaspoon/1.25 ml grated nutmeg
½ teaspoon/2.5 ml ground cinnamon
4 cardamom pods, seeds removed, and ground
5 oz/150 g natural yogurt
10 fl oz/300 ml milk
10 fl oz/300 ml water
To garnish: fresh coriander or parsley

Season the lamb with nutmeg, cinnamon, and cardamom. Process in a food processor until it is a smooth paste, adding the yogurt gradually. This will take about 3 minutes. Cover with cling film and chill for 1 hour. Take teaspoons of the mixture and poach in the milk and water with a pinch of salt for 5 minutes. Cook about six at a time. Remove with a slotted spoon and keep hot while you cook the remaining mixture. Serve garnished with coriander or parsley and accompany with Cucumber and Tomato Raita.

Serves 4

LAMB BIRIYANI

½ teaspoon/2.5 ml saffron threads
6 oz/175 g basmati rice
2 tablespoons/30 ml oil
1 onion, finely chopped
1 oz/25 g cashew nuts
½ oz/15 g blanched almonds
1 tablespoon/15 ml raisins
1 clove garlic, peeled and chopped
1 teaspoon/5 ml cumin seeds
pinch cayenne pepper
1 lb/450 g shoulder of lamb, trimmed and cubed
2-inch/5-cm piece cinnamon stick
4 cloves
2 cardamom pods, seeds removed
pinch freshly grated nutmeg
5 fl oz/150 ml chicken stock
3 tablespoons/45 ml natural yogurt

Dissolve the saffron in 3 tablespoons boiling water. Boil the rice in salted water for 10-15 minutes. Drain and reserve. Heat the oil in an ovenproof casserole and fry the onions until golden brown. Remove with a slotted spoon and drain on absorbent paper.

Add the nuts and raisins and cook until golden. Remove. Add the garlic, cumin, cayenne and the lamb and cook, stirring,

until the lamb is sealed on all sides. Add the remaining ingredients, stirring in the yogurt one spoonful at a time until combined. Stir in the saffron liquid and bake at Mark 5 — 190°C — 375°F for 10-15 minutes.

Stir in the rice and cook for a further 20-25 minutes until the meat is tender. Serve sprinkled with the reserved onions, nuts and raisins.

Serves 4-6

KASHMIRI TEA

Perfectly refreshing and fragrant.

3 teaspoons/15 ml green (unfermented) tea
6 cardamom pods, bruised
2 1-inch/2.5-cm pieces of cinnamon stick

Put ingredients into a warmed teapot and pour over boiling water. Leave to infuse for 3 to 5 minutes. Serve without milk or lemon.

Serves 4

CAULIFLOWER AND OKRA

1 medium onion
3 garlic cloves, peeled
1-inch/2.5-cm piece of root ginger, peeled
3 tablespoons/45 ml water
2 tablespoons/30 ml vegetable oil
1 tablespoon/15 ml fresh coriander or parsley
1 cauliflower, broken into florets
4 oz/125 g okra, sliced

Blend the onion, garlic and ginger with 3 tablespoons/45 ml water to a paste. Heat the oil in a heavy based pan and fry the paste for 5 minutes. Add the coriander,

cauliflower and seasoning. Cover and cook for 20 minutes. Add the okra and cook for a further 5 minutes.   ***Serves 4-6***

CORIANDER SPICED POTATOES

Potatoes are very popular in Indian cooking — here's a crunchy, mildly spiced dish.

1 lb/450 g small potatoes, washed
1 tablespoon/15 ml vegetable oil or clarified butter
1 onion, finely chopped
1 small chilli, finely chopped, with seeds removed
½ teaspoon/2.5 ml ground cumin
1 teaspoon/5 ml ground coriander
½ teaspoon/2.5 ml crushed coriander
2 tablespoons/30 ml water

Cook the potatoes in boiling salted water until tender. Drain. Heat the oil in a frying pan, and fry the onion until golden brown. Stir in the chilli, cumin and coriander and cook for a further 2 minutes, stirring. Add the potatoes, water and seasoning. Cook uncovered until the water has evaporated, and the potatoes are lightly browned.   ***Serves 4***

FRAGRANT FISH FILLETS

The Daal lake in Kashmir is a rich source of fish — especially carp. Here is a delicious, light dish using plaice with a hint of spice.

2 tablespoons/30 ml vegetable oil
6 cardamom pods
1 teaspoon/5 ml cumin
1-inch/2.5-cm piece of fresh root ginger, peeled and chopped
2 garlic cloves, crushed
1 green chilli (optional), sliced, with seeds removed
1 medium onion, sliced
4 plaice fillets, skinned
juice of 2 limes or 1 lemon

Heat the oil in large frying pan. Fry the cardamom, cumin, ginger and garlic for 30 seconds. Add the chilli, if using, and the onion. Fry until the onion is golden brown. Add the fish and lime juice. Reduce the heat and cook for 2 minutes on each side or until the flesh just flakes.

Serves 4

JAPANESE COOKING

Eating in Japan is as much an aesthetic, spiritual and social experience as a functional one to simply stave off hunger. Freshness, quality and visual appeal are most highly prized. A Japanese meal consists of tiny portions of a variety of foods selected for their shape, form and colour as much as their taste. They are always exquisitely arranged, and garnished with leaves and exotic flowers made from carrots and mooli radish. The cooking methods employed are simple and usually brief, steaming, simmering, grilling and frying, or foods are served in their purest form — raw, hence the necessity for absolute freshness. A typical simple meal will consist of a clear soup with fish, meat or vegetables floating in it, a main course such as Tempura or meat grilled on an iron plate (teppanyaki) or cubed, marinated in soy sauce, skewered and grilled (yakitori), followed by plain boiled rice and pickles. Rice wine, sake, is served hot to accompany the meal and/or bitter green tea. Desserts are rarely served, although the meal may be finished off with a platter of seasonal fruit.

SUSHI

You need a Japanese bamboo mat to shape the rolls.

12 oz/350 g Japanese rice or short grain rice

2 fl oz/60 ml sake (rice wine)

2 teaspoons/10 ml sugar

2 fl oz/60 ml rice vinegar

3 sheets sushi nori (seaweed)

Wash rice in cold water and leave to stand for ½ hour. Place rice in saucepan with 17 fl oz/500 ml water and a pinch of salt and bring to boil. Cover and simmer for 2 to 3 minutes, reduce heat further for 5 minutes. Remove from heat and leave to stand for 10 minutes. Mix sake, sugar and vinegar in bowl, add rice and stir with a wooden spatula.

Place a sheet of nori on bamboo mat and smooth 9 tablespoons/135 ml rice over, wetting fingers in water to stop rice sticking. Press rice right to bottom edge of nori, but leave 2 inches/5 cm at top. Use the bamboo mat to form sushi roll, neaten edges with a damp cloth. Make up two more rolls, allow to cool. Use immediately

or wrap in cling film and keep in refrigerator for up to 2 days.

To serve, dampen a sharp knife and cut each roll in half. Keeping the knife damp cut both halves in half again· and then again to make eight pieces per roll.

Makes 24

THE TOPPINGS

Halibut and mock caviar. Wash and skin 4 oz/125 g fresh fillet of halibut and cut into very thin strips. Cut strips into 2-inch/5-cm lengths and mix with 1 tablespoon/15 ml red lumpfish roe. Arrange a teaspoon/5 ml of mixture on each sushi piece.

Smoked salmon. Roll up ½-inch/1-cm strips of smoked salmon and place on sushi, decorate with lemon.

Herring. Cut 2 or 3 herring fillets into thin strips, place a strip on each sushi. Garnish with fresh thyme.

Cockles. Place a teaspoon/5 ml of cockles on each piece of sushi. Garnish with flat leaf parsley.

Omelette. Beat 2 eggs with 1 teaspoon/5 ml sake and a pinch of salt. Heat a lightly oiled frying pan, cook omelette, rolling it up in the pan when it has set. Cool and cut into ¼-inch/5-mm slices and place on sushi. Decorate with a dampened strip of nori, or flat leaf parsley.

TEMPURA

Tempura is best eaten immediately after cooking.

8 king size uncooked raw prawns

1 carrot

1 green pepper, cored and deseeded

4 oz/125 g mushrooms

½ aubergine

1 onion

4 oz/125 g French beans

1 sheet sushi nori

Batter:

1 egg yolk

6½ oz/190 g plain flour

good pinch bicarbonate of soda

vegetable oil plus 4 fl oz/120 ml sesame seed oil for deep frying

Wash and peel prawns without removing tails. Cut carrot into thin slices and cut into shapes with small pastry cutters. Cut

green pepper into bite-sized pieces and cut mushrooms into quarters. Slice aubergine in half lengthways and cut into 1-inch/2.5-cm pieces. Then make five or six deep slits in skin. Peel onion and cut into wedges. Trim beans, cut in half and wrap sets of three in narrow 2-inch/5-cm strips of nori.

Mix 15 fl oz/450 ml iced water with egg yolk. Add sifted flour and bicarbonate of soda, mixing roughly. Heat oil in deep fat pan or wok to 180°C — 350°F or until a drop of batter sizzles on contact. Dip prawns and vegetable pieces into batter and place in oil, not cooking more than 10 or 12 pieces in the pan at one time. Cook for 2 to 3 minutes each side until golden. Drain on kitchen paper. Keep warm in oven until all items are cooked — but eat as soon as possible.

Serves 4

TEMPURA SAUCE

In Japan, everyone would have a little bowl of sauce to eat with the tempura.

3 fl oz/90 ml sake

2 teaspoons/10 ml sugar

5 tablespoons/75 ml soy sauce

2 teaspoons/10 ml peeled and grated horseradish

2 teaspoons/10 ml peeled and grated fresh root ginger.

Mix all ingredients together in a small saucepan, heat gently and serve hot.

PEA RICE

10 oz/300 g Japanese rice or short grain rice

5 oz/150 g frozen peas

3 tablespoons/45 ml sake

Place rice in a saucepan with 16 fl oz/480 ml water and a pinch of salt and bring to boil. Gently simmer, covered, for 3 minutes, add peas and cook for a further 10 minutes. Remove from heat and allow to stand for 10 minutes, stir in sake and turn into individual bowls.

CLOCKWISE FROM THE LEFT: SUSHI, SAKE, SEASONAL FRUIT, TEMPURA SAUCE, PEA RICE, TEMPURA

CLOCKWISE FROM BOTTOM LEFT: BOEUF EN DAUBE, COQ AU VIN, PETITS POIS À LA FRANÇAISE, PÂTÉ DE CAMPAGNE, TARTE AUX ABRICOTS, GRATIN DAUPHINOISE, TARTE À L'OIGNON

CHICKEN YAKITORI

2 chicken breasts, skinned and boned
1 tablespoon/15 ml soy sauce
1 clove garlic, peeled and crushed
½-inch/1-cm piece fresh ginger root,
peeled and shredded
1 tablespoon/15 ml dry vermouth
To garnish: **2 or 3 spring onions**

Cut the chicken into ½-inch/1-cm cubes. Mix together the remaining ingredients and pour over the chicken. Leave to marinate for 1 hour, turning occasionally. Thread on to skewers and grill for 4 minutes each side. Garnish with spring onions and serve with boiled rice and salad.   **Serves 4**

FRENCH REGIONAL COOKING

BOEUF EN DAUBE
Beef with Vegetables

4 oz/125 g unsmoked streaky bacon,
rinds removed and reserved
2 tablespoons/30 ml olive oil
2 onions, roughly chopped
3 carrots, roughly chopped
4 tomatoes, skinned
2 lb/900 g shin of beef, trimmed
2 garlic cloves, peeled and bruised
½ teaspoon/2.5 ml dried thyme
1 bay leaf
few sprigs of fresh parsley
1 strip of orange rind
5 fl oz/150 ml red wine
To garnish: **fresh chopped parsley**

Chop the bacon into 1-inch/2.5-cm pieces. Place in a large earthenware pot with the oil, onions, carrots and tomatoes. Cut the beef into large pieces, about 3 to 4-inches/7.5 to 10-cm square and 1-inch/2.5-cm thick, and arrange in a layer on top of the vegetables. Scatter over the bacon rinds. Add the remaining ingredients, except the wine which must be brought to the boil in a small pan first, then poured over the meat. Cover and cook at Mark 4 — 180°C — 350°F for 15 minutes. Reduce the temperature to Mark 2 — 150°C — 300°F for 4 hours. Discard bacon rinds, sprinkle with fresh chopped parsley and serve with noodles.
Serves 4-6

TARTE AUX ABRICOTS
Apricot Tart

2 oz/50 g unsalted butter
4 oz/125 g plain flour
½ oz/15 g sugar
1 egg yolk
1 (14-oz/397-g) can apricot halves, in
natural juice
3 fl oz/90 ml double cream
1 egg
1 tablespoon/15 ml caster sugar
few drops vanilla essence

Rub the butter into the flour until the mixture resembles breadcrumbs. Stir in the sugar and then the egg yolk and enough cold water to bind. Knead lightly. Wrap in non-PVC film and chill for 30 minutes. Roll out and use to line an 8-inch/20-cm fluted flan tin. Prick well with a fork. Bake blind at Mark 5 — 190°C — 375°F for 15 minutes. Arrange the apricots, cut side uppermost, on the pastry. Bake at Mark 4 — 180°C — 350°F for 25 minutes. Beat the cream with the egg, sugar and vanilla essence, pour over the fruit and cook for a further 10 minutes. Serve warm or cold.   **Serves 4-6**

PORC A LA NORMANDE
Pork with Apples and Cream

Dairy produce characterises the cooking of Normandy as do apples, cider and Calvados — brandy distilled from apples.

1½ oz/40 g butter
1 lb/450 g pork fillet
1 large onion, sliced
1 cooking apple, peeled, cored and sliced
2 tablespoons/30 ml Calvados or brandy
8 fl oz/240 ml stock
2 fl oz/60 ml cream or crème fraiche

Melt 1 oz/25 g of butter in a pan and seal the pork fillet on all sides until brown. Remove. Melt remaining butter, add the onion and cook until softened and transparent, about 10 minutes. Add the apple and cook, stirring, until golden. Return pork with Calvados or brandy and ignite. Pour over the stock, cover and cook gently for 30 to 40 minutes. Remove the pork and keep warm. Stir the cream into the sauce and heat gently. Thickly slice the pork and serve with the sauce.
Serves 4

RAIE AU BEURRE NOIR
Skate with Black Butter

1½ lb/700 g wing of skate
1 onion, sliced
4 tablespoons/60 ml white wine vinegar
few sprigs fresh parsley
2 oz/50 g unsalted butter
1 tablespoon/15 ml capers
To garnish: **fresh chopped parsley**

Put the skate into a large frying pan and cover with cold water. Add the onion, half the vinegar and the parsley. Bring to the boil, reduce the heat and simmer gently for 15 minutes. Take out of the pan, remove the skin, take fish off the bone and cut into 4 pieces. Place in a warmed serving dish. Melt the butter in a pan and heat until it just turns rich golden brown. Add the remaining vinegar and capers and boil for 1 minute. Pour over the fish and sprinkle with parsley.   **Serves 4**

PATE DE CAMPAGNE
Country Pâté

A coarse textured, rugged flavoured pâté to serve with bread.

1 lb/450 g belly pork
1 lb/450 g lean pork
8 oz/225 g pig's liver
6 oz/175 g onions
2 cloves garlic, peeled
1 teaspoon/5 ml dried thyme
6 juniper berries
6 black peppercorns
pinch of ground cloves
2 tablespoons/30 ml red wine
2 tablespoons/30 ml brandy
4 oz/125 g streaky bacon, derinded

Mince the belly pork, half of the lean pork, liver, onions and garlic together. Roughly chop the remaining pork and combine with mince. Grind the spices and stir into the meat with the remaining ingredients, except the streaky bacon. Season well. Press into a 2-pint/1-litre terrine dish. Arrange the bacon on top. Place in a roasting tin, half filled with boiling water. Cover the terrine with foil and bake at Mark 4 — 180°C — 350°F for 1½ hours. Remove from roasting tin and allow to cool. Chill before serving.
Serves 10-12

TARTE A L'OIGNON
Onion Tart

A Lyonnais tart, which is similar to a quiche, made with sweet caramelised onions.

4 oz/125 g butter
4 oz/125 g plain flour
pinch of salt
1 egg
1½ lb/700 g onions, very finely chopped
2 egg yolks
5 fl oz/150 ml single cream
pinch of freshly grated nutmeg

Rub 2 oz/50 g butter into the flour and salt until the mixture resembles breadcrumbs. Stir in the egg and enough cold water to bind the mixture. Knead gently. Wrap in non-PVC film and chill for 30 minutes. Meanwhile, melt the rest of the butter in a large saucepan and cook the onions, covered, over a low heat until pale golden. Stir often to prevent them sticking or burning. Roll out the pastry and use to line an 8-inch/20-cm fluted flan tin. Stir the egg yolks, cream, nutmeg, freshly ground black pepper and salt into the onions and spoon on to the pastry. Bake at Mark 6 — 200°C — 400°F for 30 minutes until golden. Serve hot. **Serves 4-6**

COQ AU VIN
Chicken in Red Wine

Traditionally made with a mature cockerel — in which case, allow at least 4 hours' cooking time.

4 oz/125 g unsmoked streaky bacon, preferably in one piece, derinded
2 oz/50 g butter
1 tablespoon/15 ml oil
2 large onions, roughly chopped
2 large carrots, cut in 1-inch/2.5-cm pieces
1 (4-lb/1.8-kg) chicken, jointed
1 tablespoon/15 ml flour
3 fl oz/90 ml brandy
1 (70 cl) bottle Beaujolais
12 pickling onions, peeled
6 oz/175 g button mushrooms
¼ teaspoon/1.25 ml dried thyme
1 bay leaf
few sprigs of parsley
1 clove garlic, peeled and crushed
To garnish: fresh chopped parsley

Blanch the bacon in boiling water for 2 minutes. Drain and cut into ½-inch/1-cm pieces. Heat 1 oz/25 g butter and the oil together and fry the chopped onions, carrots and bacon for 5 minutes. Place in a casserole dish. Fry chicken until golden. Sprinkle over the flour. Heat the brandy in a small pan, pour over the chicken and ignite. Add chicken to casserole. Pour the wine into the pan and boil rapidly until reduced by half, scraping up any meaty deposits. In another pan, melt the remaining butter and fry the pickling onions until lightly coloured. Add the mushrooms and cook for a further 5 minutes. Remove and add to the casserole with the wine, herbs and garlic.

Cover and cook at Mark 4 — 180°C — 350°F for 2-2½ hours. Garnish with parsley and serve with boiled rice.
Serves 4

PETITS POIS A LA FRANÇAISE
Peas with Onions and Lettuce

1 oz/25 g butter
4 shallots or 6 spring onions, finely chopped
2 fl oz/60 ml hot chicken stock
1 lb/450 g frozen petits pois
1 small lettuce, shredded

Melt the butter and fry the shallots or spring onions over a very gentle heat until softened and transparent. Add the stock, peas and lettuce and bring to the boil. Simmer, uncovered, for 2 minutes. Serve immediately. **Serves 4-6**

GRATIN DAUPHINOISE
Potatoes Baked in Milk

Chefs dispute whether or not Gruyère cheese is a classic addition to this dish. I prefer it without. A delicious accompaniment to simple roast or grilled meat.

2 lb/900 g potatoes, peeled
1 egg, beaten
1½ pints/900 ml boiled milk
1 clove garlic, peeled
1 oz/25 g butter

If you have a food processor, use the slicing plate to thinly slice the potatoes. If not, do it very finely by hand. Mix the egg, the cooled boiled milk, and seasoning together. Rub a 2-pint/1-litre gratin dish with the garlic and then half the butter. Layer the potatoes in the dish. Pour over the milk and dot with the remaining butter. Bake at Mark 4 — 180°C — 350°F for 40 to 50 minutes. **Serves 6-8**

Entertaining for Crowds

Forward planning is the key to catering for crowds. Make lists in plenty of time and decide what food and drink must be ordered in advance. Tables, chairs, linen, china, cutlery and glasses can all be hired if you give enough notice. In this chapter, there is a finger buffet for 50, ideal for an engagement party; a sit-down buffet for 75, suitable for a wedding reception; and afternoon tea for two dozen, which could be a christening celebration. There's also a theme celebration for midsummer's night — and a Christmas feast in true Bavarian style.

● When it comes to the actual preparation, enlist the help of some extra pairs of hands and make it a team effort rather than a mad single-handed panic that leaves you exhausted for the party. Borrow fridge, oven and freezer space from friends and neighbours, and if you haven't got equipment such as food processor and mixer, borrow them too. Try to do most of the cooking the day before, allowing food to cool; then cover and store it in a cool place or the refrigerator. Serve a choice of red, white and rosé wine. For the white, choose something light and fresh — a German Riesling or Italian Soave. For the red, pick a Beaujolais, a Valpolicella or perhaps a Spanish Rioja, and offer as an alternative a fruity Rosé d'Anjou, which has a touch of sweetness. Serve the white and rosé chilled, the red slightly chilled or at room temperature (20°C, 68°F). Buy in bulk or "sale or return" if you can, and allow about half a bottle per person. Most off-licences will lend you glasses free of charge if you order your drinks from them.

● Buy some bags of ice from the supermarket or off-licence and fill a large plastic bin to chill the bottles. Provide fruit juices, alcohol-free lager and sparkling mineral water for non-drinkers. For the toasts, one 75cl bottle of champagne or sparkling wine will fill about eight champagne flutes. If you are serving a punch, don't let eager guests top it up, start from scratch to avoid headaches the next day.

KNIFE AND FORK BUFFET FOR 75

CROQUEMBOUCHE

This is a traditional French celebration cake. Its French name means "crack-in-the-mouth", an apt description of the wonderful combination of toffee crisp caramel and choux pastry.

8 oz/225 g flour
1 oz/25 g icing sugar
4 oz/125 g butter
3 egg yolks
6 quantities Choux Pastry (see page 122)
3 quantities Crème Pâtissière or 2½ pints/1.5 litres whipped double cream
1½ lb/700 g sugar
12 fl oz/360 ml water
small flowers
Caramel threads:
7 oz/200 g sugar
6 tablespoons/90 ml water
pinch of cream of tartar

Sift the flour and icing sugar into a bowl. Rub in the butter finely and stir in the egg yolks to make a firm dough. Roll the dough to an 11-inch/28-cm round and place on a greased baking tray. Bake at Mark 6 — 200°C — 400°F for 20 minutes. Cool pastry base on a wire rack.

Pipe at least 150 small choux balls on to an oiled baking tray and bake for 25 to 30 minutes. Pierce balls and cool on a wire rack. Inject each ball with a little crème pâtissière or cream, from a piping bag fitted with a plain ½-inch/1-cm nozzle.

Dissolve the sugar in the water over a gentle heat, stirring. Then bring to the boil without stirring until the syrup turns rich golden brown. Remove from the heat. Lightly oil a Croquembouche mould or a large cardboard cone. Cover with non-stick paper — but do not attach the paper to the mould, as it must slip off freely

CROQUEMBOUCHE

later. Using tongs, dip the top of each choux ball in caramel and arrange them round the outside of the mould, building up the layers to completely cover the mould. The caramel will harden quickly to hold the pyramid together. When set, very carefully slip out the mould, gently peel away the paper from the inside of the pyramid and set the pyramid on the pastry base. Just before finishing, slip small flowers in between the buns.

Decorate with caramel threads. Make a syrup, as before, using 7 oz/200 g sugar and 6 tablespoons/90 ml water, adding the cream of tartar. Boil until it becomes a golden, caramel colour. Remove from the heat immediately. Dip two forks into the caramel and quickly lift out threads and spin them round the Croquembouche. Repeat to cover completely.

GLAZED GAMMON

Cook this two days before.

10 lb/4.5 kg knuckle end gammon joint
whole cloves
5 oz/150 g soft light brown sugar
2½ teaspoons/12.5 g dry mustard
5 tablespoons/75 ml pineapple juice

Place the joint in a large pan and cover with cold water. Bring to the boil, skim, turn down the heat and simmer gently for 2½ hours. Remove the joint from the pan and cool slightly.

Cut off rind and score fat in a diamond pattern. Press cloves into intersections. Combine the sugar, mustard and pineapple juice and mix smoothly, then pour over the fat surface. Place in a roasting tin and bake at Mark 7 — 220°C — 425°F for 45 minutes, basting twice. Allow to cool completely and serve cut into thin slices.

FRUIT DIPPED IN FONDANT

2¾ lb/1.25 kg fondant icing
8 fl oz/240 ml water
10 lb/4.5 kg selected fruits in season,
washed and dried

Place the icing in a bowl with the water. Set the bowl over a pan of gently simmering water and heat gently to melt, stirring. Dip the fruit into the fondant and place on non-stick baking paper to dry.

CLOCKWISE FROM THE LEFT: GLAZED GAMMON AND PEPPERED BEEF, SELECTION OF SALADS, FRUIT DIPPED IN FONDANT, CHOCOLATE PEAR FLAN, CUCUMBER AND CHEESE MOUSSE, PEACH MELBA TRIFLES, CORONATION CHICKEN, POACHED SEA TROUT

POACHED SEA TROUT

Cook and decorate the day before.

3 (6-lb/2.7-kg) sea trout, cleaned and gutted, with heads and tails left on
1 oz/25 g parsley sprigs
8 fl oz/240 ml pink champagne or dry white wine
6 oz/175 g unsalted butter
4 lemons, sliced and quartered
1 oz/25 g aspic jelly powder dissolved in 1 pint/600 ml warm water
2 cucumbers, diced

Place each trout on a large piece of foil. Divide the parsley, champagne or wine and butter between the parcels and season. Bring the foil edges together and crimp to seal. Place on baking trays and cook at Mark 4 — 180°C — 350°F for 30 minutes or until the flesh is opaque when a knife is inserted behind the gills. Leave in foil until cold.

Place the trout on a board. Carefully strip off skin. Place on serving plates and arrange lemon slices along the length. Spoon over cooled aspic. When set, garnish with diced cucumber.

PEACH MELBA TRIFLE

60 trifle sponges
5 lb/2.3 kg raspberry jam
1½ pints/900 ml medium sherry
8 (15-oz/425-g) cans sliced peaches in natural juice, drained
2½ lb/1.1 kg ratafia biscuits
10 fl oz/300 ml brandy
8 pints/4.5 litres custard, cooled
6 pints/3.5 litres whipping cream
2lb/900 g fresh raspberries
1 lb/450 g flaked almonds, toasted

Split the sponges and sandwich together with the jam. Arrange them in large glass bowls. Spoon over sherry mixed with a little of the fruit juice, scatter over peaches, arrange ratafia biscuits in a layer on top and sprinkle with half the brandy. Spread the custard evenly over the fruit and biscuits. Whip the cream until soft peaks form, then fold in the remaining brandy. Spoon over the trifles and top with raspberries and almonds.
Fills four 6-pint/3.5-litre bowls

FROM THE LEFT: ORIENTAL SALAD, CONFETTI RICE SALAD, PASTA SALAD

CONFETTI RICE SALAD

6 lb/2.7 kg long-grain rice, cooked and
  drained
3 lb/1.4 kg sweetcorn kernels, cooked and
  drained
12 red peppers, deseeded and diced
1 lb/450 g petits pois, cooked and
  drained
2 (15-oz/425-g) cans mandarin
  segments, drained
3 bunches spring onions, trimmed and
  finely sliced
1 lb/450 g green stuffed olives, sliced
1 lb/450 g hazelnuts chopped

Combine all the salad ingredients in
large bowls. Pour over some Vinaigrette
Dressing (see recipe).

ORIENTAL SALAD

4 lb/1.8 kg bean sprouts
6 lb/2.75 kg Chinese leaves, shredded
6 bunches watercress, trimmed and
  divided into sprigs
3 lb/1.4 kg carrots, shredded
1 lb/450 g raisins

Combine all the salad ingredients in
large bowls. Pour over some Vinaigrette
Dressing (see recipe) just before serving.

PASTA SALAD

5 lb/2.3 kg coloured pasta shapes,
  cooked and drained
3 lb/1.4 kg peeled prawns
10 heads broccoli or small cauliflowers,
  divided in tiny florets, lightly blanched
1 lb/450 g black olives, stoned and sliced
12 tablespoons/180 ml finely chopped
  parsley
2 bunches snipped chives

Combine all the salad ingredients in
large bowls. Pour over some Vinaigrette
Dressing (see recipe).

PEPPERED BEEF

*You will need three joints of beef this size.
Cook the day before.*

5 lb/2.3 kg topside of beef, rolled and
  tied
2 tablespoons/30 ml black peppercorns
2 garlic cloves, peeled and crushed
3 tablespoons/45 ml oil

Place the beef in a roasting tin. Crush the
peppercorns and mix with the garlic.
Spread over meat, leave for 2 hours.
Dribble over oil. Roast at Mark 8 — 230°C
— 450°F for 15 minutes. Reduce heat to
Mark 5 — 190°C — 375°F and roast for 15

minutes per lb/450 g for rare meat, 20
minutes for medium, or 25 minutes for
well done.

CORONATION CHICKEN

5 (7-lb/3.1-kg) boiling fowl
8 large onions, finely chopped
5 fl oz/150 ml vegetable oil
6 tablespoons/90 ml mild curry powder
6 tablespoons/90 ml tomato purée
1¼ pints/700 ml dry white wine
5 fl oz/150 ml lemon juice
3 lb/1.4 kg dried apricots, soaked
  overnight
5 pints/3 litres mayonnaise
1 pint/600 ml natural yogurt
To garnish: 6 heads of chicory, finely
  pared rind of 4 oranges

Place chickens in large pans, cover with
cold water. Bring to the boil, cover and
simmer for 1½ hours. Leave to cool in the
stock. Remove chickens, reserve stock. Pull
the meat off the bones and cut into bite-
sized pieces. Discard the bones and skin.

Fry the onions in the oil (do this in
batches) until soft. Add the curry powder
and tomato purée and fry each batch
gently for 8 minutes. Stir 4 fl oz/120 ml of
the reserved stock and the wine into each
batch, with the lemon juice and

seasoning to taste. Simmer for 20 minutes. Leave to become cold.

Purée apricots in a blender, then sieve to remove skins. Place onion mixture into one large bowl and gradually add mayonnaise and apricot purée. Fold in yogurt and stir in chicken. Garnish plates with chicory, spoon on chicken mixture and garnish with orange rind.

MIXED SEAFOOD COCKTAILS

Hard-boil and peel the eggs two to three days beforehand and keep in fridge in water. The day before make up the sauce and prepare the lettuce base and lemon garnish, then cover with cling film and put in fridge.

3 tablespoons/45 ml lemon juice
2 pints/1.1 litres mayonnaise
1 pint/600 ml natural yogurt
6 fl oz/180 ml tomato purée
3 lb/1.4 kg shelled prawns
3 lb/1.4 kg crab meat (dark and white), flaked
6 (7½-oz/210-g) cans tuna, drained and flaked
24 eggs, hard-boiled, peeled and chopped
5 iceberg lettuces, divided into leaves
To garnish: **15 thinly sliced lemons, 2 punnets mustard and cress**

For the sauce, stir the lemon juice into the mayonnaise. Fold in the yogurt, and tomato purée. Add seasoning.

In large mixing bowls, combine the seafood and eggs. Gradually mix in the sauce. Arrange the lettuce leaves on large platter and spoon a portion of seafood cocktail into each. Garnish.

VINAIGRETTE

Use one-third of this quantity for the rice salad, one-third for the oriental salad and the remainder for the pasta salad. Make it one or two weeks in advance, keep in fridge.

15 fl oz/450 ml wine vinegar
8 fl oz/240 ml lemon juice
3 garlic cloves, peeled and crushed
2 teaspoons/10 ml wholegrain mustard
3 pints/1.75 litres olive oil

Beat the vinegar and lemon juice with seasonings. Gradually whisk in oil. Pour over salads, toss to coat.

CUCUMBER AND CHEESE MOUSSE

The beauty of this mousse is that it involves almost no cooking and is fresh and light to eat. Make before and chill — freezing will not improve the texture. This quantity fills two 6-pint/3.5 litre bowls.

10 cucumbers, peeled, diced
3 teaspoons/15 ml Tabasco sauce
4 lb/1.8 kg curd cheese
8 (½ oz/11 g) sachets powdered gelatine
2½ pints/1.5 litres hot chicken stock
10 fl oz/300 ml white wine vinegar
2 oz/50 g caster sugar
2 teaspoons/10 ml ground mace
2½ pints/1.5 litres whipping cream, whipped

To garnish: **5 cucumbers, sliced**

Sprinkle the cucumber with salt and leave it pressed between large plates for 30 minutes, then drain thoroughly on kitchen paper. Beat the Tabasco and seasoning into the curd cheese. Dissolve the gelatine in a little of the hot stock, then stir into the remaining stock. Blend into the cheese. Cool.

Mix drained cucumber with vinegar, sugar and mace. Fold into cheese mixture alternately with whipped cream. Turn mixture into large bowls. Chill until set. Garnish.

CHOCOLATE PEAR FLAN

You will need eight of these. You can freeze cooked flan cases before filling.

6 oz/175 g flour
2 teaspoons/10 ml cocoa powder
3 oz/75 g butter, diced
1 egg
iced water, to mix
12 fl oz/350 ml whipping cream
2 tablespoons/30 ml sweet white wine
2 tablespoons/30 ml caster sugar
2 pears, cored, sliced, and tossed in a little lemon juice
2 oz/50 g plain chocolate, melted

Sift the flour with the cocoa and a pinch of salt into a mixing bowl. Rub in the butter, then add the egg and enough iced water to bind. Shape into a ball, wrap in cling film and chill for 30 minutes. Roll out and use to line a 10-inch/25-cm flan tin. Bake blind at Mark 7 — 220°C — 425°F for 15 to 20 minutes.

Whip the cream until soft peaks form, then gradually fold in the wine and sugar. Spoon into the pastry case and arrange the pear slices on top. Put the chocolate in a piping bag fitted with a writing nozzle and drizzle chocolate over the top of the flan.

FRUIT DIPPED IN FONDANT, CHOCOLATE PEAR FLAN

FINGER BUFFET FOR 50

SPICY MEATBALLS WITH TOMATO DIP

Freeze cooked meatballs for up to three months. Thaw completely in fridge before heating through in a moderate oven, covered with foil.

3 large slices white bread, crusts removed
a little milk
3 lb/about 1.4 kg finely minced lean beef or lamb
3 eggs, beaten
1 teaspoon/5 ml cinnamon
1 teaspoon/5 ml allspice
2 tablespoons/30 ml chopped fresh parsley
2 tablespoons/30 ml chopped fresh coriander
4 tablespoons/60 ml oil
Tomato Dip:
1 (1 lb 4 oz/575 g) carton creamed tomatoes
1 small onion, grated
1 garlic clove, peeled and crushed
1 teaspoon/5 ml Worcestershire sauce
1 tablespoon/15 ml chopped fresh parsley
2 teaspoons/10 ml paprika

Tear the bread into pieces and soak in a little milk until soggy, squeeze dry. Mix thoroughly with the mince and eggs. Mix in cinnamon, allspice, parsley, coriander and seasoning. Shape into small balls. Chill for 30 minutes. Fry the balls in the oil in batches for 10 minutes. Drain.

For the tomato dip, mix all the ingredients together. Arrange hot meatballs on a platter, speared with cocktail sticks, and put the sauce in a bowl in the centre. ***Makes 120***

HERBY SAUSAGES WITH MUSTARD DIP

Oven bake 2 lb/900 g cocktail herb sausages at Mark 6 — 200°C — 400°F for 20 minutes. Drain and spear with cocktail sticks. For dip, combine 1 pint/600 ml natural yogurt with the contents of a 7¼-oz/200-g jar wholegrain mustard.

PEACH PERFECTION

10 bottles rosé wine, chilled
10 fl oz/300 ml peach liqueur or apricot brandy
5 fl oz/150 ml gin
4 oz/125 g seedless grapes
4 peaches, peeled and sliced
2½ pints/1.5 litres sparkling mineral water

Mix the wine, peach liqueur, gin and fruit. Chill for 1 hour. Just before serving add the mineral water and a handful of ice cubes.

DOUBLE HEART ENGAGEMENT CAKE

Make cake up to one week ahead. If you do not have heart-shaped cake tins, they may be hired. Or use a template to cut the shapes from round cakes — save trimmings for a trifle.

1 (12-inch/30-cm diameter) deep round sponge cake
1 (8-inch/20-cm diameter) deep round sponge cake
1 lb/450 g apricot jam, warmed and sieved
3 tablespoons/45 ml Grand Marnier
2½ lb/1.1 kg marzipan
1 (14-inch/35-cm) heart-shaped cake board
2½ lb/1.1 kg icing sugar, sifted
5 egg whites
1 teaspoon/5 ml lemon juice
orange food colouring
small fondant or silk flowers

Split each cake and sandwich together with a little of the apricot jam, mixed with the Grand Marnier. Cut sponge cakes into heart-shapes using a template.

Attach the small cake to the top of the large one with a little more jam. Set the whole cake on the board. Brush the remaining jam over the outside of the cakes.

Roll half the marzipan into two strips 21½ inches/53 cm by 2 inches/5 cm and 34½ inches/86 cm by 2 inches/5 cm for the cake sides. Press on to the cake neatly. Roll out the other half to fit the flat surfaces and press them on firmly. Allow to dry for 24 hours in a cool, airy place,

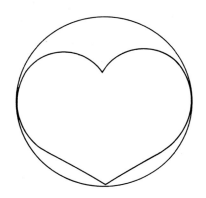

loosely covered in greaseproof paper.

Sift the icing sugar into a bowl. Break up the egg whites with a fork. Blend into icing sugar with lemon juice and beat until smooth and glossy. Add a few drops of food colouring. Spread the icing over the cake, then smooth the surface flat. Dry in a cool, airy place for 24 hours.

With the remaining icing and using a medium writing nozzle and bag, pipe dots round the top edge of each cake. Join the dots with loops of icing. Using a large shell nozzle and bag, pipe a row of shells at the base of each cake. Attach sprays of small flowers to fall across and down the cake sides.

VEGETABLE CRUDITES

4 heads of celery, scrubbed
1 lb/450 g button mushrooms, wiped
2 lb/900 g cherry tomatoes or very small tomatoes
12 oz/350 g curd cheese
12 oz/350 g taramasalata
12 oz/350 g garlic herb cream cheese
5 oz/150 g natural yogurt
8 oz/225 g blue cheese, crumbled
8 oz/225 g curd cheese
1 pint/600 ml natural yogurt

The day before, remove string from celery and cut the stalks on the diagonal into 1½-inch/3.5-cm lengths. Put into a plastic bag with a little water and store in the fridge. Remove the mushroom stalks. Cut a small slice off the bottom of each tomato, cut off the top and hollow out with a teaspoon.

Blend curd cheese with taramasalata. Pipe into the celery. Blend the garlic herb cream cheese with the yogurt and pipe into the mushrooms. Beat the blue cheese, curd cheese and yogurt together. Pipe into the tomatoes. Arrange on platters.

VEGETABLE CRUDITÉS

FROM THE LEFT: SEAFOOD PUFFS, BRIE AND GRAPE BITES, SPICY MEATBALLS WITH TOMATO DIP, PEANUT DIP, CHEESY HEARTS, COCKTAIL CHICKEN TIKKA, NEW POTATO DIPPERS WITH GARLIC MAYONNAISE, MIXED SALAD, HERBY SAUSAGES WITH MUSTARD DIP

SEAFOOD PUFFS

Open-freeze uncooked mini rolls for up to one month.

1 ½ lb/700 g cod or haddock, skinned

2 tablespoons/30 ml tomato purée

2 tablespoons/30 ml chopped fresh coriander

1 tablespoon/15 ml lemon juice

8 oz/225 g peeled prawns, roughly chopped

2 (1-lb/450-g) packets puff pastry

1 egg yolk, to glaze

2 tablespoons/30 ml grated Parmeson cheese

To garnish: prawns in shells

Mince the white fish with the tomato purée, herbs, lemon juice and seasoning. Stir in the prawns. Chill. Roll out the pastry to form a rectangle about ⅛-inch/2-mm thick. Trim the edges. Cut into long strips 3 inches/7.5 cm wide. Spoon the mixture evenly down the centre of the pastry strips. Brush the edges with a little beaten egg. Fold over one of the long edges and press together well to seal. Brush with glaze and sprinkle with Parmesan cheese. Using scissors, snip the pastry top at 1-inch/2.5-cm intervals.

Slice between cuts to make mini rolls.

To cook, place on baking trays at Mark 7 — 220°C — 425°F for 20 minutes. Garnish, serve warm. ***Makes 115***

BRIE AND GRAPE BITES

Cut a whole Brie into 1-inch/2.5-cm triangles. Spear each triangle with halved black and white grapes. You need 1 lb/450 g each of black and white grapes.

COCKTAIL CHICKEN TIKKA

20 chicken breasts, skinned and boned

2 pints/1.1 litres natural yogurt

1 tablespoon/15 ml chilli powder

2 teaspoons/10 ml ground ginger

2 tablespoons/30 ml turmeric

2 tablespoons/30 ml ground coriander

6 garlic cloves, peeled and crushed

juice of 2 lemons

To garnish: 1 lemon cut into wedges, fresh parsley

Cut the chicken into 1-inch/2.5-cm cubes. In a large non-metallic bowl, mix together remaining ingredients. Add chicken and toss well. Cover and marinate overnight in the fridge. Remove chicken from the marinade and place on a rack in a roasting tin. Cook at Mark 8 — 230°C — 450°F for 10 minutes, turning once. Garnish with lemon wedges and parsley and serve hot. ***Makes about 150***

CHEESE PASTRIES

1 ½ bunches spring onions, trimmed and roughly chopped

1 oz/25 g butter

3 lb/1.4 kg curd cheese

1 ½ lb/700 g cooked ham, diced

8 oz/225 g roasted hazelnuts, chopped

2 oz/50 g chopped fresh parsley

1 lb/450 g packet filo pastry

2 oz/50 g butter, melted

Gently fry onions in butter. Cool, mix with cheese, ham, nuts, herbs and seasoning.

Butter two roasting tins (7½ by 11 by 1½ inches/18.5 by 27.5 by 3.5 cm). Cut six sheets of filo pastry to fit each tin. For each tin, fold the six trimmed sheets in half to form a "book" and brush with melted butter, gently turning "pages". Unfold the sheets and place in the bottom of the tin. Top with the filling. Cover with

CHEESE PASTRIES

another six sheets of pastry per tin, brushing with butter as before. Cut through the top six pastry sheets to make small diamonds. Bake at Mark 6 — 200°C — 400°F for 30 to 40 minutes until golden. Cool slightly. Slice through layers, serve warm. ***Makes about 60***

EXOTIC FRUIT PLATTER

Attractively arrange on a serving platter or tray: 1 large mango, stoned and sliced; 1 Charentais melon, peeled and sliced; 1 honeydew melon, deseeded and scooped into balls; 4 kiwi fruit, peeled and sliced; 4 fresh figs, quartered; 1 lb/450 g cherries and 1 lb/450 g grapes in small clusters; 1 lb/450 g each of raspberries, strawberries and apricots.

CHEESY HEARTS

These biscuits may be stored in an airtight container for one week.

8 oz/225 g flour, sifted
4 oz/125 g fine semolina
1 teaspoon/5 ml salt
¼ teaspoon/1.25 ml cayenne pepper
4 oz/125 g mature Cheddar cheese, finely grated
1 oz/25 g grated Parmesan cheese
8 oz/225 g butter or margarine, diced

Combine the flour, semolina, salt and cayenne pepper. Add the Cheddar, half the Parmesan and butter and rub through until the mixture resembles breadcrumbs. Chill for 30 minutes. Knead the mixture to form a ball. Roll out to ¼-inch/5-mm thick and cut out hearts or other shapes with a 1-inch/2.5-cm petit four cutter. Place on baking trays and sprinkle with the remaining Parmesan cheese. Bake at Mark 4 — 180°C — 350°F for 25 minutes. Cool on a wire rack. ***Makes about 50***

PEANUT DIP

Blend 4 oz/125 g crunchy peanut butter with 4 oz/125 g quark and 15 oz/425 g natural yogurt. Garnish with peanuts.

NEW POTATO DIPPERS

Thoroughly scrub 4 lb/1.8 kg new potatoes. Boil until tender, drain. Serve with garlic mayonnaise.

EXOTIC FRUIT PLATTER

TEA FOR 24

CHEESY PUFFS

5 fl oz/150 ml water
2 oz/50 g butter
2½ oz/65 g strong plain flour, sifted
2 eggs, beaten
3 oz/75 g Cheddar cheese, grated
1 teaspoon/5 ml dry mustard
oil for deep frying
To garnish: grated Parmesan cheese

Heat water and butter gently until the butter melts. Bring to the boil. Add the flour all at once and quickly beat until smooth. Cook for 1 minute. Cool.

Gradually beat in the eggs to a smooth, glossy paste. Stir in the cheese and mustard. Drop small spoonfuls of the mixture into hot oil 190°C — 375°F and fry for 5 to 6 minutes until golden and risen. Drain. Garnish and serve hot.

Makes 32

FLORENTINES

4 oz/125 g butter or polyunsaturated
    margarine
4 oz/125 g caster sugar
4 oz/125 g blanched almonds, chopped
2 oz/50 g mixed candied peel
1 oz/25 g glacé cherries
2 tablespoons/30 ml single cream
6 oz/175 g plain chocolate, melted

Melt the butter and sugar. Add remaining ingredients except the chocolate. Drop small spoonfuls of the mixture, well spaced, on to baking trays lined with non-stick baking paper. Cook at Mark 5 — 190°C — 375°F for 9 minutes. Neaten edges with a plain pastry cutter. Lift from paper with a palette knife. Cool over a greased rolling pin. When cold, spread the back of the florentines with chocolate. Mark with a fork. Cool.

Makes 32

FAR TABLE: CHEESY PUFFS, PETITS FOURS
NEAR TABLE, ANTICLOCKWISE FROM THE LEFT:
CHEESE AND CELERY BREAD CANAPÉS,
FLORENTINES, WHITE RUM TRUFFLES, ANCHOVY
HAZELNUT BUTTERFLIES, SMOKED HAM AND SALAMI
ROLLS, FRESH FRUIT AND SAVOURY TARTLETS

FRESH FRUIT AND SAVOURY TARTLETS

CHEESE AND CELERY BREAD

8 oz/225 g self-raising flour
½ teaspoon/2.5 ml ground fenugreek
a pinch of dry mustard powder
2 oz/50 g margarine or butter
4 oz/125 g Cheddar cheese, grated
3 oz/75 g celery, coarsely chopped
1 spring onion, finely chopped
1 tablespoon/15 ml fresh parsley,
    chopped
1 egg
5 fl oz/150 ml milk

Place flour, fenugreek, mustard and
seasoning in a bowl. Rub in the butter. Stir
in cheese, celery, onion and parsley. Beat
egg and milk together and stir in. Divide
between two empty, greased baked bean
cans with one end left on. Bake at Mark 5
— 190°C — 375°F for 1 hour until risen
and golden. Cool in the cans for 20
minutes. Remove to a wire rack.
Makes two round loaves

CHEESE AND CELERY BREAD CANAPES

2 Cheese and Celery Bread loaves (see
    recipe)
2 oz/50 g butter or polyunsaturated
    margarine, softened
Turkey topping:
8 oz/225 g thinly sliced turkey (boned
    and rolled breast)
2 oranges, peeled, pith removed,
    segmented
celery leaves
Beef topping:
8 oz/225 g rare roast beef, thinly sliced
2 tablespoons/30 ml thick natural yogurt
10 baby gherkins, thinly sliced
1 tablespoon/15 ml fresh snipped chives

Cut each loaf into about 12 slices. Butter
slices. Use each topping for half the slices.
For the turkey topping, cut out rounds of
turkey using a 2½-inch/6-cm plain pastry
cutter. Place on bread. Top with orange
and celery leaves. For the beef topping,
cut out rounds of beef as for turkey. Place
on bread. Add a little yogurt, gherkin and
chives. ***Makes about 24***

SMOKED HAM ROLLS

1 lb/450 g smoked ham, thinly sliced
4 oz/125 g brown breadcrumbs
6 oz/175 g walnuts, finely ground
4 oz/125 g stuffed olives, chopped
2 tablespoons/30 ml single cream
a pinch of ground mace
a pinch of ground cinnamon
To garnish: halved stuffed olives

Cut the ham slices in half. Blend
remaining ingredients. Season with
freshly ground black pepper. Divide this
filling between the ham slices. Roll up.
Serve on cocktail sticks and garnish.
Makes about 36

SALAMI ROLLS

1 lb/450 g salami, thinly sliced
6 oz/175 g brown breadcrumbs
1 (4-oz/125-g) can salmon, drained
4 tablespoons/60 ml quark
2 eggs, hard-boiled, chopped
a few drops of Tabasco sauce
3 tablespoons/45 ml black lumpfish roe
To garnish: black lumpfish roe

Remove rind from salami. Blend together
remaining ingredients. Season with
freshly ground black pepper. Divide this
filling between the salami slices. Roll up.
Serve on cocktail sticks. Garnish.
Makes about 48

FRESH FRUIT TARTLETS

1 egg yolk
1 oz/25 g caster sugar
1 tablespoon/15 ml flour
4 fl oz/120 ml milk, scalded
a few drops of vanilla essence
6 tablespoons/90 ml quark
44 boat-shaped pastry tartlets
To decorate: a few green grapes, a few
    stoned and halved fresh cherries, 1
    peeled and sliced kiwi fruit, drained
    mandarin orange segments

Whisk egg yolk and sugar. Stir in flour,
whisk in milk. Pour into a pan and bring
to the boil, whisking. Cool for 1 minute.
Remove from heat. Add vanilla essence.
Whisk until cool, then whisk in quark. Use
to fill tartlets and decorate with fruit.
Makes 44

SAVOURY TARTLETS

Smoked Mackerel. Blend 4 oz/125 g
smoked mackerel with 6 tablespoons/90
ml thick natural yogurt and a few drops of
Tabasco sauce. Garnish with red lumpfish
roe and coriander.
Horseradish. Blend 8 oz/225 g quark with
6 tablespoons/90 ml creamed horseradish. Garnish with thin strips of pepper.
Crab. Divide 3 oz/75 g dressed crab
between the pastry cases. Top with a swirl
of natural yogurt and a sliced green olive.

Prawn. Blend 4 oz/125 g curd cheese, 4 tablespoons/60 ml natural yogurt, 2 teaspoons/10 ml lemon juice, 2 oz/50 g prawns and 3 tablespoons/45 ml chopped fresh parsley. Season with freshly ground black pepper. Garnish with prawns and lemon.

Salami. Blend 4 oz/125 g curd cheese, 1 tablespoon/15 ml natural yogurt and a few drops of Tabasco sauce. Season with freshly ground black pepper. Add a few drops of mushroom ketchup to each pastry case before filling. Top with cream cheese, salami and asparagus tips.

Makes about 60. Each flavour fills about 12 cocktail-sized pastry cases

ANCHOVY HAZELNUT BUTTERFLIES

1 lb/450 g puff pastry

1 egg yolk

1 tablespoon/15 ml anchovy paste

1 oz/25 g hazelnuts, chopped and roasted

Cut the pastry in half and roll out to a 12 by 8-inch/30 by 20-cm rectangle. Cut into four to make four 8 by 3-inch/20 by 7.5-cm strips.

Beat together the egg yolk and anchovy paste. Brush down the centre of three strips with this mixture. Place these three strips on top of each other, with the egg yolk upwards, matching the edges carefully to form a neat stack. Lay the unbrushed strip on top to seal the strips

together, press the stack down the centre (along the lines of the egg yolk) with a rolling pin. Repeat with remaining half of pastry.

Cut each stack across into ½-inch/1-cm slices (3 inches/7.5 cm long). Place the slices on a greased baking tray and fan them out at both ends in opposite directions. Sprinkle over nuts. Bake at Mark 7 — 220°C — 425°F for 15 minutes. Cool on a wire rack. ***Makes 32***

PETITS FOURS

4 eggs

4 oz/125 g caster sugar

4 oz/125 g self-raising flour, sifted

1 oz/25 g butter, melted, cooled

1 lb/450 g marzipan

1 (12-oz/350-g) jar apricot jam, warmed and sieved

1 oz/25 g glacé cherries, halved

1¼ lb/575 g fondant icing

food colourings

Whisk the eggs and sugar in a large bowl until very thick. Fold in the flour and butter. Pour into a greased and lined 10-inch/25-cm square cake tin. Bake at Mark 4 — 180°C — 350°F for 20 to 25 minutes. Cool on a wire rack.

Knead the marzipan until smooth. Roll it out to the same size as the sponge. Brush the sponge with jam. Press on the marzipan. Cut the cake into shapes using

cutters or a sharp knife. Brush the sides of the shapes with jam. Place a cherry half on top of some of the shapes, if liked. Place the shapes on a wire rack.

Melt the fondant in a bowl over simmering water. Add a little water until of a creamy pouring consistency. Colour as required and pour over the sponge shapes to coat. When dry, decorate with fine piped lines of white fondant.

Makes about 48

WHITE RUM TRUFFLES

3 oz/75 g butter

2 oz/50 g icing sugar, sifted

8 oz/225 g white chocolate, melted

1 tablespoon/15 ml white rum

2 oz/50 g ground almonds

***To decorate:* 5 oz/150 g flaked almonds, toasted**

Beat butter and icing sugar. Beat in chocolate and rum. Stir until thick and cooled. Stir in the ground almonds. Chill, shape into small balls, roll in almonds.

Makes 1½ lb/700 g

WHITE RUM TRUFFLES, PETITS FOURS

FROM THE LEFT: GREEN SALAD, FISH AND MANGE-
TOUT SALAD, WOODLAND RICE, SPINACH STRUDEL,
WINE JELLY, KIWI FLUMMERY, CHICKEN VERDI,
MIDSUMMER PUNCH

MIDSUMMER'S NIGHT MAGIC

MIDSUMMER

Midsummer's night completes the longest day of the year, marking the summer solstice which has been an occasion for celebration and revels since pagan times. With a history like that we couldn't let it die out — so we opted for a feast in the true theatrical style of Shakespeare's *A Midsummer Night's Dream*.

In your own back garden you can set the scene letting your imagination and creativity run wild. We've chosen a green and white theme to give the feeling of a woodland fantasy. Green foliage, white flowers and fresh herbs are all used as decoration to emphasise the natural look. All the food is green and white too — and I'm sure you'll think of lots more that will

fit into the colour scheme, particularly when composing a large mixed salad. If you want to be truly exotic, add a few edible flowers, such as marigolds or nasturtiums (now available in selected supermarkets), for a spectacular blaze of colour.

All the recipes are served cold and so can be prepared in advance, either the night before or on the day of the party. Keep covered in the fridge until you are ready to take the food outside. Each recipe will serve between eight and 10 people, some slightly more, but if you are planning to prepare our whole selection, you could easily feed up to 15 guests, depending on appetites.

When your guests arrive, greet them with a glass of sparkling Midsummer Punch, a deliciously light mix of wine and apples with a hint of cognac and mint. All that's left is to arrange the platters on the table and let your guests help themselves while you relax, soak up the atmosphere and, with a little luck, some golden evening sun.

GREEN SALAD

Choose a selection of your favourite leaves, such as curly endive, chicory, round, Iceberg or Webb's lettuce and combine with thinly sliced button mushrooms, finely shredded white cabbage, young courgettes cut into thin slices, spring onions and fresh herbs. Try and keep to the green and white theme.

1 fl oz/30 ml white wine vinegar
juice of ½ lemon
1 teaspoon/5 ml wholegrain mustard
1 clove garlic, peeled and crushed
pinch of sugar
4 fl oz/120 ml olive oil

Vinaigrette Dressing
Use half this dressing for the Green Salad and half for the Woodland Rice. Blend all the ingredients together except the olive oil. Season. Gradually whisk in oil until thickened. Whisk again and pour half over salad and toss just before serving.
Serves 8-10

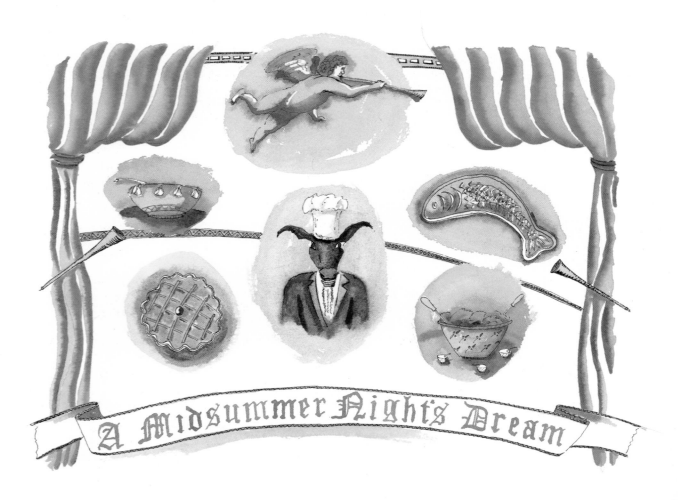

A Midsummer Night's Dream

CHICKEN VERDI

Greek yogurt, made from cow's or ewe's milk, is thicker and creamier than regular natural yogurt.

6 cooked chicken breasts
10 oz/300 g Greek yogurt
5 oz/150 g natural yogurt
1 tablespoon/15 ml water
1 bunch watercress, trimmed and
** chopped**
1 tablespoon/15 ml fresh chopped mint
1 teaspoon/5 ml fresh chopped chives
8 oz/225 g green grapes, quartered and
** deseeded**
***To garnish:* small bunch green grapes**

Remove any skin and bone from the chicken breasts. Slice the meat thinly and arrange around a serving platter. Blend the yogurt and water until smooth, stir in the watercress, herbs, half the grapes and plenty of freshly ground white pepper. Spoon the dressing over the chicken and sprinkle with remaining grapes. Chill until ready to serve. Garnish with grapes.

Serves 8-10

SPINACH STRUDEL

12 oz/350 g fresh spinach, spines
** removed**
2 lb/900 g white fish fillets, skinned
2 egg whites
1 oz/25 g butter, melted
1 oz/25 g flour
1 egg yolk
4 tablespoons/60 ml hot milk
1 teaspoon/5 ml anchovy essence
2 tablespoons/30 ml creamed
** horseradish**
grated rind and juice of 1 lemon
1 lb/450 g broccoli, separated into tiny
** florets, blanched**

Wash spinach thoroughly. Blanch in batches in boiling water for a few seconds. Plunge immediately into cold water, then drain thoroughly on kitchen paper. Spread the spinach leaves out, overlapping each other slightly, on a clean tea towel to make a 12-inch/30-cm square about 2 or 3 layers thick. Put fish and egg whites in a food processor or blender and work to a purée. Blend butter and flour together and beat in yolk and hot milk. Blend this mixture with the fish

purée, anchovy essence, horseradish, lemon rind and juice. Season with ground white pepper. Gently stir in the broccoli. Spoon the mixture along one edge of spinach square. With the help of tea towel, roll the filling up in the spinach leaves to form a long log shape. Wrap in foil and seal edges well.

Place in a roasting tin and half fill with boiling water. Cover the roasting tin with foil and bake at Mark 4 — 180°C — 350°F for 40 minutes. Remove from tin and allow to cool. Remove foil. Cover strudel and chill. Serve with green salad.

Makes 16 slices

WOODLAND RICE

1 lb/450 g long grain rice
8 oz/225 g fresh asparagus
4 tablespoons/60 ml fresh chopped
** parsley**
1 tablespoon/15 ml fresh chopped basil
2 teaspoons/10 ml fresh chopped thyme
6 spring onions, trimmed and finely
** chopped**

Cook rice in boiling water for 15 to 20 minutes until tender. Meanwhile, trim any woody stalks from asparagus and steam spears for 5 minutes. Cool slightly and slice thinly on the diagonal. Drain rice in a colander. Rinse under cold running water. Drain thoroughly. Make up the vinaigrette dressing (see previous recipe). Pour half over the rice, reserving remainder for Green Salad. Add the herbs, asparagus and spring onions to the rice and toss well. Chill until ready to serve.

Serves 8

WINE JELLY

2 ogen melons
1½ lb/700 g seedless green grapes
5 fl oz/150 ml water
5 oz/150 g caster sugar
4½ sachets powdered gelatine dissolved
** in 8 fl oz/250 ml hot water**
1¼ pints/750 ml dry white wine
2½ pints/1.5 litres white grape juice

Halve the melons and remove seeds. Scoop flesh into balls using a melon baller or small teaspoon. Remove stalks from grapes. Place water and sugar in a small pan. Heat gently to dissolve the sugar,

then bring to the boil, and boil briskly for 3 minutes. Remove from heat. Stir in dissolved gelatine. Cool. Add to the wine and grape juice.

Half fill a 4-pint/2.25-litre mould with the mixture. Chill for 1½ hours. When almost set, arrange half the grapes on the surface. Pour over another inch/2.5 cm of jelly. When almost set, again after about 30 minutes, arrange the melon balls over the jelly. Cover with another inch/2.5 cm of jelly and when nearly set, top with the remaining grapes and jelly. Leave until completely set.

Dip the base of the mould in boiling water for a few seconds and turn out on a serving dish. ***Serves 10-12***

KIWI FLUMMERY

Make the kiwi purée in advance and stir into the egg white mixture 30 minutes before serving.

8 kiwi fruit, peeled
grated rind of 2 limes
2 egg whites
***To serve:* Greek yogurt**

Press the kiwi fruit through a fine nylon sieve to make the purée. Stir in the lime rind. Whisk egg white until soft peaks form and fold into the kiwi fruit purée. Serve with a spoonful of Greek yogurt.

Serves 8-10

MIDSUMMER PUNCH

1 bottle medium dry white wine (hock or
** Mosel)**
1 pint/600 ml unsweetened apple juice
2 fl oz/60 ml Calvados (apple brandy) or
** cognac**
dash of Angostura bitters
1 (2-inch/5-cm) piece cucumber, sliced
1 bottle white sparkling wine (brut or
** sec), chilled**
1½ pints/900 ml sparkling mineral
** water, chilled**
***To garnish:* fresh mint sprigs**

In a large glass bowl, mix the medium dry wine, apple juice, Calvados or cognac, bitters and cucumber. Cover and chill for 30 minutes. Just before serving add chilled sparkling wine, mineral water and mint. ***Makes 24 glasses***

GERMAN XMAS

CARAWAY POTATOES

2 lb/900 g potatoes
1 teaspoon/5 ml caraway seeds
1 tablespoon/15 ml fresh chopped
   parsley

Peel the potatoes and boil until tender. Drain. Serve in a warmed vegetable dish sprinkled with the caraway seeds and parsley. ***Serves 6***

BAVARIAN CREAM

4 egg yolks
4 oz/125 g caster sugar
17 fl oz/500 ml milk
1 vanilla pod
2 tablespoons/30 ml powdered gelatine,
   dissolved in 4 tablespoons/60 ml
   boiling water
1 lb/450 g strawberries, sieved
1 pint/600 ml double cream
***To decorate*: whipped cream,**
   strawberries

Place the egg yolks in a mixing bowl. Add the sugar and whisk slowly to blend. Then whisk a little faster. It's better to use a hand whisk rather than electric, otherwise too much air will be incorporated and the cream will be bubbly. Bring the milk to the boil with the vanilla pod. Gradually pour on to the egg mixture, stirring continuously. Return the mixture to the pan and cook over a very low heat, stirring constantly, until thick enough to coat the back of a wooden spoon, about 15 minutes. Do not let the custard boil, otherwise it will curdle. Strain through a fine sieve. Stir in the cooled dissolved gelatine. Add the strawberry purée. Lightly whip the cream and fold into the mixture. Pour into a mould — tap the mould on the work surface to remove any air bubbles. Chill for 2 to 3 hours. To turn out, dip the mould briefly in hot water. Serve decorated with whipped cream and strawberries. ***Serves 6-8***

ROAST GOOSE

1 5-6 lb/2.3-2.6 kg oven ready goose
½ apple, unpeeled
½ onion, unpeeled
8 fl oz/250 ml beef stock
8 fl oz/250 ml red wine
2 teaspoons/10 ml cornflour

Rinse the goose but do not dry. Put the apple and onion in the cavity and stuff the neck if you wish with the stuffing below — don't forget to take the stuffing into consideration when weighing the goose. Place breast side down on a cake rack in a roasting tin, just large enough to hold the bird. Roast at Mark 6 — 200°C — 400°F for 30 minutes, reduce heat to Mark 5 — 190°C — 375°F and cook for 15 minutes per lb, basting every 15 to 20 minutes. During cooking remove excess fat from tin and reserve. After 30 minutes, turn the goose on to its back and prick the skin. Then about 30 minutes before the end of cooking, heat the stock and wine and pour over the breast.

Transfer goose to a warmed carving dish and rest in a warm place for 20 minutes before carving.

Skim fat from roasting juices and reserve. Thicken the juices, blending cornflour with vegetable water. To carve goose, remove wings and remove legs at the thigh joint. Carve the breast and serve with a little of the wing and leg meat. Cool fat, pour into jars and refrigerate for later use. Very good for roasting potatoes. ***Serves 6***

APPLE AND LEMON STUFFING

1 oz/25 g butter
1 large onion, finely chopped
2 cooking apples
2 lemons, grated rind and juice
8 oz/225 g fresh wholemeal breadcrumbs
1 tablespoon/15 ml fresh chopped
   parsley
1 teaspoon/5 ml dried thyme
1 large egg, beaten

Melt the butter in a small pan and gently fry the onion until softened but not browned, about 10 minutes. Peel, core and finely chop the apples. Mix together the apples, lemon rind and juice, breadcrumbs, parsley, thyme and egg. Add the onion, stir together well. Use to stuff the bird or bake in a lightly oiled ovenproof dish for 30 minutes.

RED CABBAGE

2 tablespoons/30 ml oil
1 onion, sliced
½ large red cabbage, finely shredded
2 cooking apples, peeled, cored and
   roughly chopped
2 tablespoons/30 ml wine vinegar
pinch of salt
1 tablespoon/15 ml sugar
¼ teaspoon/1.25 ml ground cloves
10 fl oz/300 ml stock

Heat the oil in a large saucepan and fry the onion for 1 minute. Add the cabbage and apples and fry, tossing gently, for 4 minutes. Add the remaining ingredients and reduce the heat to a gentle simmer. Cover tightly and cook for 40 minutes, shaking the pan occasionally. Season with ground black pepper before serving. ***Serves 6***